Reacting to Reality Television

The unremitting explosion of reality television across the schedules has become a sustainable global phenomenon generating considerable popular and political fervour.

The zeal with which television executives seize on easily replicated formats is matched by the eagerness of audiences to offer themselves up as television participants for others to watch and criticize. But how do we react to so many people breaking down, fronting up, tearing apart, dominating, empathizing, humiliating, and seemingly laying bare their raw emotion for our entertainment? Do we feel sad when others are sad? Or are we relieved by the knowledge that our circumstances might be better? As reality television extends into the experiences of the everyday, it makes dramatic and often shocking the mundane aspects of our intimate relations, inviting us as viewers into a volatile arena of mediated morality.

This book addresses the impact of this endless opening out of intimacy as an entertainment trend that erodes the traditional boundaries between spectator and performer, demanding new tools for capturing television's relationships with audiences. Rather than asking how the reality television genre is interpreted as text or representation the authors investigate the politics of viewer encounters as interventions, evocations and more generally mediated social relations.

The authors show how different reactions can involve viewers in tournaments of value, as women viewers empathize and struggle to validate their own lives. The authors use these detailed responses to challenge theories of the self, governmentality and ideology.

A must read for both students and researchers in audience studies, television studies, and media and communication studies.

Beverley Skeggs is Professor of Sociology at Goldsmiths, University of London. She held the Kerstin Hesselgren Professor in Gender Studies at Stockholm University and is an Academician of the Academy of the Learned Societies for the Social Sciences, UK. She has worked in the areas of Women's Studies and Cultural Studies as well as Sociology.

Helen Wood is Reader in Media and Communication, in the School of Media and Communication at De Montfort University, Leicester, UK.

Reacting to Reality Television

Performance, Audience and Value

Beverley Skeggs and Helen Wood

Routledge
Taylor & Francis Group

LONDON AND NEW YORK

First published 2012
by Routledge
2 Park Square, Milton Park, Abingdon, Oxon OX14 4RN

Simultaneously published in the USA and Canada
by Routledge
711 Third Avenue, New York, NY 10017

Routledge is an imprint of the Taylor & Francis Group, an informa business

British Library Cataloguing in Publication Data
A catalogue record for this book is available from the British Library

Library of Congress Cataloging in Publication Data
Skeggs, Beverley.
Reacting to reality television : performance, audience and value / by Beverley
Skeggs and Helen Wood.
p. cm.
Includes bibliographical references and index.
1. Reality television programs–Social aspects. 2. Reality television programs–
Psychological aspects. 3. Television viewers–Attitudes. I. Wood, Helen, 1972-
II. Title.
PN1992.8.R43S62 2012
791.45'655–dc23
2011043171

ISBN: 978-0-415-69370-7 (hbk)
ISBN: 978-0-415-69371-4 (pbk)
ISBN: 978-0-203-14423-7 (ebk)

Typeset in Baskerville
by Taylor & Francis Books

Printed and bound in Great Britain by the MPG Books Group

We would like to dedicate this book to:
Bev to Doreen, Ken and Jeremy
Helen to Max and Hannah

Contents

Acknowledgements

We would like to thank all the women who gave us their time and energy to bring this project to fruition. Especial thanks to Les Back and his family, Karen Wells, and to Nancy Thumim for her research support. Thanks especially to Margie Wetherell and Valerie Hey for invaluable support from this project's inception, and to Emily Nicholls, Lisa Taylor and Jeremy Anderson for reading the manuscript.

Thanks to the Economic and Social Research Council for funding the project 'Making Class through Televised Ethical Scenarios' (REF 148-25-0040) as part of the Identities Programme.

Bev and Helen would like to express their gratitude to Tracy James Burton for allowing us to use his artwork on the paperback cover. Amazing!

Bev would like to thank her inspirational colleagues and friends who make the pain and pleasure of writing worthwhile: Sara Ahmed, Sarah Franklin, Celia Lury, David Oswell, Kirsty Campbell, Alberto Toscano, Caroline Knowles, Ali Rooke, Michael Keith, Les Back, Lisa Blackman, Lisa Adkins, Les Moran, Jon Binnie, Pat Kirkham, Valerie Walkerdine, Rosemary Deem, Richard Phillips, Ruth Halliday, Nick Thoburn, Joanna Latimer, Joanne Hollows, Rolland Munro, Angela McRobbie, Jeanette Edwards, Sarah Green, Frances Pine, Steph Lawler, Imogen Tyler, Lauren Berlant, Elspeth Probyn, Kate Bedford, Mike Savage, Andrew Sayer, Diane Reay, Chris Griffin, Tania Lewis and Steve Cross.

I am grateful to all my friends and colleagues across Goldsmiths for producing such an interesting, quirky, challenging and stimulating environment, completely committed to real education. Included in this are my PhD students whom I have had the pleasure to supervise: Emma Jackson, Vik Loveday, Benny Lu, Sian Weston, Debbie Fallon, Kim Keith, Kim Allen, Luna Glucksberg, Patrick Turner, Mike Leary and Christy Kulz. There is nothing like the unexpected angle to keep one on one's toes. Bridget Ward and Lauren Sibley provided sanity in turbulent times for which I'm very grateful.

Thanks to Anna Loutfi and Allaine Cerwonka in Budapest for organizing visits, and to Tania Lewis in Melbourne and Elspeth Probyn for inviting me to Australia, likewise to Angel Lin in Hong Kong. Thanks to my Swedish friends who very kindly extended their hospitality and let me torture them as I developed my ideas during my stay in the superb Gender Studies Centre at Stockholm University: to Gunilla Bjeren and Birgetta Nay for making my stay possible, and thanks to Maria Karlsson, Ulrike Nillson, Annika Olsson, Fanny Ambjornsson, Ingeborg Svensson, Ulrika Dahl, Hillevi Ganetz, Johan Fornas, Sheila Ghosh, Anu Koivunen, Fateneh Farahani, Mark Graham, Tiina Rosenberg and Pia Laskar. My Danish, Finnish and Norwegian friends have also been very important to my work: Anne Dorte Christensen, Annick Prieur, Birte Siim, May-Len Skilbrei, Eeva Jokinen, Mikko Jakonen, Tuula Gordon, Harriet Allmark. My name 'Skeggs' means 'beard' in Scandinavian; I think it generates a connection. I was overwhelmed to receive honours from both Aalborg and Stockholm University. Thank you for all the invites to departments in the UK where I have also been given the liberty to try out ideas.

Thanks to my great friends Kath Moonan, Nickie Witham, Herms, Les M, NickT and Runa, Val Atkinson, Gerhard Compion, Hannelie Fourie and Debbie Coughlin.

To my amazing parents – Ken and Doreen Skeggs – who have always tried to teach me what is important and to stand against injustice: they are my inspiration. I still can't believe just how amazing is Jeremy Anderson.

And finally to Helen. We began our conversation about reality television seven years ago and have been through many turbulent times since then. But we hung on, knowing we had a project that was worth struggling over. Helen is one of the loveliest sharpest people in the world and has been a delight to work with.

Helen would like to thank colleagues at De Montfort University for providing a supportive environment to work these ideas out. Thank you especially to Diane Taylor for keeping me going. Many thanks go to Lisa Taylor for reading draft chapters and for keeping up the spirits.

Thank you for all the invitations to present this research at seminars which have contributed to this journey and to the final product. Special thanks to Katherine Sender for our conversations on audiences and for inviting me to Annenberg, Mats Trondman and Anna Lund for the invitation to Linnaeus University, Sweden, to Mikko Hautakangas for the invitation to the University of Jyvaskla, Finland, and to Diane Negra for the invitation to Dublin. Thanks to all those who attended the 'Media, Class and Value Symposium' at De Montfort in 2008 where our first rendering of the complete data was rehearsed.

Thanks to Rachel Moseley and Helen Wheatley who have put up with my endless anxieties and yet will still work with me! To Ann Gray who is still the greatest advocate of a cultural studies' approach to pedagogy.

To Vanessa Brown, Julie Hatton, Emma Rigby, Nicola Yeomans for forgiving my forgetful memory and still listening.

To my family as always, and to Pauline and Albert Wood for everything. Thanks to my beautiful boy Max and my new girl Hannah, who have brought so much to me during this journey to make it worth the while.

And finally to Bev – whose generosity, brilliance and energy is endless. I only hope I have been able to keep up. It's been emotional!

Introduction

Reacting to reality television

'The pig with the biggest mouth on TV has finally been nominated for eviction – and now **YOU** have the power to roast her.'

(*The Sun*, Showbiz Bizarre 3 July 2002)

'Jade – we hate you – the nation turns on thick racist bully'

(cited in *The Telegraph* Obituaries 22 March 2009)

'a racist pig-faced waste of blood and organs'

(TV presenter Jeremy Clarkson on Jade Goody, *Top Gear* Series 9 episode 1, 28 January 2007)

'she seems like a nasty old hag'

(*intergalacticwalrus* 4 April 2006, 11:56:39, http://www.mumsnet.com/ Talk/in_the_news/161473-lizzie-bardsley/AllOnOnePage, accessed 20 November 2011)

'Scourge of humanity who gives the majority of those who legitimately claim benefits a bad name.'

(*paolosgirl* 4 April 2006, 12:05:2, http://www.mumsnet.com/ Talk/in_the_news/161473-lizzie-bardsley/AllOn OnePage, accessed 20 November 2011)

Oh thank God. This woman is horrible – common, loud-mouthed and vile. She's the one who claimed massive amounts of benefit, a lot of it for her son who had bad asthma, but still didn't feel that it was inappropriate for her and her husband to smoke heavily around him. Who decides these people are 'celebrities'?

http://www.mumsnet.com/Talk/in_the_news/161473-lizzie-bardsley/ AllOnOnePage (Blogosphere, Mumsnet, comments on 2004 *Wife Swap* television participant Lizzie Bardsley)

The unremitting explosion of reality television across the schedules has become a sustainable global phenomenon generating considerable popular and political fervour. The zeal with which television executives seize on the easy replicability of formats is matched by the eagerness of audiences to present themselves as

television participants for others to watch and criticize. Yet it seems fairly irre-
futable that one of reality television's most notorious achievements has been to
spark fierce reaction in audiences, commentators, journalists and bloggers across
various sectors of the media sphere. The examples of vitriol above are directed
at two reality television participants – Jade Goody (*Big Brother*) and Lizzie
Bardsley (*Wife Swap*) – both white working-class women made famous via the
platform of reality television. These examples are chosen because Jade and
Lizzie appear with regularity in our conversations with British audiences about
their own reactions to reality television. But we might just as well cite the outpouring of invective towards Kate Gosselin, the 'octo-mum' (see Weber 2011),
or the love–hate reaction to *Jersey Shore* star Snooki in the USA, to see similar
emotional tirades directed at this new genre of reality-celebrity women. Headlines and posts like the above come easily to anyone doing a quick search on
reality television across the internet, but it is noticeable that it is much harder to
find similar invective directed at men.

What seems *most* distasteful about the apparent success of these women is
their ability to use the performances of their bodies, gestures and language
as themselves to their own material advantage (it was reported in the *Daily
Mail* on 8 March 2010 that Jade left her two sons £3 million on her death
in 2009). This relatively new arena of mediated self-performance is big business
at the same time that it is fraught with gender and class politics. Set Jade's
fortune, generated through a six-year cycle of post-programme celebrity magazine and programme deals, against the annual profits of the independent television production companies that make reality television, and we can see the
directional flow of most of the economic capital generated in this way. Endemol,
the makers of *Big Brother*, saw profits soar in 2005 by 30% to £57 million, which
is largely attributed to the success of *Big Brother*, with UK revenues cited at £118
million (*Broadcast* 23 February 2006). Even during the recession its company
director got a 35% pay rise to £2.8 million (*London Evening Standard* 7 July
2010) and despite Endemol hitting hard times this year (as its 2007 purchase was
handled by Lehmann Brothers and *Big Brother* has been axed from Channel 4 in
the UK) it still paid its company director 10 million euros to mark his third
anniversary in the post (*Financial Times* 24 June 2011). RDF, the makers of *Wife
Swap*, announced £5.3 million profits in 2005, largely due to the success of
Wife Swap and *Secret Millionaire* (*Broadcast* 23 May 2006). Whilst the company was
apparently hit hard after the scandal in which the documentary about the
Queen was found to have been irresponsibly edited, the parent company Zodiak
still had a revenue of £99.3 million and was still able to sell RDF for some
£52 million (Zodiak media group press archive 2010).

Of course, most reality television participants are not able to gain further
media exposure in the same way as Jade Goody and most 'ordinary' appearances on reality television are usually unpaid – participants are often given
nominal fees and perks like nice hotel rooms, champagne and taxis. Even in the
newer US reality programmes like *The Hills* and *Jersey Shore* where participants or

'person-characters' are given high fees per programme, the nature of their contracts (which are largely kept secret) means that they must remain outside of the
performers' union (Hearn 2010). The media industries have, of course, always
been keen to evoke new responses and reactions in its audiences in the interests
of finding new markets: this is its raison d'être. Reality television has opened
up this avenue further, developing numerous new exportable formats in which
non-paid actors react to a varying range of contrived situations, explicating
diverse emotions from elation to despair across our screens. This has provided
the perfect business model for a television industry struggling to find new revenue streams as it faces declining income from advertisers and competition from
the internet, among an array of digital media in which the limits seem to be
endless.

This new landscape sparked our intervention and larger research project
which form the content of this book. On one level we were curious about the
relationship between the televising of intensified emotion and the ability of producers to generate financial capital from virtually free labour, what did this
mean for our understanding of exploitation? But we were also intrigued by the
role that so called 'ordinary' people were playing in this landscape, where *self*
representation seemed to bring new sets of questions for media analysts interested in the politics of representation. Concerning us further still were the gender
and class politics that we can see at work in the vitriol that reality television
sparked across the broader media and cultural sphere. It seemed to us that many
reality television participants were being characterized as 'failing' and in need of
transformation. But whilst journalists in the US and the UK were describing this
form of television as 'class pantomimes' or old style 'class morality plays',
academics were locating the genre as part of a broader social and economic climate
of so-called neo-liberal individualization, a technology of governmentality, where
the emphasis upon spectacular selfhood often diverted attention away from
the structural conditions in which anyone can freely perform 'being themselves'.
These first observations echoed analyses of the political character of changing
class relations where arguments about class as structure were being displaced by
rhetoric about selves, souls and psychologized dispositions.

Thus we responded to a call by the UK Economic and Social Research
Council for research projects to investigate 'Identities and Social Action'. They
wanted projects which 'deepened our understanding of the processes involved in
the making of selves, groups and communities'.

> The programme focused on the attempts of people with very different tra-
> jectories and from very different contexts to build communities and 'liveable
> lives'. These were the key questions: How do people construct a sense of
> identity these days? What are the consequences of the identity paths chosen?
> How do identity choices intensify or ease social conflict? What is it like to
> build an identity in situations of social exclusion?
>
> (http://www.identities.org.uk/)

We are therefore interested in reality television as a site through which person-hood is 'made' in the interests of capital and we now seem to be in tune with some academic commentary which is arguing that these new forms of perfor-mance are changing the media's traditional relationship to representation. If, as Turner (2010) suggests, media production companies are now the ideological 'authors' of their own interests, rather than those of the state, we need to rethink the media's role in questions of ideology as presented in traditional media analysis.

The premise of the 'individualization thesis' as part of a neo-liberal politics proposed by authors like Beck (1992) and Giddens (1991) offered the starting point for many of the research projects in the ESRC programme, but it has a particular potency for our project on reality television. Television appeared to be offering lessons in individualization across our screens, exposing in numerous ways, from make-overs to game shows, incitements for 'ordinary' people to per-form their own self-awareness, self-work and ultimately self-transformation, operating as a technology of governmentality, and making the self's value visible to others. It offered instructions to audiences which are useful in a current neo-liberal epoch where the motif of self-responsibility assists in the withdrawal of state support and in generating bodies ripe for the conditions of the flexible labour market (see Ouellette and Hay 2008). But it is another step to assume that governmentality works and we wanted to interrogate this assumption, and television's role in processes of 'individualization', with audiences. The almost wholesale seduction of media analysts by ideas about governmentality we felt was problematic as it drew attention towards the individual as an insular and singular unit rather than the social as a process in formation. We are reminded of the words of Raymond Williams when he says that television 'is at once an intention and an effect of a particular social order' (1975:128).

In the empirical work we discuss here we observed a great deal of playfulness and resistance to 'lessons' of governance. During the process of the research we therefore became increasingly cautious in our use of the concept self and its association with a singular subject, changing it to the idea of personhood as the project progressed. We had already identified the self as a bourgeois political project developed to consolidate middle class interests which located the working class as its constitutive limit, and had shown how even the term subjectivity had emerged through radically different classed routes (Skeggs 2004a). We were concerned not to reproduce this history, instead using the term personhood to refer to legal, social and moral states generated through encounters with others (Bishop Merrill 1998; Munro 2005; Strathern 1991).

This presents intriguing questions around how relations of personhood are relayed and circulated through the specificities of reality television's *form* – its immediacy and its emotionality – which need to be answered in order to understand what is behind some of the force and vehemence of the reactions cited above, and whether they find fertile ground in audiences. There is some-thing deeply personal and intrusive about the new directions that reality television takes in filming participants in their most intimate of moments, which is extending what we know about the use of melodrama as a moral device. We asked, what reactions does reality television incite and are these potential reactions as divisive as it might seem? Since those on the screen were no longer 'actors' in the traditional sense, how are audiences responding to so-called 'ordinary' people on television? How do we react to so many people breaking down, fronting up, tearing apart, dominating, empathizing, being humiliated and shamed and seemingly laying bare their raw emotion for our entertainment? Do we feel sad when others are sad? Or are we relieved by the knowledge that our circumstances might be better? As reality television extends into the experiences of the everyday, it makes dramatic and often shocking the mundane aspects of our intimate relations, inviting us as viewers into a volatile and visceral arena of mediated morality.

It is useful just to remind ourselves of the various layers involved in the verb 'react' evident from its entry in the *OED*.

1. Produce reciprocal or responsive action (esp. action and reaction); (Chem. and Phys) reacting of one substance etc. with another; CHAIN reaction.
2. Response of organ etc. to external stimulus; responsive feeling (*what was his reaction to the news?*); immediate or first impression.
3. Occurrence of condition after interval of opposite (e.g. glow felt after cold bath, depression after excitement).
4. (Mil.) counter-stroke.
5. Tendency to oppose change or return to former system esp. in politics.
6. Propulsion by emitting jet of particles etc. in direction opposite to that of desired motion.

Reaction thus refers to an action set in motion by a trigger, and importantly that response is registered physically. It is most often *immediate* and instantaneous and it resides in *bodily* form, in order to be *felt*. At some level reaction also occurs in the interaction between opposing forces, propelling elements to different 'sides'. Therefore, in thinking about 'reactions' to reality television we are trying to think with another register to that usually adopted by media audience research that addresses how audiences cognitively 'read', 'make meaning' and 'interpret' media texts. Whilst we draw on audience research which has used the framework of emotion to understand meaning, we want to take this a stage further in order to understand how reality television's particular form of dramatic mediation – with its emphasis upon the immediate, the everyday and the indeterminate – locates its reactions *within* the reactions of audiences. Thus we are interested in the workings of 'affect' as a force in the social relations between audiences and television. As our research developed we realized that affect, through its various forms of transmission, makes people do/not do things. Although we know of the huge body of literature that debates the precise meaning of affect, for the purposes of this book we define affect as the feelings that produce an effect, and we deploy Deleuze's (1978) reading of Spinoza. Spinoza notes how some social encounters can leave us feeling diminished, thereby reducing our capacity to act, whilst others may make us feel joyful and powerful. For Deleuze the body is an ensemble of relations composed via the power of being affected. We use the term emotion to refer to the codification of affect, when feeling (being affected) becomes translated and attached to an idea, such as fear or joy. The codification process (the translation of an affect into an idea) became key to how we understood the relationship between audiences and text, but more importantly, the connections between people and other people.

Therefore, if the boundaries of audience and performer are being eroded in television's new landscape, and reality television is charged by intensified affect, we want to think about how reactions abound and rebound through the social experiences of viewers. This is not a complete re-writing of the scripts of audience research, but it is we think, a distinct re-emphasis, charged to us by the very form of reality television. The subtitle of this book is 'Performance, Audience and Value' – these are elements of a critical sensibility which we think are all captured by that verb, 'react'. To hyphenate re-act is to emphasize 'act' again which points us to reactions' relationship to notions of performance. Nigel Thrift (2004) develops Marcuse's (1964) 'performance principle' to detail the media's extensive involvement in making and capturing spaces for emotional performance. For instance, he notes how politicians have to be extremely careful as most aspects of their lives are now subject to performance review and measurement: remember when George Bush emoted wrongly at the news of 9/11? If people are expected to constantly *perform* their value, and many social sites are theatres for the scrutiny of that performance, we need to understand how the media makes areas of life that were previously invisible visible and subject to public judgement.

Of course any performance requires an audience and we are interested in the ways in which audiences are invoked into this level of intimate display. We acknowledge that conducting audience research itself involves inviting certain performances from our respondents as part of the specific research encounter. Thus our research involves analyses of performances *on* reality television, but also performances produced *in* reaction to television, *in* interviews, text-in-action viewing sessions and in focus groups. This performance actually led to us recognizing a specific affective reaction which led to the development of a new method to understand people's relationship to television: the affective textual encounter. If 'performance' is to the twenty-first century what Foucault's 'discipline' was to the twentieth, as John McKenzie (2001) suggests, this book attempts a new agenda for combining social and media theory.

Finally, and perhaps most importantly, our third structuring principle in this book relates to questions of value, how it is produced, distributed, extracted, claimed and performed. We problematize and develop traditional understandings of value. The first is straightforward: it is the value that is extracted from people (usually through paid labour) and turned into financial capital. Just as others have shown how television has found new ways of exploiting people and extracting value from the commodification of surveillance (Andrejevic 2004, 2010, 2011) and the promotion of moral entrepreneurship (Hollows and Jones 2010; Illouz 2003, 2007; Illouz and Wilf 2008), we show how 'free' enforced performances enable the commodification of bodies and practices. Paradoxically reality television has found a formula for extracting profit from the people with the least person-value.

But it is not just the extraction of economic value that interests us. Nor do we draw on the traditional distinction between the economic and the moral (Graeber 2001); rather we look at how the economic works through the moral and the cultural, entwined through value practices and ideas about what makes a person. Our second value configuration examines how reality television requires participants to perform their value, generating a semiotics of value that invites us as viewers into modes of evaluation. Gayatri Spivak (1985) calls for an expanded understanding of 'the textuality of value' to see how expressions of value move through different circuits of value, from the abstract to the concrete, from the person in their material relational location to the different expressions of value. To understand the value of a person's performance we begin our analysis with the model we had previously developed (Skeggs 2004a, 2011) from Bourdieu's (1987) metaphors of capital. We used this to identify the different forms of cultural, economic, social and symbolic capital which people *accrue over time in different volumes and compositions*, noting how only some people can access the capitals which can be converted into value. Value is only known when people enter fields of exchange for capital conversion and the value is realized. When reality television participants enter arenas for exchange, value is extracted from them through their performance, but they also have to display their value to others through the conditions created by programme formats. It is in the identification of lack of capitals that the format of self-transformation operates, requiring people to reveal their deficit in order to learn how to accrue. But, just like Bourdieu's schema, on reality television it is only high cultural capital that carries value, everything else is a zero-sum.[1]

But what Bourdieu cannot account for is how those, excluded from the opportunities to access, realize and invest their capital, generate value for themselves. Are they as represented on reality television (reference the vitriolic comments earlier) always the zero-sum of culture – the constitutive limit to what is 'normatively' recognized as valuable? What about the intimate fields of exchange that represent a great proportion of our lives? As many feminist critiques of Bourdieu have noted (Adkins and Skeggs 2004; Lovell 2000, 2003; McNay 1999; Moi 1991) gender does not work in the same way as class, as a field of exchange, and cannot simply be reduced to a minor form of cultural capital.

The gendered fields of the family, femininity and motherhood are key sites for value formation where capitals have a different significance and exchange value, as has been noted by feminist television scholars such as Charlotte Brunsdon (1981), who first pointed out how the viewing pleasures of soap opera are contingent upon the culturally constructed skills associated with femininity and the conduct of personal life, whilst Tania Modleski (1983) posited that the multi-faceted nature of the soap required multiple identifications of the viewer which were akin to the 'ideal mother'. Television has often been associated with women's cultural competences which have been prized in genres that sit comfortably with the form as a domestic medium (Ang and Hermes 1996; Brunsdon 1991, 2003; Gray 1992; Hobson 1990; Wood 2009). Lifestyle or 'women's television' carefully calibrates the value of women's lives, establishing the terms for exchange of labour and investment in practices such as appearance and care, but it is dismissed in the dominant symbolic register of cultural taste as 'trash' in the same way as reality television. Hence we want to understand how female television audiences understand their own and others' value through the textual mediation of the value practices that make up their own lives.

Our third configuration of value therefore examines relational value, which in the personal sphere is gained through conditional temporal transactions – the affective and the aesthetic. We say temporal because women's aesthetic value depreciates over time and emotional labour such as love and care has to be continually performed. Likewise, this temporal analysis demonstrates the complex forms of exchange that cut across gender and class: for instance, women who have invested aesthetically in their bodies (and bodies can be a value that can be capitalized) can produce a return through the exchange relation of marriage to access economic security. But this security may be precarious as the capitalization of femininity de-values over time and lack of constant investment in the exchange through emotional and domestic labour may result in the woman also losing economic value following divorce. Investment in the future aestheticization of bodies for exchange may or may not pay off, it is not straightforward future accrual of value (in the Bourdieu model) although it is institutionalized and legitimated through the marriage contract and hence property law. It is also normalized for to not be feminine, married and/or a mother is to be pathologized. This is about being positioned as the constitutive limit to value in the dominant symbolic, although for many people to be non-feminine, unmarried and childless may be highly pleasurable and a rich source of relational value outside of the dominant symbolic. We need to be clear that relational value traverses the accrual and relational forms, often offering an alternative source of value for those denied access to field for exchange accrual in many cases throughout our research.

So, to our understanding of the extracting, performing and relating aspects of value we add two temporal dimensions. First, making sure *one does not lose* value. The prevention of loss is central to the understandings of those who only have very limited access to the fields of exchange for converting capitals. Investment in value practices may not just be about moving forward through social space, as Bourdieu imagines, but about resisting a reverse trajectory back into past conditions, or about *holding fast to the present*. But second, thinking *beyond* the exchange value form, into practices that cannot be converted into value, that just are, non-exchangeable values. This enables us to escape from the traditional theoretical constraints of thinking within an accrual model of capital and expand our understanding of value into other dimensions of life that offer other sources of value to people (Skeggs 2011). Working out these formations was absolutely central to our research as performances of relationality were key to our respondents as they displayed their own value-claims in reactions to texts. This also enabled us to see how class and gender transact, as our respondents' affective authority claims in one sphere were used to offset devaluation in another.

Through our interviews we mapped not only our respondents' access (or not) to capitals, but how they defined, defended and performed value-practices outside of the traditional fields for exchange. We were also interested in how these practices materialized in the current historical conjuncture of 'performing oneself' – which means displaying ones' value publicly, a feature considered central to contemporary legitimacy. We thus wanted to place all forms of value practices, claims and conversions alongside each other, to generate a broader picture of the circulation of value more generally, to see where value circulates and is realized by public performances and reactions that eventually consolidate as 'person value' (See Skeggs 2011 for a full development of this model).

Through our audience findings we demonstrate how television participants *and* audiences are located within these extended 'circuits of value', helping us to see why it is that vitriolic reactions 'stick' where they do, and why certain figures and bodies are loaded with more invective than others. But also to identify the challenges that are made to attempts to make only certain forms of personhood appear with value.

The book therefore works with three different spatial and temporal configurations of value: a model of *extraction from the person* (surplus value extraction from labour power – time and energy, the traditional model of capitalism), a model of *accruing value to* the person (noting the time and energy spent on self development in the making of the 'subject of value' of most theorists of self and subjectivity, including Bourdieu[2]), including defence of value, and *relationality* (time and energy with and for others, which can include dispersal of value to others and alternative forms of value). If we pay attention to how these operate empirically we can see how a mediated economy of personhood takes shape. One of the benefits of this multi-dimensional of value is that it enables us to understand ambivalence – how people hold contradictory positions in their responses to television (and life more generally), which is a feature so often problematized but rarely fully theorized in television audience research. How do we explain the love/hate relationships that we have with (reality television) texts where we experience pleasure and disapproval simultaneously? One way to interrogate this may be through a broader understanding of how we navigate circuits of value. Attempts to gain value from capitals are rational imperatives. No matter how much Bourdieu (1992) denies that his is a rational action model, the future propelling subject that works on accruing capitals is premised on a knowing self-interested subject (Sayer 2005; Skeggs 2004a, 2004b). Whereas, the model of person value that we propose can be accruing, defending and relational and is based on connecting to others not just, or even for, social or (moral) cultural capital, but for affective reasons, for connection beyond self-interest – for love, care and connection. The dispositions to continually invests in one's self (accrual) and to relationality (when not operating in the interests of accruing social capital) are not necessarily compatible, but a person is likely to operationalize a range of value practices in which the limits will be set by access to social and cultural space and possibilities for investments over time.[3] We can see this most vividly, enabled by our methodology, in the contradictory reactions a viewer can have to the same television participant, as they see the different value practices contained within a person's value performance. Our audience respondents revealed the intensity of their connections to these different investments, which depend upon the circuits of value in which they are already located, enabling us to identify how class and gender both constitute and disrupt investments in value practices. And as we argue more fully in the conclusion to the book, stabilizing this ambivalence through these investments is a key imperative to the workings of ideology.

The book therefore has two interconnected frameworks. The first draws upon television and media studies to map the debates into which the book enters, including issues about format, reality, performativity and spectacle. The second framework enters debates in social, cultural and feminist theory about public intimacy, personhood and value. By bringing these two frames together we extend the discussions about the significance of performance, the aesthetics of value, and the role of capital and governance in an understanding of new (mediated) political formations. The incitements and techniques used on reality television by which people are expected to perform their own person value can be seen to have a wider purchase across sites of work, welfare, law and other forms of public and popular culture, enabling us to locate reality television within a wider social realm.

We therefore want to tease out the relationship between new mediated incitements to perform with the broader social relations in which value is made. Our fundamental questions are: in what ways are television participants called to perform themselves and what reactions are invited? How should we understand the circulation of feeling generated through reality television in terms of its impact upon our forms of social life? Does it generate more divisiveness, as in the tabloid and blogosphere examples above, or potentially more understanding as we see people fall apart? What capacity is there for connecting to others in this new mediated theatre of person-performance? And importantly, what do investigations of these questions tell us about the configuration of gender and class relations in the current conjuncture?

Chapter outlines

In the opening chapter, 'From representation to intervention', we make a pathway through the now extensive literature about reality television and discuss the genre's role in effecting a significant shift in television culture, whilst firmly keeping in view the form's continuities with older traditions. We set up the debates which form a large body of the critical work on the genre that discuss its relation to the 'real' through connections to documentary forms and to melodrama. We make a case for considering the politics of performance via sensation and emotion. As we have noted many writers locate the genre within the current emphasis on neo-liberal governance, with an imperative to self-work through the pedagogic and surveillance aspects of the genre. Whilst this makes sense, these trends are not new but part of longer gendered and classed histories of mediated telling, display and observation, which complicate the 'nowness' of some explanations of reality television. Theories of governmentality do not wholly account for what has been seen as most radically suggestive of reality television – its emphasis upon immediacy, intimacy and indeterminacy. Reality television has been described as a genre involved more in 'intervention' than 'representation' (Bratich 2007; Brunsdon 2003), because of its emphasis upon affect and reaction over any determined meaning. This was certainly the case for our research where audiences as potential performers are located in a different relationship with texts as they broker a new interaction between relations on television and their own social experiences. We show how reality television in refiguring reaction urges us to forge an approach which is sensitive to developments in both media, social and cultural theory and it is to the latter that we turn in Chapter 2.

In Chapter 2, 'Performance and the value of personhood', we map out a broader historical social and cultural context into which the current televised emphasis upon performing personhood enters. By understanding reality television as a new form of public intimacy we reveal it to be an emotionally saturated site for the display and establishment of a person's value. Initially we turn to social theory to help explore this phenomenon as theories of individualization and identity have become central to a great deal of social theorizing. For instance, the idea of reflexive biography has been promoted as the technique to narrativize our sense of self to gain and display authority and value (Beck 1992; Giddens 1991). Other theorists, have suggested that we are now in a period of 'compulsory individuality' where the terms of moral legitimacy have shifted from traditional sources of authority (religion, the patriarchal family and the state) to the ability of the self to tell itself as a source of moral good (Strathern 1992; Taylor 1994). Thus the opening out of the self to public judgement is one of the ways in which personhood becomes evaluated. All of this feeds into the numerous ways in which the performance of behaviour is increasingly incited but also regulated across fields such as law, sexuality and the media where performances can have certain 'returns'.

We propose a framework in which the opening out of intimacy produces a new form of economy – an economy of personhood – in which intimate bodies, parts and practices are opened out to evaluation and exploitation, generating what counts as worthwhile with value. This is an economy that not only produces value through traditional forms of exploitation and labour (providing audiences for advertisers and delivering intimate surveillance knowledge to corporations, as identified by Andrejevic (2004)), but also by making the performance of intimacy into a commodity (Illouz 2007). We detail the intricate flow between calculation, expectation and return in the spheres of public and 'private', especially in the arenas of sexuality and motherhood, where the textual terms of exchange have a long history in developing 'models for mating' in many cultural forms (such as literature).

The repeated incitements to demonstrate one's moral interiority as a sign of value is also shown to be a product of a particular history, in which discourses from psychoanalysis and religion value-code certain modes of telling as valuable in order to legitimate middle class moral authority and interests. These insights are used to explore the role of reality television in the circulation of 'person value' detailing the significance of performance to the social relations of affect, in order to consider how both television participants and audiences are implicated. Many of the literatures drawn upon here do not often make it into current analyses of reality television, and throughout we regularly point to the suggestive connections these theories have with various programmes and sub-genre. We use both Chapters 1 and 2 as a framework for the forthcoming textual and audience analyses.

In Chapter 3, 'Textual intimacies', we offer up textual mapping and close textual analyses to interrogate the social dynamics of person-performance. We analyse the exponential rise of reality television during our research period (2004–8) by counting and charting the various types of format across the numerous intimate fields in which reality television intervenes, showing how personhood is made into economically useful 'units' which can be exchanged in the textual development of formats for the reality television economy. Detailing the programmes we analysed and the ones we watched with our respondents, we describe how programme formats and their 'engines', or conceits, contribute to how the telling and performance of the self is circumscribed by class and gender relations.

We also reveal the significance of the organization of time to the shaping of the good and bad (classed) person. Some programmes such as *Wife Swap* call on participants to 'react' to contrived situations immediately. In these moments time and space is compressed and participants are divorced from any understanding of their histories or emotional and cultural resources, letting them appear baffled, confused and unable to control the situation. In contrast, other programmes such as *Get a New Life* use a documentary style, developed over much longer stretches of time and space to follow a protagonist who is able to reflexively narrate and demonstrate control over their destiny in a more complete and morally authored 'architecture of the self' (Bennett 2003). In this chapter we also discuss *Faking It,* which by intense focusing in on gestures and bodies, paradoxically displays how cultural capital cannot be acquired by a quick fix but requires time, possibilities for investment and access to specific spaces to develop. We demonstrate how the affects of confidence and entitlement are almost impossible to simulate, showing how (following Bourdieu) skills must always be connected to the 'how' knowledge (the episteme) that underpins their use.

This forensic focusing on bodies and practices, particularly in make-over programmes like *What Not to Wear* and *You Are What You Eat,* extends the melodramatic sensibility and our analysis of time further. The forensic detailing of parts of bodies, modes of deportment, style and aesthetics come to stand in for a self that has *not* invested in itself. We call this attribution of value 'metonymic morality', which through prolonged visual attention invites our judgement as audiences. Our judgement is also incited by the close-up. The long-held close up invites a reaction *to* reaction which we can see is taken up by our audiences. These relays of reaction enable us to identify the points at which our audiences evaluate participants alongside themselves; evaluations that can often reach beyond some of the dominant symbolic coding of reality television participants. These textual features become the clues to exactly where, how and why our audiences responded. The forensic detailing and evaluation of everyday intimate practices is one of the ways reality television explodes the normative nature of gender by visualizing every element of the performative, making conscious that which is usually an unconscious habitual performance. In the next chapter we detail the methods we used to align our textual analyses with our audience research.

This chapter, 'Reacting to reality television: methodology', explains how we were able to make the connections between text and audience. We outline our empirical research material which was drawn from four different groups each containing ten women from different ages and social backgrounds (Black, South Asian and white, working-class and middle-class). To supplement our textual analysis we used multi-methods: interviewing to socially locate respondents and understand their media usage, 'text-in-action' viewing sessions (a method developed by Wood 2007) to locate key moments and types of engagement with the programmes, and focus groups to analyse the way public discussion proceeds on issues raised about reality television by the previous methods. Our multi-method approach enabled us to see how different methods *create* alternative platforms through which research participants could resource their responses and reactions. It also allowed us to understand responses to the materiality of the television object temporally and spatially: some hide the television, some have it on 24/7.

We do not take our research respondents to be representative but indicative of how people engage with the televised imperatives for person-performance. We were interested in the forms and types of connection they made with the television: enabling us to examine how people place themselves within the drama of the programmes; how they insert themselves into, or distance themselves from, the intimate relationships displayed; how they feel about characters on television in relation to themselves, friends and family; and how they enact their reactions to the participants. The way in which our respondents articulated their relationship to the television and to the reality television genre replayed some of theoretical assumptions about access to the cultural resources people can use to *tell* and *perform* themselves, in this case to the researcher. But we also found profound differences in the relationships that the groups had to television: a working class nonchalant relationship that is more integrated into family and sociability, whilst the middle class displayed the need to control their viewing as part of their regulation of their time which they needed to invest wisely.

We were interested in all reactions and even minimal linguistic responses enabled us to tease out 'the affective textual encounter'. By interpreting *all* the affective responses our audiences made, their tuts, gasps, minimal responses, etc., we were able to align these responses with the manipulation of affect in texts. The three different methodological encounters with our respondents enabled us to capture immediate reactions, linguistic responses *and* the post-hoc rationalizations that can be collected in interviews and via the public forum of focus groups. These multiple reactions and responses can also be understood in relation to the social location of the respondent and offer alternative means for our audiences to mobilize the cultural resources and discourses which shape their reactions. By drawing upon such detail we can see how viewers move between affective reactions to cognitive judgement, revealing investments and channelling ambivalence, in ways which tease how out how reactions are both *provisional* and yet *located*. It is to the contingent and social aspects of these encounters that we now turn in Chapters 5, 6 and 7, which detail some of our empirical findings.

Chapter 5, entitled 'Affect and ambiguity, not governmentality', begins to detail how the affective and emotional attachments of our audiences to reality television participants present a complex, powerful and shifting set of dynamics. We begin with a discussion of affect as a process, which involves movement between the sensual and the material. Our findings are used to complicate arguments drawn from textual analyses which suggest that reality television incorporates viewers into governmentality, inviting the audience to take part in its lessons as 'viewer-pupils'. Only one of our groups seemed to consistently acknowledge any type of learning from television and on closer inspection we saw how the discourses of life-learning seem to be inculcated more to re-evaluate a past, a narrative produced through the experience of migration. Much more frequent across our groups was a rejection of the aspects of pedagogic instruction in television, taking pleasure in resisting the positions of experts, or sometimes enjoying the 'happiness' of participants.

Thus, we argue, the affective dimensions of viewing intervene in the pedagogic invitation. An affective connection can offset some of the negative symbolic inscription of television participants. We show how by making a 'constitutive actualisation', by placing oneself 'as if' in the same situation our respondents were able to 'look through' the image to make a situated connection to television participants. This connection may disrupt any straightforward interpretation of 'meaning' associating instead with 'mattering' (Kavka 2008). However, we are not arguing that this means reality television's affect works beyond the social in ways that only perpetually individuate (as in some arguments about the power of affect) since affect is a social force. Rather, we argue for a sustained analysis of the 'movement' between affect and cognition and the ambiguities produced. What we find is that the women are involved in complicated processes of emotional management which have long histories in women's culture and which suture the affective to the moral. Our viewers can move seamlessly between showing empathy and care on the one hand and judgement and condemnation on the other, revealing their investments in the different configurations of value as they locate themselves 'as if' in the same predicaments as the television participants. Whilst in this chapter we show how affect generates ambivalence in relation to a gendered politics of care, in the next chapter we look at how audiences attempt to generate ontological security and certainty by attaching affective states to moral authority.

Chapter 6, 'From affect to authority: the making of the moral person', then discusses the ways in which reality television invites audiences to take sides and to produce themselves as persons of value. We discuss the way in which our respondents speak *schadenfreude* to assuage the uncertainties set in motion by affect, reassuring themselves that their lives 'are not like that'. We then discuss some of the patterns of reactions that emerge from our text-in-action data. Our middle class women often produce commentary displaying their ability to perform abstract speculation and draw upon their own cultural capital to critique television experts and the television production, but also to show care for participants. They were much less likely to be drawn into the drama, having learnt to 'read representations' and hold the form at a distance. Two of our groups seemed to offer the most emotive responses in relation to gaining value through asserting authority. They used their investment in relationships and experience of motherhood to interact with the programmes in the present, 'as if' they were in the situation, sometimes even entering the frame of programme, performing and re-animating aspects of the drama on television. Our most verbally vitriolic reactions came from working class mothers towards women most like themselves (in terms of capitals and resources) but who had made different 'choices' re investments in the future.

We are reminded of the arguments about the relations of proximity that produce affect – where a point of contact must be felt in order for the pulling away that an affect like disgust involves. In these heightened moments our respondents directly share the same deictic frame as the television, so close to the image that they take part in a class 'masquerade'. We use Mary Ann Doane's (1982) term here and adapt it to account for the women's feelings as they react to their over-presence in the image (in a programme like *Wife Swap*) in acts of masochism expressed as maternal martyrdom. These acts can be understood within current UK neo-liberal politics whereby full-time mothers are depicted as a drain on the nation and encouraged to go to work. For those who have invested in the full-time care of their children as a source of moral authority and the 'unlikely' opportunity (high unemployment rates) to access low-wages and long hours, defending their choice against accusations of value degradation is understandable. Therefore we can understand how defensive reactions (to the impossibility of capital accrual): the refusal of that which is refused, according to Bourdieu, can be pleasurable public performances of person value in which a position on the moral high ground is taken and authority asserted. We then explain these differences through an analysis of 'affective economies' (Ahmed 2004) that are ultimately *socially* distributed, which align some groups and interests with and against others, but which also explains the intensities between feelings and social location evoked by the text.

The final empirical chapter, 'The productive person: recognizing labour and value', pulls together data from all three elements of the empirical research to consider the feminist debates on the expansion of public cultures and intimacy (Berlant 1997, 2000, 2008) by asking what it means to explicitly visualize feminized domestic and emotional labour on television. On the one hand such a visualization legitimates women's experience but it also simultaneously reconfigures women's responsibilities and worth in new terms: such as new demands for the 'concerted cultivation' of children (Gillies 2005; Lareau 2003); communication with and attention to partners; increased attention to appearance; disciplining the body; and developing performance at work. We examine the relationship between longer moral historical legacies towards 'labour' and newer governmental imperatives to perform the 'self-work ethic' (Heelas 2002). Spending time, investment and energy on aesthetic and affective labour was central to the expert advice promoted on most reality television programmes. Finding out about the women in our study and their relationship to television we discovered very different time uses: our middle class respondents were concerned never to waste time. We realized time, energy and capacity use (labour) was absolutely central to the judgements our respondents made about television participants, themselves and others. For instance, by making 'constitutive actualizations' of their own experiences the self-work initiative was repeatedly challenged through an evaluation of the real time that self-investment takes. Similarly in relationship programmes like *Wife Swap* the women question the emotional management and practical labour put into relationships as wasted time, recognizing the gendered power dynamics of domestic labour. Whilst neo-liberalism encourages us all to re-orient ourselves around the labour market, enterprising ourselves 'up' (du Gay 1986), the moral authority gained from motherhood, often acts as a powerful refusal to the call.

Class distinctions also became apparent in the way our working class participants often valued the uncomplaining and indefatigable performance of the labour of reality television participants for, 'just getting on with it', an assessment tied to earlier findings about reality television audiences detecting authenticity and pretentiousness. Our middle class respondents expressed antagonism towards reality television participants who received 'something for nothing' by just being themselves, without the investment of time and energy through traditional routes such as education and work. In contrast there was a good deal of defence of infamous working class participants such as Jade Goody for using the 'opportunity structure' of television to gain economic value, in order to offset the daily 'ducking and diving' required to put food on the table.

Finally, we discuss how reality television's ultimate conceit in expounding the self-work ethic is to deny the cultural knowledge required to put skills into practice – separating out the logic of skills from their underlying episteme. When our middle class viewers see this unhinged in *Faking It* they initially feel empathy for the reality television participant as they connect with his struggles to perform, recognizing their own experiences in similar work-placed situations. But in their post-hoc rationalization of the programme, however, we see them re-align his failure to *perform* with his failure to *do* properly and begin to question his abilities, allowing us again to see the difference between 'immanent' affective connections made to participants and retrospective cognitive assessments which might otherwise support the overall thesis of governmentality. If reality television is involved in pedalling an ideology of self-work then it is met by our audiences in diverse ways where they authorize themselves from within their own circuits of value. This economy of personhood has a long classed and gendered history, allowing us to see the nuances between our textual and audience analysis.

And finally we draw these arguments together in the conclusion challenging current understandings of governmentality, performativity and ideology, showing how engaging audiences in tournaments of value is key to reacting to television. Our audiences have enabled us to cut through some of the debates that assume that television works in a particular way. The purpose of the book is to detail what television does as it intervenes in people's lives.

Notes

1 Morality may operate as a form of cultural capital if it can be traded to gain a realizable capital value. For instance, we have previously shown how in struggles over 'queer' space propriety can be converted into property (Moran and Skeggs 2001; Moran *et al.* 2004).
2 (Skeggs 2004c) maps out all the dominant theories of the self which are premised upon an understanding of the subject that *can* accrue capital value.
3 Huge thanks to Jeremy Anderson for patiently thrashing this idea out over time.

References

Adkins, L. and Skeggs, B. 2004 *Feminism After Bourdieu*, Oxford: Blackwell.

Ahmed, S. 2004 'Affective Economies', *Social Text* 22(2): 117–39.

Andrejevic, M. 2004 *Reality TV: the Work of Being Watched*, Oxford: Rowman and Littlefield.

——2010 'Reading the Surface: Body Language and Surveillance' *Culture Unbound: Journal of Current Cultural Research*, Vol. 2, Linkoping: Linkoping University Electronic Press.

——2011 'Managing the Borders: Classed Mobility on Security-Themed Reality TV', in H. Wood and B. Skeggs (eds) *Reality Television and Class*, London: BFI/Palgrave.

Ang, I. and Hermes, J. 1996 'Gender and/in Media Consumption', in J. Curran and M. Gurevitch (eds) *Mass Media and Society*, 2nd Edition, London: Arnold.

Beck, U. 1992 *Risk Society: Towards a New Modernity*, London: Sage.

Bennett, T. 2003 'The Invention of the Modern Cultural Fact: Toward a Critique of the Critique of Everyday Life', in E. B. Silva and T. Bennett (eds) *Contemporary Culture and Everyday Life*, Durham: Sociology Press.

Berlant, L. 1997 *The Queen of America Goes to Washington City: Essays on Sex and Citizenship*, Durham and London: Duke University Press.

——2000 'The Subject of True Feeling: Pain, Privacy, Politics', in S. Ahmed, J. Kilby, C. Lury, M. McNeil and B. Skeggs (eds) *Transformations: Thinking Through Feminism*, London: Routledge.

——2008 *The Female Complaint: The Unfinished Business of Sentimentality in American Culture*, London and Durham: Duke University Press.

Bishop Merrill, S. 1998 *Defining Personhood: Toward the Ethics of Quality in Clinical Care*, Amsterdam: Rodopi.

Bourdieu, P. 1987 'What Makes a Social Class? On the Theoretical and Practical Existence of Groups', *Berkeley Journal of Sociology* 32: 1–17.

Bourdieu, P. and Waquant, L. 1992 *An Invitation to Reflexive Sociology*, Chicago: University of Chicago Press.

Bratich, J. Z. 2007 'Programming Reality: Control Societies, New Subjects, Powers of Transformation', in D. Heller (ed.) *Makeover Television: Realities Remodelled*, London: I.B. Taurus.

Brunsdon, C. 1981 '*Crossroads* – Notes on a Soap Opera', *Screen* 22(4): 32–38.

——1991 'Pedagogies of the Feminine: Feminist Teaching and Women's Genres', *Screen* 32(4): 364–82.

——2003 'Lifestyling Britain: The 8–9 Slot on British Television', *International Journal of Cultural Studies* 6(1): 5–23.

Deleuze, E. and Deleuze, J. 1978 'Giles Deleuze: Lecture Transcripts on Spinoza's Concept of *Affect*', Vol. 2006: http:/www.webdeleuze.com/php/sommaire.html.

Doane, M. A. 1982 'Film and Masquerade: Theorizing the Female Spectator', *Screen* 23 (3–4): 74–88.

du Gay, P. 1986 *Consumption and Identity at Work*, London: Sage.

Giddens, A. 1991 *Modernity and Self-Identity; Self and Society in the Late Modern Age*, Cambridge: Polity.

Gillies, V. 2005 'Raising the Meritocracy; Parenting and the Individualisation of Social Class', *Sociology* 39(5): 835–55.

Graeber, D. 2001 *Toward an Anthropological Theory of Value: The False Coin of our own Dreams*, New York: Palgrave.

Gray, A. 1992 *Video Playtime: The Gendering of a Leisure Technology*, London: Routledge.

Hearn, A. 2010 'Reality Television and the Limits of Immaterial Labour', *Triple C* 8(1): 60–76.

Heelas, P. 2002 'Work Ethics, Soft Capitalism and the "Turn to Life"', in P. du Gay and M. Pryke (eds) *Cultural Economy*, London: Sage.

Hobson, D. 1990 'Women Audiences and the Workplace', in M. E. Brown (ed.) *Television and Women's Culture: the Politics of the Popular*, London: Sage.

Hollows, J. and Jones, S. 2010 '"At least he's doing something": Moral Entrepreneurship and Individual Responsibility in *Jamie's Ministry of Food*', *European Journal of Cultural Studies* 13(3): 307–22.

Illouz, E. 2003 *Oprah Winfrey and the Glamour of Misery*, New York: Columbia University Press.

——2007 *Cold Intimacies: The Making of Emotional Capitalism*, Cambridge: Polity.

Illouz, E. and Wilf, E. 2008 'Oprah Winfrey and the Co-production of Market and Morality', *Women and Performance: A Journal of Feminist Theory* 18(1): 1–7.

Kavka, M. 2008 *Reality Television, Affect and Intimacy*, Basingstoke and New York: Palgrave Macmillan.

Lareau, A. 2003 *Unequal Childhoods: Class, Race and Family Life*, Berkeley, CA.: University of California Press.

Lovell, T. 2000 'Thinking Feminism with and against Bourdieu', *Feminist Theory* 1(1): 11–32.

——2003 'Resisting with Authority: Historical Specificity, Agency and the Performative Self', *Theory, Culture and Society* 20(1).

McKenzie, J. 2001 *Perform or Else; From Discipline to Performance*, New York and London: Routledge.

McNay, L. 1999 'Gender, Habitus and the Field: Pierre Bourdieu and the Limits of Reflexivity', *Theory, Culture and Society* 16: 95–119.

Modleski, T. 1983 'The Rhythms of Reception: Daytime Television and Women's Work', in E. A. Kaplan (ed.) *Regarding Television: Critical Approaches*, Los Angeles: American Film Institute.

Moi, T. 1991 'Appropriating Bourdieu: Feminist Thought and Pierre Bourdieu's Sociology of Culture', *New Literary History* 22: 1017–49.

Moran, L. and Skeggs, B. 2001 'Property and Propriety: Fear and Safety in Gay Space', *Social and Cultural Geography* 2(4): 407–20.

Moran, L., Skeggs, B., Tyrer, P. and Corteen, K. 2004 *Sexuality and the Politics of Violence and Safety*, London: Routledge.

Munro, R. 2005 'Partial Organisation: Marilyn Strathern and the Elicitation of Relations', in C. Jones and R. Munro (eds) *Contemporary Organisation Theory*, Oxford: Blackwell.

Ouellette, L. and Hay, J. 2008 'Makeover Television, Governmentality and the Good Citizen', *Continuum: Journal of Media and Cultural Studies* 22(4): 471–85.

Sayer, A. 2005 *The Moral Significance of Class*, Cambridge: Cambridge University Press.

Skeggs, B. 2004a *Class, Self, Culture*, London: Routledge.

——2004b 'Introducing Pierre Bourdieu's Analysis of Class, Gender and Sexuality', in L. Adkins and B. Skeggs (eds) *Feminism After Bourdieu*, Oxford: Blackwell.

——2004c 'Exchange Value and Affect: Bourdieu and the Self', in L. Adkins and B. Skeggs (eds) *Feminism After Bourdieu*, Oxford: Blackwell.

——2011 'Imagining Personhood Differently: Person Value and Autonomist Working Class Value Practices', *Sociological Review* 59(3): 579–94.

——2012 'Feeling Class: Affect and Culture in the Making of Class Relations', in G. Ritzer (ed.) *The Wiley-Blackwell Companion to Sociology*, Oxford: Blackwell.

Spivak, G. C. 1985 'Scattered Speculations on the Question of Value', *Diacritics* winter: 73–92.

Strathern, M. 1991 *Partial Connections*, Maryland: Rowman and Little.

——1992 *After Nature: English Kinship in the Late Twentieth Century*, Cambridge: Cambridge University Press.

Taylor, C. 1994 'The Politics of Recognition', in D. T. Goldberg (ed.) *Multiculturalism: A Critical Reader*, Oxford: Blackwell.

Thrift, N. 2004 'Intensities of Feeling: Towards a Spatial Politics of Affect', *Geografiska Annaler* 86B(1): 57–78.

Turner, G. 2010 *Ordinary People and the Media: The Demotic Turn*, London: Sage.

Weber, B. 2011 'From All-American Mom to Super Bitch from Hell: Kate Gosselin and the Classed and Gendered Politics of Reality Television', in H. Wood and B. Skeggs (eds) *Reality Television and Class*, London: BFI/Palgrave.

Williams, R. 1974 *Television, Technology and Cultural Form*, London: Fontana.

Wood, H. 2007 'The Mediated Conversational Floor: An Interactive Approach to Reception Analysis', *Media, Culture and Society* 29(1): 75–103.

——2009 *Talking with Television: Women, Talk Shows and Modern Self-Reflexivity*, Illinois: Illinois University Press.

Chapter 1

Reality television

From representation to intervention

Big Brother, I'm a Celebrity and *The X Factor* are components of the most rigorously moral genre on modern television. It gives people in general, and children in particular, absolutely the right idea about what is acceptable behaviour ... This is how it works. A bunch of people go into a house, a music studio, or a jungle. They are filmed so intensively, over such a long period, that (despite occasional prejudicial editing) their true characters cannot be hidden from view. At that point the British nation's moral spine goes rigid. The bad characters are punished and the good rewarded ... the sermon of right and wrong is as simple as that of Enid Blyton, Harry Potter or Superman.

(*The Observer* 2005)

Introduction

As Su Holmes and Deborah Jermyn (2004) point out in the introduction to their collection *Understanding Reality Television,* the broader debates about 'cultural value' which surround reality television programmes are often shaped by notions of 'quality' which are themselves couched in discourses of social hierarchy and class. With appropriate pomposity Salman Rushdie (2001) called reality television an 'inverted ethical universe where worse is better' as he confidently announced its existence as heralding the 'death of morality'. Other commentators were quick to point out how so many ordinary people laying themselves bare on television persistently relay hackneyed myths about social difference and conventional morality. For instance, Zoe Williams (2003) in *The Guardian* newspaper argued that *Wife Swap* is 'an old school morality tale that starts off with how frightful the working classes are, then winds us round to the inevitable conclusion that, they may be poor, but they're good and happy'. This quote cues us into two things about the relationship between reality television and social distinction: first, the genre supplies theatrical performances of ethics; and second there is nothing inherently 'new' about such tales of morality. This chapter will outline many (though not all) of the extensive debates about how reality television has effected a significant shift in the form of contemporary television and media culture. It will also hold in tension arguments about the consistencies the form has with older (gendered and classed) cultural traditions. By keeping both the push of change and the pull of continuity in view, we use this chapter to set up our analytic framework in which reality television enters into *established* forms of sociality through a *reorganized* set of principles around the performance of a mediated ethical self.

Reality, sensation and politics

A great deal of research maps how reality television is a product of political economy, where the commercial pressure to chase exportable 'formats' (ideally with increased interactive potential and alternative revenue streams) determines programme content (Moran 2005). Chad Raphael (2004) discusses the US context where the restructuring of television distribution, the growth of cable, and the dilution of advertising spending in the face of increased audience fragmentation, meant that reality television was the solution to an economic crisis. The explosion of reality television can be traced to its commercial success in generating audiences through low production costs. As long as networks need to fill the hours around expensive dramas and sitcoms, reality television will always survive in the service of televisions' more worthy assets. This registers the inferiority of the genre in terms of financial investment and its location in cultural hierarchies. In the European context reality television has provided the solution to previously expensive public service commitments to 'factual programming'. Its relatively high ratings are used to justify 'public interest'. Annette Hill (2007) charts how in the UK, for some public service channels 'general factual' was the dominant genre for peak-time schedules (46% for BBC2 and 35% for Channel 4 according to a 2005 Ofcom Report). One of the grave fears is that the spread of 'factual entertainment' is driving out the space for traditional documentary output. Hill thus charts a more general trend towards the 'restyling of factuality' in the face of changing relations of television and democracy in public culture.

Fears around reality television's challenge to accepted notions of a 'proper' public culture in liberal democracies, often revolve around the relationship of reality television to the traditional project of documentary television. Although acknowledged as experimental, documentary was oriented around a particular expository mode related to a world-view with a strong sense of social responsibility, subscribing to what Bill Nichols (1991b) refers to as a discourse of sobriety. Although the relationship between documentary as art form and its commitment to social realism has always meant a set of uneasy tensions between the factual and the fictional, the public project of documentary was generally seen to work in the interests of informing the citizen rather than entertaining the consumer (Corner 1996). Interpreted in this vein, the entrance of reality television comes to represent not just the restyling, but rather for some, the bastardizing and denigration of the documentary form.

A great deal of early work on reality television was concerned with its claims on the 'real'. This led John Corner (2002) to suggest that new forms of reality television and their various morphings with game-shows, soaps, lifestyle make-overs, etc., are indicative of a 'post-documentary culture' where the entertainment drive towards diversion and a performative playfulness upset the categories of the 'real', the 'social' or even the 'public' which were once hard-fastened to the documentary form. His position resonates with writers like Richard Kilborn (2003) who suggest that rather than a commitment to represent the world 'out there', these lucrative genres put increasing pressure upon programme makers to 'stage the real' through formulaic contrived situations. Paul Watson, the British documentary film-maker responsible in the 1970s for the observational documentary *The Family*, has vehemently resisted responsibility for spawning reality television in the UK, suggesting instead that the rise of reality docu-soaps using observational filming techniques is an entirely different beast, offering a flood of cheap series that merely '[point] a camera at someone wanting self-promotion' (Watson 1998 cited in Bruzzi 2006).

Here, the implication is that any documentary should have at its core, some purchase or claim on 'truth' as a relatively objective, observable phenomenon, notwithstanding the variation in the presence of the voice of the film-maker. This preserves a clear distinction between what constitutes fact and fiction. Critics of the staging of reality television, its emphasis upon narrative editing, the selection of participants, the prominence of personalities and plot, suggest that the 'fakeness' of the reality which it purports to represent is the problem. Importantly for the democratic polity, this intervenes in questions of 'trust' between the audience and programme-makers. The more audiences become used to the idea of the constructedness of reality, the less credible genuine attempts at social intervention become and the less film-makers will be attached to a sense of social responsibility, since it is simply no longer expected of them. These arguments are at the root of those where reality television straight-forwardly represents the tabloidization and therefore debasement of contemporary culture which abound in both academic and journalistic accounts.

The problem with this reading is that documentary's grasp on the 'real' as authentic 'truth' has always been more fragile and ambiguous than these accounts tend to suggest – as John Grierson's (the father of UK social-realist documentary) description of documentary as the 'creative treatment of actuality' betrays. Bill Nichols (1991a) offers us the now almost normative evolutionary framing of documentary developments from expository to performative modes as a series of historical shifts – away from a grasp upon the objective truth towards a subjective 'less real' emphasis upon sensation and performance. Here 'spectacles of particularity' run directly counter to any socio-political project, replacing the rational exploration of macro socio-economic issues, with emotive instances of the micro, the particular and the personal. But, for Stella Bruzzi (2006) Nichols' ideals hinge on a utopian myth (particularly via the observational mode of documentary) whereby representation *can* easily map onto reality. It is far more honest, she claims, to reveal the various modes of construction and acknowledge the elements of performance, as in some contemporary documentary and 'formatted' reality television, in order to enter into a dialogue with audiences over what constitutes the real.

Commentators on reality television must therefore also concentrate their attention on these fictional elements. The intermingling of performance with naturalism is part of Corner's (2002) formulation of a 'post-documentary context' which he is keen to be interpreted as a call for broadening out notions of what we accept as factual programming, rather than heralding the demise of the documentary form completely. For him the post-documentary context is a contradictory cultural environment, where viewers, participants and producers are less invested in absolute truth and representational ethics and more interested in the space that exists between reality and fiction, in which new levels of representational play and reflexivity are visualized.

However, the issue here is that the discussion of performance is still rendered as separate from, and potentially as impairing, elements of the 'real'. Whereas for Bruzzi, these shifts must instead force us to interrogate the performative further and not dismiss its presence as 'only' entertainment. This is especially the case since there is a more complicated history of performance in documentary than can be accessed via Nichols' genealogy. Bruzzi cites UK drama documentaries such as *Cathy Come Home* and *Who Bombed Birmingham?* that brought about social change, but she also points to a more fundamental critique of the function of documentary. Drawing upon Judith Butler's (1993) notions of performativity, she argues that we can apply those concepts to documentary. Butler's notion relies on Austin's separation of an utterance into its constative and performative elements. To understand meaning in language we should consider not just the content of language but what is performed in its expression such as 'I now pronounce you man and wife' which institutionalizes and brings into view the structural relationship of the organization of gendered property interests. For Bruzzi documentary, like language, works as an *act*:

> A parallel is to be found between these linguistic examples and the performative documentary which – whether built around the intrusive presence of the film-maker or self-conscious performances by its subjects – is the enactment of the notion that a documentary only comes into being as it is performed because it is given meaning by the interaction between performance and reality.
>
> (2006:186)

Helen Wood (2009a) has previously argued that a great deal of broadcasting works in a similar way, where meaning is generated in the establishment of communicative acts between programmes and audiences, as well as through traditional models of representation and semiotics, a point from which our methodological debate departs in Chapter 4.

To draw our attention to elements of drama and performance as having a purchase on reality in terms of what they *enact* is to register the latent gendering of these debates around what constitutes the political. There is a longer history of feminist writing around the politics of melodrama where the emphasis upon the personal and subjective world is always both an intervention and a constitution of what we know as 'real' lived social experience. This calls into view the well established arguments around the distinction between fact and fiction as inherently gendered fields, where mass culture is coded as feminine against the modernist project of masculine rationality (Huyssen 1986). It also registers the continuity with discussions of the talk show whereby subjective accounts of experience with their own truth claims are prioritized over the more abstract notion of institutional evidence offered via a Habermasian account of public debate (Shattuc 1997). Lisbet Van Zoonen (2001) writing about *Big Brother* discusses how original critiques of the programme were embedded within bourgeois notions of the distinction between the private and public sphere, attacking *BB* in favour of keeping the distinction intact, whilst the huge audiences that it attracted suggested a widespread rejection of such a divide.

The focus on the banal and minutiae can also be seen in trends from make-over and lifestyle television of the 1990s: the rise of lifestyle and its insistence on the exploration of the personal and intimate has given momentum to these changes in documentary formats. One of the prevailing techniques from the make-over show is where the camera is more interested in the *re*action to the situation, rather than the action – what Charlotte Brunsdon (2003) calls 'the changed grammar of the close-up' (p.10). Reality television evokes rather than represents. Rachel Moseley (2000), writing about the arrival of make-over television at the end of the nineties describes how:

> Make-over shows ask the audience to draw on a repertoire of personal skills, our ability to search faces and discern reaction (facilitated by the close up) from the smallest details – the twitch of a muscle, an expression in the eye – a competence suggested by Tania Modleski as key to the pleasure of soap opera's melodramatic form. These programmes showcase the threatening excessiveness of the ordinary ... These are precisely, instances, of powerful spectacular uber-ordinariness.
>
> (2000:314)

The regularity and importance of the close up across all reality programmes, coupled with ironic music and juxtapositional editing, register the close proximity reality programming has to melodrama and its manipulation of affect. In discussing the rise of lifestyle TV, there is no doubt in Brunsdon's (2003) mind that 'this is melodramatic television' in contrast to earlier hobbyist forms of instructional television which operates in a realist mode (p.11). Private lives are transformed into public spectacle through an emphasis upon drama and performance over information. Helen Piper (2004) usefully offers us the phrase 'improvised drama' to describe how the banal observations in a series like *Wife Swap* are turned into moments of dramatic intensity. According to Bruzzi (2006), the emphasis upon emotion and character in formatted documentaries now fill the slot vacated by traditional drama across our schedules.

For a documentary commentator like Nichols (1991a) when objectivity and rationality give way to subjectivity and sensation in this way any potential mode of engagement in public culture is closed down: 'Spectacle is more properly an aborted or foreclosed form of identification where emotional engagement does not extend as far as concern but remains arrested at the level of sensation' (p.234). He further notes (1994) that the sensations produced by reality television have no public purpose or political connection:

> The very intensity of feelings, emotion, sensation, involvement that reality TV produces is also discharged harmlessly within its dramatic envelope of banality. The historical referent, the magnitudes that exceed the text, the narratives that speak of conduct in the world, of face-to-face encounters, bodily risk and ethical engagement ground themselves harmlessly in circuits devoted to an endless flux of the very sensations they run to ground.
>
> (p.57)

But for feminist writers this is *precisely* a site where socio-political questions of the national and the moral are shaped (Ahmed 2004; Berlant 1997, 2000, 2004, 2006) and/or for situationists and/or Deleuzians it is precisely sensation and spectacle that offers new ways for thinking about what constitutes, and how to generate, the political (Debord 1967/1994; Deleuze and Deleuze 1978; Deleuze 1969/1990; Massumi 1996).

These debates have long been argued out in relation to melodrama, where Thomas Elsaesser (1987) notes there may be a different kind of 'truth' than that at work in traditional forms of documentary: 'Even if the situations and sentiments defied all categories of verisimilitudes and were totally unlike anything in real life, the structure had a truth and life of its own' (p.64). This resonates with Ien Ang's (1985) discussion of viewers of *Dallas* whose attachments to the soap opera fiction are generated through an 'emotional realism' – a recognition of the interpersonal dramas of everyday life (a discussion we develop in Chapter 4 through our viewers' reactions).

Christine Gledhill (1987, 2000) maintains that melodrama brings a type of realism which enables television and film to visualize the morally good and bad people of the nation. Thus it is the connection to the moral (so clearly identified by journalists writing about reality television above) that gives reality television some purchase on the social. For Peter Brooks (1976/1995) melodrama repre-sents the moral 'reaffirmation of society' and for Linda Williams (2001) melo-drama shapes the form that race relations take in the US. She argues that without understanding melodrama we cannot understand contemporary config-urations of race in which moral legitimacy is produced through the spectacle of racialized bodily suffering. Likewise, it is representations of women's suffering that Berlant (2008) argues works to obscure the possibility of political agency.

Melodramatic suffering reduces the violence of everyday life into individualized emotion thereby occluding the workings of broader social and historical structures. So for Berlant, understanding the ambivalence of sentiment is crucial to understanding how politics works. Hence we argue that techniques involved in the production of melodrama, sentiment, sensation and spectacle (all deployed across reality television) are essential for understanding how reality television contributes to the broader political climate.

Whilst for some the structural formulae of reality television renders it 'apolitical', for others the focus on domestic and banal observations of everyday life may instead represent an 'opening out' of political relations by making public the very fields that are considered as private. As feminists have argued for a long time the private *is* public and of course *always* politicized. When John Corner (2006) re-evaluates *Wife Swap* he suggests that it 'exposes some of the rhythms, tensions, and contradictions of everyday living and indeed the structures of wealth, class and culture in ways not open to more conventional [documentary] treatments' (p.73). Deborah Jermyn and Su Holmes' (2008) analysis of the ambiguities present in the same series suggest that the focus on the struggles of the individual and their everyday labours reveal the very constructedness of 'typical' gender identities. Participants then are at least opening themselves up to the possibility of re-imagining the routine and the everyday as they wrestle with aspects of discontent. Therefore, throwing the spotlight on the ritual acts of intimate and domestic life and allowing for indeterminacy creates room for a feminist politics.

Indeterminacy and unpredictability are central to the appeal of reality television, regardless of the format. There is a tension over the unknowable: How will people react in a certain situation? What will happen when X meets Y? For some therefore, it is the unscripted nature of events that allows space for more open readings that have the potential to resist dominant ideologies. Christopher Pullen (2004) argues that it was exactly in the unscripted action between gay and straight housemates in MTV's *The Real World* that space for a more open dialogue on sexuality emerged, even if that was not part of the producer's intent or any authorial voice. The unpredictability of non-professional actors offers potential interest beyond the formulae that we all know and recognize.

Thus far the discussions over reality television have concentrated on its relationship to the 'real', which are ultimately invested in well established gendered arguments over the public politicizing of the personal. What counts as 'real' is still a gendered battlefield. Reality and 'truth' are tied to external socio-political 'authored' argument and rationality on the one side, whilst the personal, emotional and subjective speak to an alternative 'truth' which relies on the melodramatic and the indeterminate on the other. The central question is whether instances of the particular have anything to say about the more general, the political or the social. This leads us to another set of questions: If the particular moral codes on offer are universal and eternal then what can they tell us about the current historical conjuncture? How do instances of melodramatic intensity reveal anything about the broader socio-political climate?

Self-governance, advice and the 'talking cure'

As we develop in detail in Chapter 2, it is important to understand just how socio-political trends in western societies have been re-organized around what Charles Taylor (1989, 1991) and Marilyn Strathern (1992) define as 'compulsory individuality', where people have to perform their own social worth to others rather than looking to 'higher' authorities such as religion and the state to provide legitimation for their lives. The 'individualization thesis' put forward by Ulrich Beck (1992) and Anthony Giddens (1991) suggests that in contemporary modernity, the emphasis upon the individual and the promotion of the biographical project of the self is the new way in which the social is being reproduced. For Beck, 'the individual himself or herself becomes the reproduction unit for the social in the life-world' (p.130), and 'class loses its sub-cultural basis and is no longer experienced' (p.98). In these instances therefore, traditional modes of identification related to class, race or gender for example are in decline in a 'reflexive modernity' where the process of the self is simply worked upon and 'made' reflexively, 'we are not what we are but what we make of ourselves' (Giddens 1991: 75).

We suggest that 'compulsory individuality' has partly enabled the explosion and relative success of reality television. This is not to suggest that questions of social structure are not relevant, but that they are *re*-invested through discourses of selfhood and self-responsibility (Wood and Skeggs 2004). The familiar trope of 'lifestyling' in advanced capitalist consumer-driven societies coupled with the industrial economic changes in the television industry, mean that shifts in factual television have come to represent neo-liberal political economic structures. A now huge body of social theory argues that these are new ways in which personhood is (per)formed where claims to legitimacy and rights are enacted through instancing the personal and particular (see Chapter 2). For Jon Dovey (2000) the move to 'first person' television represents an emphasis upon 'spectacular subjectivity' whereby reality television is characteristic of political neo-liberal shifts in a new form of 'life-politics' and 'emotional democracy'. Thus the focus on the personal and the particular and the emphasis upon self-work and self-inspection in many make-over and reality formats seems to make perfect sense in an epoch where the lifestyling of identity is part of a commercialized and commodified project of the self. Here the individual is made responsible for their life choices whilst the intervention of the state is rolled back in terms of welfare support.

Nikolas Rose's (1999) theories of contemporary governmentality suggest that power in society is not metered centrally but is diffused amongst subjects through bodily practices whereby the citizen-subject productively engages in forms of self-regulation. Gareth Palmer (2003) first pointed to evidence of these trends on UK television, citing examples from crime documentaries where a story that would once have been presented in terms of civil liberties is now framed through the logic of personal risk management. He sees the rise of *Big*

Brother, where contestants submit to a central authority with no contact with the outside world, as the ultimate experiment in governance. Likewise Laurie Ouellette and James Hay (2008) demonstrate how television is being instrumentalized as part of programmes of social service, social welfare and social management in the US. They describe how television is being reinvented as an instructional template for taking care of oneself, further enabling the state to decrease its social responsibilities. Showing how reality television is a pedagogic cultural technology through which subjects come to monitor, improve, motivate, transform and protect themselves in the name of freedom, enterprise and social responsibility, they develop theories of governmentality whereby the self is called to regulate itself. They describe how across formats from as variable as *What Not to Wear* to *American Idol*, reality television operates as the ultimate cultural technology in neo-liberal self-governance.

Particular programmes include the US court-room mock set up *Judge Judy* which intervenes in family and personal disputes where instructions are exercises in self-governance (Ouellette 2004). In the UK *Honey We're Killing the Kids* typifies a focus on how personal failure can be passed on to one's family (Biressi and Nunn 2008), and *Supernanny* and *Nanny 911* exemplify how intervention in parenting skills can promise to improve family life (Becker 2006). The plethora of personal make-over programmes such as *Extreme Makeover* and *The Swan* advance the cause of cosmetic surgery and promise to improve femininity and 'self-esteem' (Gailey 2006); and *Queer Eye for the Straight Guy* remodels masculinity through improving modes of consumption and self-inspection (Lewis 2007; Miller 2006). Many of these shows operate via a new army of television cultural intermediaries – or 'lifestyle experts' (Bonner 2003, 2008).

Brenda Weber's (2009) research on a host of make-over programmes in the US further extends our understanding of the trend of 'transformation' in relation to contemporary concerns of self-identity whereby intensified affective registers allow participants to gain access to contemporary citizenship. In the 'makeover nation' the self is subject to numerous 'illogics', circa Judith Butler (2004), whereby seemingly incompatible narratives make sense: such as that of an 'inner self' which is ultimately remodelled; an essential femininity which is found and 'remade'; or a 'unique individual' is created which can conform to normative class, gender and racial expectations. These illogics are held in balance, so much so that the phrase from one contestant, 'they're going to transform me into the person I really am!', seems to make perfect sense (p.130). Whilst Weber's reading draws on Rose's theories of governmentality in terms of the workings of power, she also points to an 'affective currency' in which participants' shame is met with experts 'care' in what she calls 'affective domination'. Valerie Walkerdine (2011) discusses the gender and classed historical transmission of shame which she says contextualizes its affective use in much make-over and reality television. In Chapter 5 we suggest that rather than extending the workings of governmentality, affect is much less straightforward and disruptive, often involved in revealing and challenging the workings of power.

Within this picture, the culture of governance often goes hand in hand with a culture of increased surveillance, part of what Rose (1989) refers to as evidence of new 'scopic regimes'. For instance Weber (2009) describes the make-over participants' ultimate subjection to the gaze of others. It is no coincidence, as Palmer (2003) points out, that many different reality television formats make use of surveillance technology such as CCTV and webcams, from crime shows (*Crimewatch, America's Most Wanted*) to shows about health and hygiene (*How Clean is Your House, Too Posh to Wash*). In a broader discussion of the changing social relations of surveillance, Thomas Mathiesen (1997) suggests a revision of Foucault's ideas about the panoptican, where the few watch the many, to a new 'viewer society' where the many watch the many. Trends in reality television are thus seen to parallel the increase in surveillance of public and private space in contemporary Western cultures, where CCTV is a ubiquitous part of modern living.

Mark Andrejevic (2004) in *Reality TV: The Work of Being Watched* suggests that in taking part in reality television we allow our intimate experiences to be harnessed as forms of consumer labour in the advancement of the capitalist economy. By submitting ourselves as the viewer to the observation of lifestyle choices in the interests of market knowledge and the accumulation of capital we are acculturating ourselves into new levels of surveillance. In this description performance is ultimately commodified and the democratic myth of participation is recapitulated into processes of mass customization which, as Andrejevic (2002) notes, 'serves as a form of acclimatisation to an emerging economic regime predicated on increasingly unequal access to, and control over, information' (p.267). For Andrejevic (2002, 2004) the synchronous relationship between surveillance and reality television is realized through the development of digital media and the extension of television as it reaches across alternative platforms (the internet), searching for new ways of engaging with audiences and ultimately new sources of revenue. Thus reality television is a contemporary phenomenon in which the political economy of the industry fits well with the ideologies of surveillance and control. Here television occupies a position as *the* cultural technology of the neo-liberal age, at the heart of cultural citizenship, in which 'a project of government at a distance is well and truly in place' (Miller 2007:26).

But also, the exposition of personal life is revealing of the relationship between domestic and political life and of course women have long been subject to surveillant regimes. We are thus reminded of the domestic labour debate from the 1980s that addressed the value of women's domestic and emotional labour (their time and energy) for capitalism. Arlie Hochschild (2003) draws attention to the complex relationship between feminization and commodification where she argues that certain aspects of the Women's movement have entered into the mainstream in the commercialization of intimate life. However, only the parts of feminism which fit with capitalism and individualism have been adopted, rather than any real structural change to the system to really enhance the cause of women (McRobbie 2009; Negra and Tasker 2007; Skeggs 1997).

This process of generating self-surveillance and then mobilizing self-management in response has become more intense in relation to the needs of contemporary capitalism where the worker must demonstrate their flexibility in the job market. Now, all forms of time and energy expenditure become a pre-requisite to personal and to professional success: self-fashioning becomes a form of self-enterprising. Ouellette and Hay (2008) note a paradox in make-over TV in that: 'It prepares the worker to take on burdens of insecurity and disposability in the name of his or her own freedom, and provides them with the tenuous resources for navigating the impossibility of this task' (p.101). A relay therefore develops between the affective and emotional labour for the family and its performance at and for work. Aesthetic labour on oneself becomes tied to one's tradable value in the occupational structure. Working on oneself becomes part of a more generalizable 'self-work ethic' which Heelas (2002) identifies as part of the current conjuncture, a new form of 'soft-capitalism' which involves a 'turn to life'. This assumes that paid-work makes us not just more effective as a worker but as a person more generally, by which our life is enriched through enhancing commitment and motivation.

The emphasis on self-work circulates between the worlds of the domestic and the occupational. No longer is the performance of affect restricted to the sphere of the 'private' (see Thompson in Chapter 2) but it is now also a requirement of most forms of service work (and see debate on our audience discussions of labour in Chapter 7). According to McRobbie (2009) it is women, and young women in particular, who have been offered incitements and enticements through faux-feminist language like empowerment to perform the self-work ethic, by which 'she is congratulated, reprimanded and encouraged to embark on a new regime of self-perfectibility' (p.62). The sphere of paid work figures large as a theatre for performance whereby women's movement into the workforce has been managed in such a way that it complies with the new requirements of individualized subjectivity in employment, sexuality and in consumer culture more generally.

Thus we want to argue that the politics of gender and class do not disappear as self-governance comes into effect, rather they are re-enacted *through* modes of personalization and individualization. This is because they still carry with them the legacies of structural disadvantages, such as access to cultural resources and the ways in which people can operationalize the techniques required for the development of the self-project (Skeggs 2004). These inherited and renewed inequalities of how to make 'the self' as the moral individual are often ignored in subscribing to a position which only attends to the 'nowness' of the individualizing neo-liberal phenomenon. Therefore we want to take account of the historical trajectories into which reality television enters as a means to help us position the form firmly within the politics of gender and class.

Gendered histories: expertise and taking advice

Whilst the emergence of reality television at the end of 1990s represents a proliferation of 'ordinary' people appearing in the media, there are older trends which alert us to the gendering of modes of self-representation. Griffen-Foley (2004) charts the history of participatory media from the late nineteenth century discussing periodicals which featured reader contributions (what was called the 'New Journalism') to build mass circulation and allow for more personalized editor/reader interaction. The year 1919 saw the rise of 'confessional magazines' predicated on viewers' personal life stories written in the first person. Whilst at first many of the advertisements addressed men, by the 1930s it was women's stories that dominated the pages and confessional magazines adopted a distinct address to the female consumer. From here the rise of mass circulated women's magazines continued to adapt many forms of reader contribution, from recipes and fashion to be followed at home, to intimate advice columns and problem pages. Jane Shattuc (1997) in her account of the 90s phenomena of the talk show suggests that the talk show is as old as American broadcasting and 'borrows its basic characteristics from nineteenth century popular culture, such as tabloids, women advice columns and melodrama' (p.3).

The classed and gendered history of the advice column forges a relationship between practical and moral guidance. In Europe upper class women provided 'expert advice' in an early attempt to promote self-governance through a broader 'civilisation project'. Leonora Davidoff and Catherine Hall (1987) note how in the UK in the 1840s a culture of domesticity (strongly influenced by Evangelical religion) was established by middle class women to legitimate them-selves by operating as relay mechanisms of manners and morality in 'the minu-tiae of everyday life' by passing their influence and standards to others. Since the late nineteenth century childhood became perhaps the most intensely governed sector of personal existence (Rose 1989) and it was mothers who were given the responsibility for this government (see David 1980 for how this responsibility became enshrined in law). In the 1900s 'ordinary' women began to appear in popular culture: 1920s talk back radio typically featured a combination of host experts and 'ordinary citizens' in conversation, and radio advice shows in detail every aspect of home management targeting a female audience – what Barnard (1989) calls 'housewife radio' (and see Mitchell 2001).

By the 1920s women giving and getting advice on behaviour, replete with expositions of middle class morality, was standard fare across newspaper, radio and book publishing industries (Shattuc 1997). The extension of advice and responsibility brought with it increased monitoring of standards, as if working class women could never be fully trusted, a legacy developed in 'women's genre' television. Mary Beth Haralovich (1992), for instance, documents how 1950s US sitcoms detail female failure, re-positioning domesticity from a practice in which pleasure was previously taken, to one in which they 'need to try harder', a trend which is repeated across other women's genres (Hermes 1993; Shattuc 1997). This shift was significant as it brought into vision a different object: from the middle class 'polite and proper' family to the dysfunctional working class family. In the UK, Su Holmes (2008a) in her archival research of 1950s BBC television, describes a show called *What's Your Problem?* in which (usually working class) women tell tales of their personal dilemmas in order to gain advice from a clergy member, a university Vice Chancellor and a politician. Daytime schedules of the 1990s in UK and the US offered a direct address to the female consumer (Rapping 1995). Features of audience participation in daytime magazine programmes through phone-ins, texts, letters and appearing on television promoted a gendered mode of personal disclosure which is mutually undertaken by audiences and television presenters alike (Wood 2009a). It has been women who have taken up the call to demonstrate their value by having their personal stories recognized and judged in public, perhaps not surprisingly given their traditional exclusion from other forms of public culture.

Telling one's stories for public recognition was also part of the 1970s feminist attempts at consciousness-raising, which encouraged women to verbalize the extent of their suffering through their gendered experience. Wendy Brown (1995) has called this disclosure the 'wounded attachment', whereby the pain and suffering of the personal world can gain public recognition, a technique we see regularly performed on the talk show (Illouz 2003; Masciarotte 1991; Shattuc 1997). Similar debates have been rehearsed over the talk show, where on the one hand programmes which have privileged women's personal voices have been heralded as a feminist public sphere, whilst others have been more critical of the evocation of the personal at the expense of the social and economic (McLaughlin 1993). However, recently talk shows have developed a more demonstrable emphasis upon argument and entertaining spectacle. Programmes like *Jerry Springer* in the US and *The Jeremy Kyle Show* in the UK, although different in style, have shifted the emphasis on telling in keeping with a moral agenda which has marked participants as 'beyond' these structures of 'good citizenship'. Rather than telling one's story to claim political or public recognition, telling here marks its limit: abjection, with participants often described as 'trash'.

The more recent obsession with lifestyle and make-over television registers the migration of daytime schedules which deployed these gendered techniques to prime-time television. Brunsdon (2003) recognizes this process as the 'feminisation' of prime-time partly engendered through the rise of women in the workforce, the increased number of women working in the television industry, and the professionalization of what were once previously domestic skills and labour – as homes, gardens and clothes parade across our television screens in need of improvement. Tania Lewis (2008) describes this contemporary shift as a 'reframing of things previously gendered, domestic and ordinary' into a lifestyle phenomenon 'underpinned by the individualistic, consumption-oriented conception of the relationship between selfhood and the social' (p.5). For Ehrenreich and English (2005) the most recent incarnation of a cultural turn to domesticity is part of a 'domestic nostalgia' in the US which dovetails with a renewal of conservative moral values. This re-labelling of domestic labour also accompanies the trend towards its outsourcing, as professional women are pressed for time (McRobbie 2002) but also as Western middle class women become increasingly reliant on global outsourcing that provides care and domestic labour from developing countries (Anderson 2000; Ehrenreich and Hochschild 2004).

Whilst there is not space to wholly do justice to these histories, they serve to contextualize women's longer and more ambiguous relationship to elements of standardization and self-disciplining via the ambivalent gesture of disclosure than is available through an explanation of reality television via the contemporary neo-liberal context. Ros Gill (2007) discusses how women's bodies have long been open to the discourses of re-modelling in ways which predate the current consumer emphasis on lifestyle and cosmetic culture. Attempts to modify motherhood through self-governance in particular have a long history in English culture (Dyhouse 1976, 1977) potentially replicated in the numerous reality programmes which emphasize instructions in 'parenting' skills: *Supernanny*, *Nanny 911*, *House of Tiny Tear-Aways*, *Bank of Mom and Dad* and *My Teen's a Nightmare* to name just a few. Weber (2009) points to an emphasis in make-over program-ming of 'yummy mummies' as dowdy moms are ridiculed, simultaneously signalling and rejecting the tolls of motherhood on women's bodies and self-confidence. Thus the current over-representation of women as consumers of the self-help industry highlight their well-established unequal relationship to self-governance (Blackman 2004; Shattuc 1997).

The gendered pressures of monitoring and modification are also infused with classed discourses. For instance David Bell and Joanne Hollows (2005) point out how nineteenth century etiquette and taste manuals make the home the space for performing social status and class distinction, where women bear the responsibility for the symbolic representation of a bourgeois identity (Bourdieu 1986; Langland 1995). In Tania Lewis' (2008) substantial overview of the lit-erature on Victorian etiquette and home manuals in the making of the moder-nist project involving the rationalization of domestic labour, issues of moral responsibility come to bear on women around questions of taste and aesthetics (Veblen 1899/2008). Aesthetics, Terry Eagleton (1989) argues, is the space that mediates between property and propriety in the making of class. It is the means by which structures of power become structures of feeling. He describes how manners operated as the crucial hinge between ethics and aesthetics in which the meticulous disciplining of the body enabled the conversion of morality to style, thereby aestheticizing virtue. Coupled with women's take up of engagement in the media these histories provide the architecture upon which the opening out of the intimate world on reality television depends.

'Ordinary' performances of class

Participation on television has also been framed in terms of the excessive repre-sentation of the 'ordinary'. Infusing debates about the democratization of access to television are another key set of themes around the representation of the working class. We must remind ourselves of the political history behind the term 'ordinary' as we use the phrase to describe the category of non-actors or non-professionals that enter the media world. As Roger Bromley (2000) writing about the UK notes, the term 'ordinary' was one of the euphemisms to emerge as a substitute for the term 'working class' within a socio-political context in which class structures were politically denied (see Chapter 2). Likewise Barbara Ehrenreich (1990) documents how ordinary is a term that applies to the respectable Black and white working class in the US: 'poor' and 'trash' are terms reserved for those without proximity to respectability. And empirical research has detailed how the term ordinary is often deployed to deflect associations of privilege and inequality (Savage *et al.* 2001; Sayer 2002).

Early social-realist documentary in the UK in the 1940s, influenced by the Griersonian tradition was largely committed to exposing everyday life – a mode in which 'authenticity' was firmly associated with working class experience. Biressi and Nunn (2005) detail the relationship reality television had with these public service traditions where capturing reality through observational camera techniques combined both a sociological and aesthetic agenda, and television became the new site for depicting the working class. Consider the debates about reality with which we opened this chapter – in this documentary tradition the 'real' was constituted *as* working class life: 'realism became measured through the subject matter … and that realism depends upon notions of suffering, raw experience and personal struggle as emblems of the real' (Biressi and Nunn 2005:36). Yet if we examine the etymology of authenticity in British culture we can see how it is used to naturalize class and race differences (Gilroy 1987; Kahn 2001).

Moreover, the literary representations of 'everyday life' also reveal an association with working class practices, as life in which nothing interesting happens, and in which banality is the habituated norm (Bennett 2003). The British comedy programme *The Royle Family* attempted to satirize this bourgeois perspective, encapsulating working class everyday life as routines of doing nothing much but sitting in front of the television. But for some this programme was often tragically misunderstood as a 'real' representation of how the working class lived (Medhurst 1999).

The 1970s observational documentaries, *The Family* (1974) and *An American Family* (1973) in the UK and the US respectively, generally regarded as precedents of what we now understand as reality television, were both expositions of 'ordinary' working class lives. Anthropologist Margaret Mead famously described *An American Family* as a social scientific breakthrough, and Anna McCarthy (2004) charts how 1950s' hidden camera shows like Allen Funt's *Candid Camera* were understood as part of a public service ethos in the interests of the production of public knowledge about the social world. These liberal social-realist intentions contained a pedagogic moral agenda in which 'reality television served as a place where popular culture and social science overlapped via a realist ideal in which social norms, mechanisms of conformity, ritualized scripts, and modes of interaction were put on display' (p.22).

As interventions in social experimentation and liberal education these forms therefore are not so far away from other state-led forms of social intervention into working class life. In Chapter 2 we discuss Carolyn Steedman's (2000) research which details the historical rise of the 'telling self' as establishing a precedent in the attainment of poor relief where redemptive narratives become a measure of a respectable and 'worthy' citizen, marking the distinction between the deserving and undeserving poor.

It is hardly surprising therefore that class themes emerge as some of the dominant conceits in many contemporary versions of reality television. Pygmalion narratives (from female pauper to proper lady) structure many shows like *Ladette to Lady*, *From Asbo Teen to Beauty Queen*, class conflict is set up in *Wife Swap* and *Holiday Showdown* or class passing is encouraged in a show like *Faking It*. *Secret Millionaire* is a Channel 4 format in which a millionaire goes undercover in a poor community to decide who deserves his/her help in the form of large quantities of money, revealed at the end of the show in emotive moments of tears and gratitude, which resonates with earlier narratives of the deserving poor. Clearly the difference here is the intervention of the production company and the independently wealthy entrepreneur, rather than the state, but some of the moral conditions around the performance of worth, as some members of the community are deemed 'beyond help', clearly resonate around older traditions of applauding the 'authentic' and therefore deserving working classes. In the current epoch, both Andrejevic (2004) and Brunsdon (2003) point out that in the US and UK respectively, it comes as no surprise that the modes of democratization offered by the accessibility of reality television to the 'ordinary' person through the display of aspirational consumption, come at the same time as the gap between rich and poor widens, and the minute social mobility that did exist grinds to a halt. Depictions of 'reality' increasingly figure the fantasy of social possibility detached from social conditions.

The journalists cited at the opening of the chapter all comment on the idea of reality television as some kind of morality play, part of televisions' ethical turn (Hawkins 2001). Just as Rose (1989) points to the fact that a governing self must be aware of 'doing the right thing', the explosion of lifestyle and reality television makes visible ethical choices as solutions to contemporary problems. Annette Hill's (2005) research with audiences of reality television provides evidence that reality formats encourage viewers to judge good and bad conduct organized around a relatively conservative consensus of 'the family' and 'responsibility'. Whilst this is important research, we must also be aware that there is not a universalized moral consensus about family shapes and standards. As Andrew Sayer (2005) points out, questions of morality are always embroiled in class politics as 'differences in the distribution of respect, envy, resentment or condescension and deference are partly a product of inequalities in economic distribution' (p.225). Class is always a moral category and is historically shaped through national moralities (such as Puritanism) (Skeggs 2004). As we hope is becoming clear 'doing the right thing' is a social division of labour, a classed practice that is *at the same time* presented as a personalized project.

Therefore, writers on reality television have pointed out how class distinctions mediate the representations of consumption in many lifestyle shows: the 'new you' of the make-over is a bourgeois you where the symbolic markers of class taste are neutralized. McRobbie (2004) talks of the symbolic violence at work in a programme like *What Not to Wear* where vicious animosities of class and gender are re-enacted, whilst Deborah Philips (2005) discusses the reinforcement of the culturally superior knowledge of class capital of the make-over expert. Similarly Lisa Taylor (2005) argues that in the garden make-over 'the depth of personal [working class] meaning must be sacrificed to the cleansing agency of design aesthetics' (p.119). Weber (2009) has gone on to outline the toning down of classed excesses in the 'make-under' as upward mobility is written onto the body. Palmer (2004) asserts that in *Changing Rooms, House Invaders, What Not to Wear* and *Would Like to Meet,* participants are taught how to appropriate taste and embody middle classness, drawing upon Bourdieu's arguments about class capitals and habitus and resurrecting the trend in nineteenth-century etiquette and advice discussed earlier. Thus, whilst lifestyling is promoted as a signal of the demise of class and the potential attainability of a more affluent (individualized) consumer self, the process itself works to devalue working class culture and taste and instate the middle class as the 'particular universal class' (Savage 2003:536 – also see Chapter 2). Some of the research on reality television also reproduces the classed distinctions that structure the genre, in the same way that Jon Cook (2000) proposes about Bourdieu's work, by suggesting that only high culture constitutes cultural capital and working class culture is located as value-less (Skeggs 2011).

Whereas in the social-realist documentary tradition representations of working class life were couched in valorized discourses of community culture, now the emphasis upon the individual in reality television has been psychologized and premised on personal failure (Ringrose and Walkerdine 2008). Classed ways of life are presented as blockages to progress because they represent a lack of investment in the enterprising neo-liberal self (Doyle and Karl 2008). Thus often those 'ordinary' people most useful to the dramatic narrative of transformation are framed as outside of the consumerist self-improvement game. Elayne Rapping (2004) discusses how in US programmes like *America's Most Wanted* the representation of crime is taken out of any historical context to represent the perpetrators as pathological, as deviants without location, motivation, or any connection to civil culture. Played out against tougher criminal sentences for working class African Americans in particular (Gilmore 2007), US reality cop shows come to represent the socially excluded as aliens and sub-humans. Similarly, in UK television, shows like *Ibiza Uncovered* which detail the unreflexive, sexualized and hedonistic ethnographic display of working class youth on holiday abroad, represent the abject as the constitutive limit to a universalized and ultimately middle class sense of propriety. We have argued previously that many shows whilst presenting 'new ethical selves' as solutions to the structurally inherent problems of contemporary everyday life only represent class and gender antagonisms in new ways (Wood and Skeggs 2004) and we return to a more extended discussion of these debates through our textual analyses in Chapter 3.

The politics of intervention

It is therefore incumbent upon us to keep the politics of gender and class firmly in view, whilst at the same time the intensification of affect and opening out of intimacy in the televisual form urges us to hone our tools for the forthcoming text and audience analysis. In the arguments over reality television's relationship to the documentary form reality television is considered to fail to make any gains in public culture because it lacks the responsible 'authored' voice of the film-maker with a clear point of view and sensibility (Nichols 1991b), suggesting that emphasis on spectacle can only function at the expense of 'message'. However, what this fails to acknowledge is that reality television does not work within the same parameters of representation that were established in documentary tradi-tions, namely reality television has a different temporality and spatiality: it is the drama of the moment, imminent and evocative. We must therefore think through a new relationship between the performative and the social rather than accept one that is structured through the traditional politics of representation.

The issue for us is that reality TV is 'more intervention than representation' (Bratich 2007). It is a constituting technology: according to Jack Bratich (2007) it 'does not *represent* the current conjuncture – it interjects itself into the con-juncture and enhances particular components required by it' (p.7) Recall Stella Bruzzi's (2000) point that documentary in any case does not just work at the level of the constative (representative) but also at the level of the performative: through 'acts' which intervene in the social world. It is for this reason that in this book we attempt to account for reality television through an appropriate sociological *and* media analysis which foregrounds the increasing mediation of self-performance.

In Nichols' (1991b) discussions of documentary it is the performative elements of factual programming that cause a blockage to the functioning of the form in relation to public culture. But for us the very point of self-performance incited through reality television is more intriguing than his dismissal allows. To make successful television, participants need to be able to tell, and increasingly *show*, how they feel. What does this concentration on the performative enact in rela-tion to contemporary social relations, given that inequalities are increasingly structured through a new emphasis upon personal performance? For us, as with many feminist theorists, the move towards the performative *is* constitutive of the political as reality television operates as an intervention into contemporary operations of power. For instance, if participating in reality television can now begin to constitute a 'job' (Jost 2011) what does that signal about the economic imperative to perform oneself as a form of labour? Reality television participants can be bound into exploitative contracts with production companies over their life stories (Collins 2008) and Alison Hearn (2008) writes of reality television's incitement into various forms of impression management where 'branding' the self is a new form of labour and self-performance is now an ultimately commodified endeavour.

Nick Couldry (2003) in his discussion of media rituals gives us the concept of 'media selves' to help explain personhood *as* a mediated phenomenon, one in which most social subjects habitually engage. This reaffirms the media's power in that it ritualizes a 'myth of the mediated centre'. What is significant here is the way in which the mediation of self-disclosure is taken for granted, and yet this is what Couldry discusses as ' … the most puzzling aspect of this whole landscape' (p.116). To be able to perform well at mediated selfhood is applauded in contemporary culture, making sense of the way celebrity – being someone through the media – has become so central to contemporary popular culture. This era of performing personal intimacy has opened out so that the once previously limited access that the public had to being in the media has been extended.

Graeme Turner (2010) describes television in particular as having evolved from representing cultural identities to now 'authoring' identities for profit – a move which must produce far reaching social and cultural effects. He argues that media organizations (in the West) no longer work to represent the interests of other bodies, such as the state, but operate almost *like* a state because it 'legitimates forms of identity that are primarily invented in order to generate commercial returns' (p.23). Reality television 'makes' cultural identity in its own interests, 'operating like an ideological system without an ideological project' (p.25). But as we go on to detail in this book, we are interested in what kind of ideological project this is if it configures its relationship with its audiences in new ways.

Transformations in media at the turn of the century (participation in media forms across alternative platforms) have meant categories like 'text' and 'audience', once discrete in media analysis, are now much more problematic (Tinknell and Raghuram 2002). In reality television the audience often has an interactive role in determining the programme content (as in voting), but also through the possibility of the being in the text (Holmes 2004; Holmes and Jermyn 2004). Whilst Tinknell and Raghuram (2002) are rightly sceptical about assuming that interactivity or participation necessarily equates with resistive activity, these developments offer suggestive implications for understanding a new participatory relationship between the viewer and the screen. Holmes (2008b) suggests that reality television now deploys a 'self-conscious relay between the positions of "performing" and "viewing"' (p.14). Nick Abercrombie and Brian Longhurst's (1998) description of changing audience relations in media saturated societies, suggests that 'we are audience and performer at the same time' (p.57). Holmes points out that this does not equate to open and democratic modes of engagement, and similarly Graeme Turner (2004, 2010) cautions against seeing access as a democratic turn akin to action, substituting the phrase with 'demotic turn'. Likewise, we want to place at the centre of our discussion an exploration of how the very construction of intimacy and immediacy underscores the media's workings of power.

We might see reality television's play with immediacy representing a triumph of the medium (Kavka 2008; Skeggs and Wood 2008). According to Margaret Morse (1998), television's temporal and spatial organization of 'liveness' means that it operates as a fiction of 'presence' rather than as a medium of *re*-presentation. But as Jane Feuer (1983) and Jerome Bourdon (2000) both have pointed out television's claim on 'liveness' is ideological and works to concretize the power of the medium and television's institutions via its grasp on a relatively flexible claim to truth (a debate developed in Chapter 3). Thus the affective aspects of television – the *feeling* of 'being there' – help to account for how the real of reality television becomes meaningful. As Misha Kavka (2008) points out, viewers find truth not in the transparency or erasure of the media frame, but rather in the social or inter-subjective truths that arise out of the frame of manipulation. Here the interactive relations between audience and texts are more significant than systems of representation (Dovey 2000), more suggestive of an 'extended social/ public realm' (Biressi and Nunn 2005).

Reality television may be less an aesthetic genre than a set of techniques and social experiments in which the audience are not so much engaged through the modes of escapism usually associated with fiction, but are ensconced in practices of 'incapism' – a mediated immersion into everyday life (Bratich 2007). This immanent relationship is also embroiled in the debates about the genre's social intervention in questions of ethics. In Hill's (2005) work with audiences she finds that they often make judgements of participants based upon authenticity, on how 'true' they are being to their 'real selves'. Richard Kilborn (2003) points out that:

> There is a sense in which we are made to feel that those who appear as on-screen protagonists actually represent the interests and pre-occupations of the audience. Viewers relate to these persons both as characters in a special made for TV even *and* as real individuals with flesh and blood characteristics. Rather than being allowed to remain at a safe critical distance, viewers are drawn into the world that these performers inhabit.
>
> (2003:52)

Thus there is a double articulation at work here – audiences are both aware of the nature of the constructedness and conventions of the form *and* are also at once immediately implicated in 'flesh and blood' social relations. This sets up an affective set of relations in which emotional attachments may be heightened and which may involve some element of danger, rather than *safe* critical distance. Hill (2007) talks about audience's evocation of a language of shame for watching and for taking part in voyeurism which we return to later in the book. As we maintained throughout this opening chapter, the feminization of the genre and the workings of emotion and melodrama elevate the affective currency of immediacy over the signifying practices of representation (Gorton 2009; Kavka 2008). Misha Kavka (2008) suggests that this amplification of feeling and incorporation of the viewer into the community of the programme offers potential for analysis beyond the over-easy dismissal of viewers having false consciousness. Kavka's textual analysis suspects that 'viewers find their experiences are not quite their own because they are shared by others, hence amplified and all the more real' (p.28). Thus it is *significance* not signification that we tease out in this book. Our research showed how research respondents placed themselves in the same circuits of value to those of the television participants, as if they too may be subject to similar judgements (see Chapter 4). The performance of labour (work, emotional and domestic) became immanently subject to performance review, as if our respondents were under the same demands as the television participants.

Thus we are concerned with what is at stake in this concentration on drama and affect in these new relationships between text and audience. Rather than the emphasis upon the personal in reality TV remaining arrested at the level of affect (circa Nichols), we will see in the next chapter how the circulation of affect *enacts* power relations and thus intervenes in the current socio-political conjuncture. Precisely how does the play on intimacy and immediacy serve to intervene in social relations where the affective and the performative are now so central to the politics of class and gender? Thus we draw our attention to the dangers, politics, and pleasures of getting involved.

This chapter has provided one framework that we develop into analysis through our empirical and textual research later in the book. In the next chapter we explore in more detail the debates in social and cultural theory that have also framed our analysis, extending the issues of intimacy, personhood and performance that we have introduced here.

References

Abercrombie, N. and Longhurst, B. 1998 *Audiences: A Sociological Theory of Performance and Imagination*, London: Sage.

Ahmed, S. 2004 *The Cultural Politics of Emotion*, Edinburgh: Edinburgh University Press.

Anderson, B. 2000 *Doing the Dirty Work? The Global Politics of Domestic Labour*, London: Zed Books.

Andrejevic, M. 2002 'The Kinder, Gentler Gaze of Big Brother: Reality TV in the era of Digital Capitalism', *New Media and Society* 4(2): 251–70.

——2004 *Reality TV: the Work of Being Watched*, Oxford: Rowman and Littlefield.

Ang, I. 1985 *Watching Dallas: Soap Opera and the Melodramatic Imagination*, London: Routledge.

Barnard, S. 1989 'On the Radio: Music and Radio in Britain', Buckingham: Open University Press.

Beck, U. 1992 *Risk Society: Towards a New Modernity*, London: Sage.

Becker, R. 2006 'Help is on the Way! Supernanny, Nanny 911 and the Neo-Liberal Politics of the Family', in D. Heller (ed.) *The Great American Makeover: Television, History, Nation*, New York: Palgrave Macmillan.

Bell, D. and Hollows, J. (eds) 2005 *Ordinary Lifestyles: Popular Media, Consumption and Taste*, Maidenhead and New York: Open University Press.

Bennett, T. 2003 'The Invention of the Modern Cultural Fact: Toward a Critique of the Critique of Everyday Life', in E. B. Silva and T. Bennett (eds) *Contemporary Culture and Everyday Life*, Durham: Sociology Press.

Berlant, L. 1997 *The Queen of America Goes to Washington City: Essays on Sex and Citizenship*, Durham and London: Duke University Press.

——2000 'The Subject of True Feeling: Pain, Privacy, Politics', in S. Ahmed, J. Kilby, C. Lury, M. McNeil and B. Skeggs (eds) *Transformations: Thinking Through Feminism*, London: Routledge.

——(ed.) 2004 *Compassion: the Culture and Politics of an Emotion*, London and New York: Routledge.

——2006 'Cruel Optimism', *Differences: A Journal of Feminist Cultural Studies* 17(3): 20–36.

——2008 *The Female Complaint: The Unfinished Business of Sentimentality in American Culture*, London and Durham: Duke University Press.

Biressi, A. and Nunn, H. 2005 *Reality TV: Realism and Revelation*, London: Wallflower Press.

——2008 *The Tabloid Culture Reader*, New York: McGraw Hill.

Blackman, L. 2004 'Self-help, Media Cultures and the Production of Female Psychopathology', *Cultural Studies* 7(2): 219–56.

Bonner, F. 2003 *Ordinary Television: Analysing Popular TV*, London: Sage.

——2008 'Fixing Relationships in 2-4-1 Transformations', *Continuum: Journal of Media and Cultural Studies* 22(4): 547–57.

Bourdieu, P. 1986 *Distinction: A Social Critique of the Judgement of Taste*, London: Routledge.

Bourdon, J. 2000 'Live Television is Still Alive', *Media, Culture and Society* 22(5): 531–56.

Bratich, J. Z. 2007 'Programing Reality: Control Societies, New Subjects, Powers of Transformation', in D. Heller (ed.) *Makeover Television: Realities Remodelled*, London: I.B. Taurus.

Bromley, R. 2000 'The Theme That Dare Not Speak its Name: Class and Recent British Film', in S. Munt (ed.) *Cultural Studies and the Working Class: Subject to Change*, London: Cassells.

Brooks, P. 1976/1995 *The Melodramatic Imagination: Balzac, Henry James, Melodrama and the Mode of Excess*, New Haven and London: Yale University Press.

Brown, W. 1995 'Wounded Attachments: Late Modern Oppositional Political Formations', in J. Rajchman (ed.) *The Identity in Question*, New York and London: Routledge.

Brunsdon, C. 2003 'Lifestyling Britain: The 8–9 Slot on British Television', *International Journal of Cultural Studies* 6(1): 5–23.

Bruzzi, S. 2000 *New Documentary: A Critical Introduction*, London and New York: Routledge.

——2006 *New Documentary*, 2nd Edition, London and New York: Routledge.

Butler, J. 1993 *Bodies That Matter: On the Discursive Limits of 'Sex'*, London: Routledge.

——2004 *Undoing Gender*, New York and London: Routledge.

Collins, S. 2008 'Making the Most out of 15 mintues: Reality TV's Dispensable Celebrity', *Television and New Media* 9(2): 87–110.

Cook, J. 2000 'Culture, Class and Taste', in S. Munt (ed.) *Cultural Studies and the Working Class: Subject to Change*, London: Cassell.

Corner, J. 1996 *The Art of the Record: A Critical Introduction to Documentary*, Manchester: Manchester University Press.

——2002 'Performing the Real: Documentary Diversions', *Television and New Media* 3(3): 255–69.

——2006 'Analysing Factual TV: How to Study Television Documentary', in G. Creeber (ed.) *Tele-visions: An Intoduction to the Study of Television*, London: BFI.

Couldry, N. 2003 *Media Rituals: A Critical Approach*, London: Routledge.

Coven, V. 2005 'If you want to see Morality tune into *Big Brother*', *The Observer* 23 January 2005.

David, M. 1980 *The State, the Family and Education*, London: Routledge and Kegan Paul.

Davidoff, L. and Hall, C. 1987 *Family Fortunes*, London: Hutchinson.

Debord, G. 1967/1994 *The Society of the Spectacle*, London: Verso.

Deleuze, E. and Deleuze, J. 1978 'Giles Deleuze: Lecture Transcripts on Spinoza's Concept of *Affect*', Vol. 2006: http://www.webdeleuze.com/php/sommaire.html.

Deleuze, J. 1969/1990 *The Logic of Sense*, New York: Columbia University Press.

Dovey, J. 2000 *Freakshow: First Person Media and Factual Television*, London: Pluto.

Doyle, J. and Karl, I. 2008 'Shame on You: Cosmetic Surgery and Class Transformation in 10 Years Younger', in G. Palmer (ed.) *Exposing Lifestyle Television*, Ashgate: Aldershot.

Dyhouse, C. 1976 'Social Darwinistic Ideas and the Development of Women's Education in England 1880–1920', *History of Education* 5(2): 41–58.

——1977 'Good Wives and Little Mothers: Social Anxieties and the Schoolgirls' Curriculum 1890–1920', *Oxford Review of Education* 3(1): 21–35.

Eagleton, T. 1989 'The Ideology of the Aesthetic', in P. Hernadi (ed.) *The Rhetoric of Interpretation and the Interpretation of Rhetoric*, Durham and London: Duke University Press.

Ehrenreich, B. 1990 *Fear of Falling: The Inner Life of the Middle-Class*, New York: Pantheon.

Ehrenreich, B. and English, D. 2005 *For Her Own Good: Two Centuries of the Expert's Advice to Women*, New York: Anchor Books.

Ehrenreich, B. and Hochschild, A. 2004 *Global Women: Nannies, Maids and Sex Workers in the New Economy*: Henry Holt and Co.

Elsaesser, T. 1987 'Tales of Sound and Fury: observations on the Family Melodrama', in C. Gledhill (ed.) *Home is Where the Heart is: Studies in Melodrama and Women's Film*, London: BFI.

Feuer, J. 1983 'The Concept of Live Television: Ontology as Ideology', in E. A. Kaplan (ed.) *Regarding Television: Critical Approaches – An Anthology*, Los Angeles: American Film Institute.

Gailey, E. A. 2006 'Self-made Women: Cosmetic surgery shows and the construction of female psychopathology', in D. Heller (ed.) *Makeover Television: Realities Remodelled*.

Giddens, A. 1991 *Modernity and Self-Identity; Self and Society in the Late Modern Age*, Cambridge: Polity.

Gill, R. 2007 *Gender and the Media*, Cambridge: Polity.

Gilmore, W. R. 2007 *Golden Gulag: Prisons, Surplus, Crisis, and Opposition in Globalizing California*, Berkeley and Los Angeles: University of California Press.

Gilroy, P. 1987 *There Ain't no Black in the Union Jack*, London: Hutchinson.

Gledhill, C. 1987 *Home is Where the Heart is: Studies in Melodrama and Women's Film*, London: Routledge.

——2000 'Rethinking Genre', in C. Gledhill and L. Williams (eds) *Reinventing Film Studies*, London: Arnold.

Gorton, K. 2009 *Media Audiences: Television, Meaning and Emotion*, Edinburgh: Edinburgh University Press.

Griffen-Foley, B. 2004 'From Tit-Bits to Big Brother: A Century of Audience Participation in the Media', *Media Culture and Society* 26(4): 533–48.

Haralovich, M.-B. 1992 'Sit-coms and Suburbs: Positioning the 1950s Homemaker', in
L. Spigel and D. Mann (eds) *Private Screenings: Television and the Female Consumer*,
Minneapolis: University of Minnesota.

Hawkins, G. 2001 'The Ethics of Television', *International Journal of Cultural Studies* 4(4):
412–26.

Hearn, A. 2008 'Variations on the Branded Self: theme, invention, improvisation and
inventory', in D. Hesmondhalgh and J. Toynbee (eds) *The Media and Social Theory*,
London and New York: Routledge.

Heelas, P. 2002 'Work Ethics, Soft Capitalism and the "Turn to Life"', in P. du Gay and
M. Pryke (eds) *Cultural Economy*, London: Sage.

Hermes, J. 1993 'Media, Meaning and Everyday Life', *Cultural Studies* 7: 493–506.

Hill, A. 2005 *Reality TV: Audiences and Popular Factual Television*, London: Routledge.

——2007 *Restyling Factual TV: Audiences and News, Documentary and Reality Genres*, London:
Routledge.

Hochschild, A. 2003 *The Commercial Spirit of Intimate Life and Other Essays*, San Fransisco and
Los Angeles: University of California Press.

Holmes, S. 2004 '"But this time you choose!" Approaching the interactive audience in
reality TV', *International Journal of Cultural Studies* 7(2): 213–31.

——2008a *Entertaining Television: The BBC and Popular Television Culture in the 1950s*,
Manchester: University Press.

——2008b 'The Viewers have ... taken over the airwaves? Participation, reality TV and
approaching the audience-in-the-text', *Screen* 49(1): 13–31.

Holmes, S. and Jermyn, D. (eds) 2004 *Understanding Reality Television*, London: Routledge.

Huyssen, A. 1986 'Mass Culture as Woman: Modernism's Other', in T. Modleski (ed.)
Studies in Light Entertainment: Critical Approaches to Mass Culture: Indiana University Press.

Illouz, E. 2003 *Oprah Winfrey and the Glamour of Misery*, New York: Columbia University
Press.

Jermyn, D. and Holmes, S. 2008 '"Ask the fastidious woman from Surbiton to hand-wash
the underpants of the aging Oldham Skinhead ... ": Why not Wife Swap?', in
T. Austin and W. De Jong (eds) *Rethinking Documentary: New Perspectives and Practices*,
Oxford: Oxford University Press.

Jost, F. 2011 'When Reality TV is a job', in M. M. Kraidy and K. Sender (eds) *The Politics
of Reality Television: Global Perspectives*, London and New York: Routledge.

Kahn, J. S. 2001 *Modernity and Exclusion*, London: Sage.

Kavka, M. 2008 *Reality Television, Affect and Intimacy: Reality Matters*, London: Palgrave
Macmillan.

Kilborn, R. 2003 *Staging the Real: Factual TV Programing in the Age of Big Brother*, Manchester:
Manchester University Press.

Langland, E. 1995 *Nobody's Angels: Middle Class Women and Domestic Ideology in Victorian
Culture*, Ithica, NT: Cornell University Press.

Lewis, T. 2007 'He Needs to Face His Fears with these Five Queers!: Queer Eye for the
Straight Guy, Makeover TV and the Lifestyle Expert', *Television and New Media*, 8(4):
205–311.

——2008 *Smart Living: Lifestyle Media and Popular Expertise*, New York: Peter Lang.

Masciarotte, G.-J. 1991 'C'mon, Girl: Oprah Winfrey and the Discourse of Feminine
Talk', *Genders* 11 (Fall): 81–110.

Massumi, B. 1996 'The Autonomy of Affect', in P. Patton (ed.) *Deleuze: A Critical Reader*,
Oxford: Blackwell.

Mathiesen, T. 1997 'The Viewer Society: Michel Foucault's "Panoptican" Revisited', *Theoretical Criminology* 1(2): 215–34.

McCarthy, A. 2004 '"Stanley Milgrim, Allen Funt and Me": Post war Social Science and the "First Wave" of Reality TV', in S. Murray and L. Ouellette (eds) *Reality TV: Remaking Television Culture*, New York: New York University Press.

McLaughlin, L. 1993 'Chastity Criminals in the Age of Electronic Reproduction: Re-viewing Talk Television and the Public Sphere', *Journal of Communication Enquiry* 7(1): 41–55.

McRobbie, A. 2002 'From Holloway to Hollywood: Happiness at Work in the New Cultural Economy', in P. du Gay and M. Pryke (eds) *Cultural Economy*, London: Sage.

——2004 'Notes on "What Not to Wear" and Post-Feminist Symbolic Violence', in L. Adkins and B.Skeggs (eds) *Feminism after Bourdieu*, Oxford: Blackwell.

——2009 *In the Aftermath of Feminism: Gender, Culture and Social Change*, London: Sage.

Medhurst, A. 1999 'The Royle Family' *Material Cultures* conference, Coventry.

Miller, T. 2006 'Metrosexuality: See the Bright Light of Commodification Shine! Watch Yanqui Masculinity Made Over!', in D. Heller (ed.) *The Great American Makeover: Television, History, Nation*, New York: Palgrave Macmillan.

——2007 *Cultural Citizenship: Cosmopolitanism, Consumerism and Television in the Neo-liberal Age*, Philadelphia: Temple University Press.

Mitchell, C. 2001 *Women and Radio*, London and New York: Routledge.

Moran, A. 2005 'Configurations of the New Television Landscape', in J. Wasko (ed.) *A Companion to Television*, London and Victoria: Blackwell.

Morse, M. 1998 *Virtualities: Television, Media Art, and Cyberculture*, Indianapolis, IN: Indiana University Press.

Moseley, R. 2000 'Makeover Takeover on British Television', *Screen* 41(3): 299–314.

Negra, D. and Tasker, Y. (eds) 2007 *Interrogating Postfeminism: Gender and the Politics of Popular Culture*, Durham: Duke University Press.

Nichols, B. 1991a *Representing Reality*, Indiana: Indiana University Press.

——1991b *Representing Reality: Issues and Concepts of Documentary*, Bloomington and Indianapolis: Indiana University Press.

——1994 *Blurred Boundaries: Questions of Meaning in Contemporary Culture*, Indianapolis IN: Indiana University Press.

Ouellette, L. 2004 '"Take Responsibility for Yourself" Judge Judy and the Neo-liberal Citizen', in S. Murray and L. Oullette (eds) *Reality TV: Remaking Television Culture*, New York: New York University Press.

Ouellette, L. and Hay, J. 2008 *Better Living Through Reality Television*, Oxford: Blackwell.

Palmer, G. 2003 *Discipline and Liberty: Television and Governance*, Manchester: Manchester University Press.

——2004 '"The New You": Class and Transformation in Lifestyle Television', in S. Holmes and D. Jermyn (eds) *Understanding Reality Television*, London: Routledge.

Philips, D. 2005 'Transformation Scenes: The television interior make-over', *International Journal of Cultural Studies* 8(2): 213–29.

Piper, H. 2004 'Reality TV, Wife Swap and the Drama of Banality', *Screen* 45(4): 273–86.

Pullen, C. 2004 'The Household, the Basement, and The Real World: Gay Identity in the Constructed Reality Environment', in S. Holmes and D. Jermyn (eds) *Understanding Reality Television*, London: Routledge.

Raphael, C. 2004 'The Politcal Economic Origins of Reali-TV', in L. Ouellette and S. Murray (eds) *Reality TV: Remaking Television Culture*, New York: New York University Press.

Rapping, E. 1995 'Daytime Inquiries', in G. Hines and J. M. Hume (eds) *Gender, Race and Class in Media*, Thousand Oaks, California, London: Sage.

——2004 'Aliens, Nomads, Mad Dogs and Warriors: the Changing Face of Criminal Violence on Reality TV', in S. Murray and L. Oullette (eds) *Reality TV: Remaking Television Culture*, New York: New York University Press.

Ringrose, J. and Walkerdine, V. 2008 'Regulating the Abject: The TV Make-over as a site of Neo-Liberal Reinvention, towards Bourgeois Femininity', *Feminst Media Studies* 8 (3): 227–46.

Rose, N. 1989 *Governing the Soul: The Shaping of the Private Self*, London: Routledge.

——1999 *Governing the Soul: the Shaping of the Private Self*, Second Edition, London: Free Association Books.

Rushdie, S. 2001 'RealityTV: A Dearth of Talent and the Death of Morality', *The Guardian*, 9 June 2001.

Savage, M. 2003 'A New Class Paradigm? Review Article', *British Journal of Sociology of Education* 24(4): 535–41.

Savage, M., Bagnall, G. and Longhurst, R. 2001 'Ordinary, Ambivalent and Defensive: Class Identities in the Northwest of England', *Sociology* 35(4): 875–92.

Sayer, A. 2002 'What are you Worth? Why Class is an Embarrassing Subject', *Sociological Research Online* 7(3).

——2005 *The Moral Significance of Class*, Cambridge: Cambridge University Press.

Shattuc, J. 1997 *The Talking Cure: TV Talk Shows and Women*, New Jersey: Lawrence Erlbaum.

Skeggs, B. 1997 *Formations of Class and Gender: Becoming Respectable.*, London: Sage.

——2004 *Class, Self, Culture*, London: Routledge.

——2011 'Imagining Personhood Differently: Person Value and Autonomist Working Class Value Practices', *Sociological Review* 59(3): 579–94.

Skeggs, B. and Wood, H. 2008 'The Labour of Transformation and Circuits of Value "around" Reality Television', *Continuum: Journal of Media and Cultural Studies* 22(4): 559–72.

Steedman, C. 2000 'Enforced Narratives: Stories of Another Self', in T. Cosslett, C. Lury and P. Summerfield (eds) *Feminism and Autobiography: Texts, Theories, Methods*, London: Routledge.

Strathern, M. 1992 *After Nature: English Kinship in the Late Twentieth Century*, Cambridge: Cambridge University Press.

Taylor, C. 1989 *Sources of the Self: The Making of the Modern Identity*, Cambridge: Cambridge University Press.

——1991 *The Ethics of Authenticity*, Cambridge, Mass: Cambridge University Press.

Taylor, L. 2005 '"It was Beautiful Before you Changed it all": Class, Taste and the Tranformative Aesthetics of the Garden Lifestyle Media', in D. Bell and J. Hollows (eds) *Ordinary Lifestyles: Popular Media, Consumption and Taste*, Maidenhead: Open University Press.

Tinknell, E. and Raghuram, P. 2002 'Big Brother: Reconfiguring the "Active" Audience of Cultural Studies?', *European Journal of Cultural Studies* 5(2): 199–215.

Turner, G. 2004 *Understanding Celebrity*, London: Sage.

——2010 *Ordinary People and the Media: The Demotic Turn*, London: Sage.

Van Zoonen, L. 2001 'Desire and Resistance: *Big Brother* and the Recognition of Everyday Life', *Media, Culture and Society* 23(5): 667–9.

Veblen, T. B. 1899/2008 *The Theory of the Leisure Class*, New York: A. M. Kelly.

Walkerdine, V. 2011 'Shame on you! Intergenerational Trauma and Working-class Femininity on Reality Television', in H. Wood and B. Skeggs (eds) *Reality Television and Class*, London: BFI/Palgrave.

Watson, P. 1998 *The Daily Mail*.

Weber, B. 2009 *Makeover TV: Selfhood, Citizenship and Celebrity*, Durham, NC: Duke University Press.

Williams, L. 2001 *Playing the Race Card: Melodramas of Black and White from Uncle Tom to O.J. Simpson*, Princeton: Princeton University Press.

Williams, Z. 2003 'Bride and Prejudice: Tonight's celebrity edition of *Wife Swap* is proof that the programme is more about class than couples', *The Guardian* (Media), 11 November.

Wood, H. 2009a *Talking with Television: Women, Talk Shows and Modern Self-Reflexivity*, Illinois: Illinois University Press.

Wood, H. and Skeggs, B. 2004 'Notes on Ethical Scenarios of Self on British Reality TV', *Feminist Media Studies* 4(2): 205–8.

Chapter 2

Performance and the value of personhood

In this chapter we introduce the social and cultural theories that inform our analysis. Taking on board arguments from media theory we suggest that media 'normalize' their own power by *creating* models for the distribution of value as they extend their reach into everyday life and intimacy. We extend the analytic frame of Chapter 1 to understand the social and cultural context which frames the mediation of performance. We draw out a framework for the co-extensive social relationships into which reality television enters, suggesting a more reverberative enactment between social relations and media power than is currently available.

Nick Couldry's (2006) discussion of the new media landscape of reality television suggests that 'the most puzzling aspect' is 'the notion that the media provide a "central" space where it makes sense to disclose publically aspects of one's life that one might not otherwise disclose to anyone' (p.16). We show here which social factors give force to this imperative to self-disclosure and unpack the 'puzzle' demonstrating the extension of modes of telling oneself into new modes of self-performance. First, we develop the discussion in Chapter 1 in more detail by demonstrating how trends in social theory have led to the dominant interpretation of television's current focus on the self as a technique of individualization and governance. We then move to think beyond these models of a 'singular self' through an analysis of the techniques for performing personhood. We challenge the focus on the singular and insular self of individualization or governmentality theory through an analysis of value, performance and affect, which we show to be resolutely social and relational, staged through class and gender legacies.

Beginning with historical research we detail how performing personhood is always connected to ideas about value (economic, moral, affective). Previously social space was organized and idealized into a highly valued gendered male public and a lesser valued affective female private sphere. However, the imperatives of quantification and calculation that were associated with the former and the qualitative emotions associated with the latter have now shifted terrains, permeating each other and producing on one hand *new* ideas about what it means to be a proper person, but also moving techniques between the two domains so that the 'private' affective domain became subject to calculation and quantification, whilst the public economic sphere was infused with methods for using affect to extract value. These legacies of techniques for calculation and relationality as forms of value are carried into the present and as we show are complicated by structures of class and gender.

We are thus interested in the circulation and distribution of value on reality television. As we noted in the introduction we are working with a model of person value that is based on accruing, defending and affecting (relating to others). Only the former works within the traditional classed politics of the 'possessive individual' where people can own property in themselves. The other value formations are about investments and actions, whereby in the former people defend the value they can access in order to legitimate and put a floor on their circumstances; in the latter they connect to others as a gift and source of value. It is only when we move into understanding value in the abstract do we make the connection to how this person value works for capital more generally. Western neo-liberalism (extending the politics of the possessive individual) encourages us to think of ourselves as 'human capital' (Feher 2009), as do some theories of subject formation as we show. We have also been encouraged to think of ourselves as having value contained within us, a psychic property of the self and a form of moral interiority, something that reality television programmes work hard to visualize. In this chapter we detail how attention to self-accrual (for future reward) and the metaphorical inner (generated from past investment) deflects analysis away from present inequalities, away from the social relations and value circuits we inhabit.

All performance is ultimately predicated upon it having an effect on others and thus many commentators discuss contemporary social and political relations as built through the distribution of affect, through 'affective economies' (Ahmed 2004a). Therefore we turn our attention to what affect is and how it works, always with the potential to disrupt the normative performative, and offering the potential for connections to be made to audiences. But also for understanding how affect became a source of value for women. Because affect is always the unpredictable element in a social encounter, we explore how it offers great entertainment potential, but also how it cannot be subject to regulation (although 'feeling rules' are a staple of much reality television), and thus opens up ways to move beyond traditional understandings of governance and representation.

The singular self as a classed imperative

The now full-blown emphasis upon *self*-representation across television has meant that television analysts have turned to the burgeoning literature on self-hood across social theory. There has been a plethora of writing on the increased significance of the self as an aesthetic project. Beginning with Michel Foucault's description of the modernist 'aesthetic self', which operates as the base line from which most other models develop: we also have the 'postmodern self' outlined by Mike Featherstone (1991) where the self is expected to display its own value through the acquisition of cultural objects and knowledge; the 'enterprising self' of Paul du Gay (1996) where the self turns itself into a project of cultural investment in order to become employable; or the branded self as described by Tom Peters (1999) and Alison Hearn (2008) where self-promotion is the name of the game. There are also other culturally resourced selves such as the 'mobile self' proposed by John Urry (2000); the 'possessed self' of Arthur Kroker (1992); and the 'prosthetic self' of Marilyn Strathern (1992) and Celia Lury (1998). The self has also been described by the methods by which it reveals itself. The 'reflexive self' of the risk society described by Ulrich Beck (1992) and the individualization thesis of Anthony Giddens (1991) describe how a 'new' self requires specific methods of narration and biography in advanced capitalism. Bourdieu's (2000) habitus is also a description of self figured through the conversions of capital it can or cannot make across time and space. Many of these proposed selves are underpinned by an abstract understanding of the 'rational actor', a trope of selfhood that gets repeated throughout history as an explanation for self-interested economic acts (Fine 2001), but by which social responsibility is located at the site of the singular individual rather than the collective social.

When putting all these formulations of self from social theory together, a model of self emerges, a self that is constantly engaged in increasing its potential for exchange-value: in converting its potential or capacity into social movement in the present *and* in the future (Skeggs 2004c). These are all models of selves on the move and on the make, which display their value, in order to be recognized by others. They provide descriptions of a self that can *access* cultural resources, can *move* across social space and can *invest* in its self. Actually they describe the different shapes that the middle class self takes in contemporary conditions, be it adaptation to the new immaterial technical opportunities in the economy, gaining moral worth in a competitive arts market, or dispersing value via inheritance and accrual by loading their children with competitive advantage through educational/cultural experience.

It is not surprising therefore that research on reality television has often drawn on this more recent literature on the self to describe its spectacularization (Dovey 2000). As discussed in Chapter 1 many accounts see the televised pedagogic advance for better living as about improving oneself in the interests of the nation, adopting modes of governance as a neo-liberal initiative that works alongside the repeal of the state provision (Heller 2006; Lewis 2008; Ouellette and Hay 2008; Weber 2009). Others construct a more positive image of the democratic ability to freely construct oneself from numerous (mediated) resources. For instance John Hartley's (2004) 'DIY self' suggests a potentially liberating form of cultural citizenship. Either way there has been some consensus on the rising cultural significance of what Rachel Moseley (2000) calls 'the makeover takeover'.

The problem is that some of the work on reality television, which straightfor-wardly adopts social theories of the self, does so without adequate attention to the classed dynamic of this call to self-accrual, display and recognition. Move-ment through social space offers ample opportunity for the middle class self to constantly amass and attach value to itself and its inheritors. Historically it is the culture, morals and aesthetics of the middle class that are regarded as legitimate and thus can operate as forms of symbolic capital. Terry Eagleton (1989), for instance, describes the emergence of the middle class as a specific aesthetic moral project, one that was able to legitimate its own interests through the institutions of education, law, welfare and the promotion of a particular form of 'superior', 'high' culture. However, the working class is purposely excluded from access to these forms of symbolic authority. For instance, descriptions of the British working class in the dominant media and political rhetoric reveal them to be represented as at a distance from the normative. Chris Haylett (2001) in the UK demonstrates how the white working class are repeatedly and regularly described as 'useless subjects' an atavistic drain on the nation, as ungovernable and as a blockage to the development of cosmopolitan global capitalism. Likewise in the US accusations of laziness, irresponsibility and stupidity are attached to the white and black working class, making personal dispositions the measure of structural inequality, using the epitaph 'trash' to literally position the working class as waste (Hartigan 2005). These examples show how the supposed lack of volition to work on one's self is politically rhetoricized as a lack of aspiration and ambition in which the person is shown to lack the capacity to accumulate value. Bad behaviour is coded as an issue of psychology, a faulty disposition and a personal failure: bad culture equals bad choice. But at birth one inherits differential *access* to the space and resources required to *acquire* and *convert* capitals.

When Pierre Bourdieu (2000) describes the self-accruing bourgeois habitus that constantly accumulates capital as it moves across social space, he is both describing and critiquing the process. These descriptive critiques are useful when they connect to empirical specificity: the enterprising self, for instance, can indeed be seen as a new form of worker commodification in the new media/high tech middle class occupations; the 'post-modern' self describes the development of a new cultural intermediary, a faction of the professional middle class, and Bourdieu provides a vivid study of how the bourgeois habitus reproduces itself through French education, academic, and art/culture (taste) structures (Bourdieu 1984 [1979], 1988, 1990 [1965], 1996). Yet most theorists of the self propose their models as universal when in fact they are specific, Western, historical, class/race/gender formations (and usually that of the theorist), with little recognition of the conditions of production of their own theories. For instance, Giddens (1991) and Beck (1992), without any empirical research, propose the decline of class cultures and the rise of individualization and reflexivity as a Western universal. Beck maintains that the self chooses the structural forces on which to act and which to ignore, enabling them to live out the diversity of the social relations that surround them, generating a self-narrativizing biographical self in a condition of reflexive modernity. Likewise, Giddens describes the self as constantly reflecting on its actions in order to plan its future. For both theorists the method (of narrating the self) is the key to self-production: the self communicates with its self in order to enhance its future potential and interests.[1] The method is evoked as if neutral, as if telling oneself is a technique freely available to all (Adkins 2002; Skeggs 2002). Many of these perspectives present the narration of the interior self as 'new', rather than a re-working of Adam Smith's (1757) classic promotion of the subject of capitalism where he sets out the model for the perfect subject of profit who invests (via religion) through reflecting on his own self-interests (Skeggs 2004a). These are theories and methods that represent the lives, interests and perspectives of the middle class and against which the working class are measured. It is not surprising therefore that the working class is found lacking, making the theories themselves rather limited in their explanatory capacity (Aguiar 2011; Skeggs 2011).

As we know from the histories of the generation of working class subjectivity, reflexivity and telling are specific cultural-linguistic resources available and structured through race, class and gender relations, connected to sources of authority such as religion, the state, and capital (Steedman 2000; Vincent 1981). Therefore if reality television foregrounds an emphasis upon the self, it must also foreground class, even if the ties to structural inequality are not always made explicit. As we suggested in the last chapter some writers on reality television point to the over-representation of working class subjects as figures of failure in need of transformation, and to the symbolic violence done to participants as their culture is erased. The viewer is most often offered a place of class-based and taste-based superiority (Moseley 2000) as the 'middle class normative', which Savage (2003) describes as now occupying the dominant cultural ground, and which fits neatly into the messages of ethically good selfhood on television. It was precisely for this reason that we wanted to extend our analysis of economies of personhood (Skeggs 2004a, 2011, 2012b), of how value is distributed to persons, into the arena of reality television, as the significance and spectacularization of the self – its fashioning, telling, performance and labour – dramatically take centre stage.

However, before we proceed we need to define what we mean by class. We begin with Bourdieu's (1987, 1989) analysis of capitals. Along with economic capital he also identifies the following.

- *Cultural capital*: this can exist in three forms: in an embodied state i.e. in the form of long lasting dispositions of the mind and the body; in the objectified state, in the form of cultural goods and in the institutionalized state, resulting in such things as educational qualifications. Bourdieu defines cultural capital as high culture.[2]
- *Social capital*: resources based on connection, networks and group membership: who you know, used in pursuit of favour and advancement.

- *Symbolic capital*: the form the different types of capital take once they are perceived and recognized as legitimate. Legitimation is the key mechanism in the conversion to power. Cultural capital has to be legitimated before it can have symbolic power. Capital has to be regarded as legitimate before it can be capitalized upon, before its value is realizable.

All capitals are context specific and their value depends upon the fields in which they are exchanged/converted. Thus, according to Bourdieu, all people are distributed in the overall social space according to: the global *volume* of capital they possess; the *composition* of their capital, the relative weight in their overall capital of the various forms of capital and *evolution over time* of the volume and composition according to their *trajectory* in social space. Thus when we talk about class we are talking about the different compositions and volumes that people carry as they are distributed across social space. This enables us to explain how cultural resources such as language and emotions can be seen to be classed, as they are forms of capital that are limited in distribution: not everybody has access to the same culture, to capital, to social networks and to forms of legitimation. It also enables us to see how class, race and gender constitute and disrupt each other through their capital composition.

Classed moral techniques

One might argue that the visualization of self-work reveals its classed dimensions, but on the whole reality television denies the historical structural inequalities which leave some participants bereft of the appropriate skills to cope in the new conditions afforded by television. Models of the self most generally encouraged on reality television are versions of the aesthetic, enterprising, reflexive and prosthetic selves, promoted through a self-work ethic (Heelas 2002) (see also Chapter 7). The prosthetic self is based on experimentation, on playing with knowledge, objects and culture and is thus the perfect model for reality television and we discuss in Chapter 3 the way in which the opening out of intimacy and selfhood is compatible with the mutation of television formats. The prosthetic self, historically and empirically detailed as resolutely middle class by Marilyn Strathern (1992), moves through social space converting aspects that previously seemed (naturally or socially) fixed (such as gender) into sites of strategic decision-making. For instance, male managers using emotional management techniques to manipulate workers in order to gain rewards (Adkins and Lury 1999). In adopting/adapting a prosthesis, the person is constituted in the relation 'I can, therefore I am' (Lury 1998) and the emphasis is placed upon 'doing' and knowing what to use to enhance self-value. As we go on to discuss, reality television constantly places participants in situations not of their own making, creating the drama out of their reaction and ultimately their ability or not to 'manage' themselves.

Even more crucial to the study of reality television, is the understanding that this 'play' with prosthetic selfhood involves the individual in performance. In her study of prosthesis Strathern (1992) points out that the opportunity for forms of self-enhancement from the choosing and 'putting on' of parts (prosthesis) is also ultimately dramatic and performative (see also Munro (1996)): for instance, acting out caring for somebody in order to achieve rewards by deploying the 'right' emotional dispositions. We choose which dispositions to hide and display depending on the encounter and the audience. On television, reality participants are expected to display themselves through prosthetic enhancement where we see them trying to perform different capacities, through the taking on and off parts, knowledge, relationships and ways of being. For instance *Faking It* directly asks participants to become another entity far removed from their own experience – a burger bar worker tries to pass as a professional chef, or a factory worker must become a fashion designer. *Wife Swap* asks women to take on the role of another wife and mother, to see what they might learn from someone else's experience. *Ladette to Lady* puts working class women into an old fashioned finishing school to see if they can learn to 'become' a lady. Much of reality television is constantly about testing individuals in new theatres of experience to capture the right per-formance for the circumstances (although the circumstances from which the TV participant emerges are usually occluded).

This process enables us to see how elements of behaviour – dispositions, aes-thetics, emotions, intentions, relations – are known through the distribution and attachment of value to each. For instance, Weber (2009) describes how make-over television makes explicit what should be left behind and what should be carried into the future in order to establish a more valuable self – the mobile 'after body'. Performing 'doing' responsibility displays one's capacity for it. The pressure to reflexively construct one's biography through telling and performing the stabilizing narratives of the family, for instance, by demonstrating the desire to be a better wife, mother, carer, enables the display of moral responsibility on reality television (and elsewhere); it is an act of *value production*.

Some reality television therefore extends the model of a middle class self and offers it as a model for working class subjects to achieve when they are always/already positioned through recruitment as in need of transformation. Class relations are not just premised upon attempts to impose middle class *standards* but also about deployment of *techniques* (such as reflexive telling of moral inter-iority) that are mainly accessible to and operate in the interests of the middle class. These techniques are attached to institutionalized *moral* narratives that legitimate middle class forms of organization such as the nuclear family.[3]

The moral imperative of reality television, so freely identified by journalists and academics alike and discussed in Chapter 1, requires some considerable historical contextualization if we are to fully take account of reality television's intervention in social relations. Historically, classes in Britain had access to very different gendered and classed ways of telling themselves: Middle class men were expected to tell their value through narratives of property and adventure in the tradition of the possessive individual, whereas middle class women were expected to express domestic and moral purity and responsibility. Certain forms of subjectivity, such as 'the knowing self' with interiority, were attributed to the bourgeois subject. Carolyn Steedman (2000) points to the significance of the tradition of the 'great European novel' to show that *what* we tell and *how* we tell our selves has been influenced through the technique of literary production. David Vincent (1981), in a study of English working class autobiography in the nineteenth century, describes how working class experience was coded through the display of respectability by morally inspiring pieces of work encouraged by religious evangelists. The working classes were only offered the position of self if they could fit into a particular mode of telling morally redemptive narratives. This work also demonstrates how the concept of a recuperative self was developed from an early age in working class children, making morality central to self-production *and* child development (Steedman 1990; Walkerdine and Lucey 1989).

Steedman further traces how certain forms of subjectivity were formed through relations with state administration in the distribution of poor relief and legal decisions about social worthiness. Most well known of these are stories of the 'deserving poor' and the gendered variant of the recuperable fallen woman, who reiterates the narrative of seduction, betrayal and redemption. (As we have discussed in Chapter 1 this trope is repeated in programmes like *Secret Millionaire* or *Poor Little Rich Girl* where the state is replaced by the entrepreneur or the television production company.) The way in which the self can be told therefore is highly regulated. Legal questions structured the forms of telling and recorded accounts remove the interlocutor as the self emerges through its answers to legal questions. Steedman notes:

> By these means, multitudes of labouring men and women surveyed a life from a fixed standpoint, told it in chronological sequence, gave an account of what it was that brought them to this place, this circumstance now, telling the familiar tale for the justices clerk to [...] transcribe.
>
> (2000:29–30)

If we substitute 'the justices clerk' for the talk show host we get some sense of how these techniques have been carried into the present. By making people accountable through the telling of themselves, moral character is revealed. We must therefore be aware of the traditions of the performative structuring of speech because they have a history of bringing gendered and classed selves into effect to be recognized as with or without moral value.

Techniques for telling the self have expanded into the full-blown performance of the self on reality television, conditioned by the new forms of media organization in which the mediation of selfhood is ritually acknowledged. Under many reality formats the self comes under pressure to 'choose' which way to present themselves, to experiment and act. Yet many of the participants selected for reality television make-over and self-transformation programmes (the types of programmes used for our research) are unlikely to have a great range of resources upon which to draw. The techniques for self-performance therefore become a means by which participants are asked to display their lack of technical/linguistic skill for entertainment. Talk show precedents like *The Jerry Springer Show* (US) and *The Jeremy Kyle Show* (UK) offer the most vivid examples of inappropriate behaviour: when shouting and screaming display an inability to reflexively demonstrate control over the telling of the self. As Wood (2001, 2009) observed talk show hosts incite narratives using combative strategies to generate the best dramatic spectacle as a condition of good television. Forms of telling are therefore also structured and transformed by the entertainment drive of television (see Tolson 2011).

We can see this carried over into reality formats, not just via the transformation narrative of the make-over but also through the antagonistic formats which pit obvious (class) backgrounds against one another, such as *Wife Swap, Holiday Showdown*, etc. Yet this lack of access to linguistic capital often appears as if it is both a personality disposition and the choice of the person, rather than as a result of structural inequality heightened by the production process. It appears as though participants have *chosen* to behave in such an excessive way, rather than to give time to, or acknowledgement of, a different rather than deficient culture. Our textual analysis in Chapter 3 thus draws attention to the techniques that incite the display of a lack of access to resources that are rendered as a result of bad choice *and* bad culture. This lack is compounded by the performance expectations of how the proper self should perform in public, hence why the further the deviation from standardized moral value, the more likely the amplification of drama and humour in the television economy.

Establishing value and measuring relationships

Moral value is intricately interwoven into the formation of the normative codes and discourses of gendered behaviour and relationships. James Thompson's (1996) study of the history of the modern English novel examines how the concept of value came to be understood in eighteenth-century England through the relationship between two emerging and divergent discourses: political economy and the novel. By looking at the relationship between these two developing forms (finance and romance), Thompson demonstrates how value came to have such different but intimately connected meaning in different realms of experience – moral and economic – generating gendered separate spheres of public and domestic life and allocating men's and women's concerns to different objects: emotion and money.

In novels characters are inserted into the plot as variables are inserted into an algorithm and both return a value on a scale (a technique we can see developed on reality television with its various formulas). Thomson documents how in the eighteenth century finance and romance become dialectically related so that the presence of one calls on the absence of the other. Both rely on different methods: *accounting of* counting and *accounting for* character via narrative and both models and methods set up *expectations* (of what one can reasonably expect to happen in certain circumstances). Accounting for and expectations are crucial to how we are now expected to explain relationships, as we can see in the explosion of relationship counselling available through popular media. Thompson (1996) argues that novels indulge individual subjects' expectations about what might happen: why they should get married (governance), to whom (exchange), how it may happen (narrative) and how they are supposed to feel about it (affect). They offer up a general model against which the individual can measure and judge her own circumstances. This is a performance measurement template which establishes what makes investment in a relationship worthwhile but also creates fantasies of a better life that may/or may not be possible in the future. He makes clear that this is the model of value that has most influenced contemporary culture and we might see this as a symbolic template for the assessment of expectations and feeling as expanded and visualized across reality television. The interest in domestic situations, *Wife Swap*, *Who Rules the Roost*, or the route towards romance and marriage, *The Bachelor*, *Temptation Island* as some of the numerous dating permutations on reality television, all point to an emphasis upon the management, performance and accounting for relationships that is now turned into entertainment and 'played' out across reality television.

Behavioural expectations were also traditionally coded through spatial metaphors as middle class women attempted to gain some power in the domestic domain in order to legitimate their position. Nancy Armstrong (1987) notes how by the early nineteenth century middle class writers and intellectuals use the 'virtues' embodied by the bourgeois domestic woman as standards against which to measure working class women's culture. The bourgeois feminine ideal paradoxically generated a new form of political authority for middle class women. Moral superiority (from the radical Protestant dissenting tradition) became a source of political power enabling women to dominate over the objects and practices in the domain of affect that we now associate with intimate life. Armstrong details how literature devoted to producing the domestic woman appeared to ignore the political world run by men whilst recognizing a new moral template of value:

> Of the female alone did it presume to say that neither birth nor the accoutrements of title and status accurately represented the individual: *only the more subtle nuances of behaviour indicated what one was really worth*. In this way writing for and about the female introduced a whole new vocabulary for social relations, terms that attached precise moral value to certain qualities of mind.
>
> (Armstrong 1987:4 our emphasis)

As the nineteenth century develops these 'subtle nuances of behaviour' become more controlled by the public sphere of rational calculation. In a study of Australia between 1880 and 1940 Kerreen Reiger (1984) details how the principles of scientific forms of calculation and management were brought to bear on the home though the influence of a new group of 'experts': 'members of the medical profession, teachers and kindergarteners, domestic guidance and child guidance specialists' representing modernizing, scientific and rationalizing forces.[4]

The emphasis upon domestic interrogation throws the spotlight on motherhood as women become the predominant bearers of these new forms of regulation. As Rose (1989) has pointed out the dominance of child psychology has normalized specific *mothering* practices over the twentieth century. Walkerdine and Lucey (1989) suggest the mother has become the guarantor of the 'liberal democratic order' where a healthy nation has been irrevocably mythologized through the 'natural' connection between mothers and their children. Walkerdine and Lucey (1989) and Lawler (2000) demonstrate how these norms serve to pathologize working class families as lacking in 'normative' modes of care enabling the figure of the single mother to become the key figure of blame for the (immoral) state of the nation. They refer to the expectations of 'domestic pedagogy' that regulate middle class women into incorporating the mental development of the child into their household activities. Thus women are offered a model of motherhood that must at once be 'rewarding and persecuting' (Rose 1989: 15), as the line between one's own needs and the child's can never be drawn.

Matt Briggs (2009) notes how these imperatives have been intensified in debates about children's television, in which mothers are often vilified for not providing the 'right' educational development, in which every form of play must have an educational value. Buckingham and Scanlon (2003) note how the BBC both responds to and reproduces this imperative through its pedagogic form of address to parents which 'curricularize' television. This address is also repeated across a range of sites such as journalism, healthcare advice, parentcraft courses and advertising. Kathy Pitt (2002) describes the ways in which maternal pedagogy is maintained as a discourse by family literacy campaigns in the service of a capitalist economy, whilst Hey and Bradford (2006) describe the way in which the New Labour government's Sure Start campaigns restated the responsibility for the failing community onto the 'responsibility' of the individual mother. That parenting programmes now extend across our screens does not surprise us as *Supernanny, Nanny 911, The House of Tiny Tearaways, Honey We're Killing the Kids* all use psychology to give advice on how to handle and *develop* our children. They all operate with a model of the good parent who labours on their own conduct in order to reproduce the value-loaded child. Briggs (2009) maintains that 'simple unreflexive parenting in insufficient. Rather, parents themselves should aspire to the status of "experts"' (p.31), making decisions on how to spend their own and their families' time and energy.

If mothering has been subject to struggles to establish value in different spatial domains then so too has biological reproduction. Herbert Marcuse (1955) noted how the scientific management of instinctual needs became a vital factor in the reproduction of capitalism as sexuality became sublimated to the interests of calculative rationality. Sexuality has always been seen as something in need of 'management', a 'sexual mode of production' (Hawkes 1996), or a form of consumption in which the body 'spends' its energy (Heath 1982) and where performance measures of efficiency and outcome come to the fore (e.g. achieving rather than having orgasm). Stevi Jackson and Sue Scott (2004) note how modernist sexuality is a governmental self 'project' that has to be worked upon as part of a pedagogic approach to the management of everyday life and Melissa Tyler (2004) traces the movement from a Fordist rationality into a post-Fordist sexual ethic whereby sexuality is unhinged from reproduction and characterized instead by pluralization, experimentation and choice. Angela McRobbie's (1996) research on young women's magazines identifies the promotion of a 'knowing sexual subjectivity' in which young women are *expected* to treat sexuality as a site for experimentation, play and parody (hence prosthetic culture). Paul du Gay and Graeme Salaman (1992) argue that everyday life has fallen prey to the 'totalising and individualising' effects of the imperatives of economic rationality. For the enterprising self all social relations come to be perceived as exchange relations and the language of enterprise has traversed traditional limits and 'colonized our interiors'.[5]

There has therefore been a creeping intensification of the way intimate lives are managed in relation to the economy and Viviana Zelizer (2005) makes this process explicit through an understanding of law. She explores the ways in which care, household commerce, coupling etc. are inextricably interwoven into the workings of capitalism. She argues that intimacy always bears a moral charge because different sorts of intimacy vary in their moral qualities and quantities thereby constantly re-drawing the boundaries between proper and improper intimacy. In her analysis of law there is explicit quantification and adjudication of the value of selves in intimate relationships. The law establishes the monetary worth of intimacy by matching the right sort of (literal) monetary value with the social transaction in hand. Law courts perform a distinctive variety of relational work, calling up a matrix of possible relationships and evaluating these by distinguishing the value of these relations from others. Lawyers then match economic transactions and expectations and connect the disputing couple under examination to their matrix (asking moral questions such as: 'should people be treated in such a way?' 'Is his behaviour justified?' 'Can she expect that from him?', etc.). Law makes visible, institutionalizes and legislates for the incorporation of moral and economic value on the basis of the properties involved and the quantity and quality of the relation. It is a matrix evoked through a great deal of women's popular culture and on many reality television programmes that focus on relationships.

Therefore reality television thrives in a culture in which value is performed through intimate and domestic relationships. The value of intimate relationships is also enshrined in social, political, as well as legislative structures. When different forms of adjudication come together with the techniques of revealing, confessing and telling in performance we can see infinite possibilities for the calculation and evaluation of intimate practices. The present incitement to per-form one's person value in front of the nation suggests that the emphasis may have shifted from the subtle nuances of behaviour to the obvious display of behaviour in all its glory. This leads us to turn our attention to the increased significance of performance.

As we discussed in Chapter 1, writers on make-over and reality television remind us that participants are always called upon to excavate, reveal and dis-close interior narratives of the self. There is always some appeal to an inner or paradoxically 'true' self, whilst at the same time participants have to reflexively recognize their need for self-improvement. A programme like *How to Look Good Naked* purports not to change the outside but the inside, so that if you *feel* that you look good naked then you will, as Gok Wan's catchphrase reminds us: 'It's all about the confidence.' But again it is important to set this imperative against historical evidence, which shows that moral interiority is not an equally available resource, which therefore sets limits upon the way it can be performed.

Extending moral interiority and inequality

As Foucault (1979) details, the confession is central to the development of the modern subject. Those earlier narratives of (working class) moral redemption charted by Steedman and Vincent have now been extended by psychological discourses into various forms for displaying moral rectitude and responsibility (Rose 1989). But according to historians of psychoanalysis, only certain groups were considered to have an interior (Jackson-Lears 1981; Rieff 1966). Joel Pfister (1997) describes how the rise of 'therapeutic culture' is allied historically and ideologically to the ascendancy of the white middle class: 'This class's invention of a therapeutic culture has also been tied to its strategy to establish its "inner" ("human") value over the working class and over subordinate ethnic and racial groups' (p.23). Likewise, David Lubin (1997) details how pre-existing discourses of religious suffering, medical interrogation and the social defeat of marginalized Americans, were crafted into a psychological rhetoric of middle and upper middle class nervous interiority and class superiority. Whilst John Kasson (1990) details the increasing significance the middle class placed on aesthetics, etiquette *and* emotional control and maintains that this desire for control was linked to the insecurities of an uncertain market place which was experienced as disorderly and alien. Pfister and Schnog (1997) also note how it became fashionable amongst the upper middle classes to become neurotic as it displayed psychological depth:

> Members of the twentieth century middle and upper classes, having adopted psychological and therapeutic discourses (which had nineteenth century lit-erary and domestic origins), affirmed their social superiority or potency by elevating the cultural value of anxiety, sexual conflicts, and family tensions. Put differently, an increasing number of persons who belonged to these

classes re-signified anxiety as affirmation, emotional turmoil as subjective potency, and familial ambivalence as psychological capital.

(p.40)

Moreover, not only did psychoanalysis enable the promotion and development of a particular middle class formation of subjectivity, but it also influenced understandings of personhood in European social theory, promoting specific ideas about the working class as a susceptible mass, unable to be reflexive and critical (Blackman 2007). As psychology extends its influence it also extends its range of techniques where the 'private' self comes to be recognized as a public form. For instance 'the coming out' narrative is enacted through the technique of telling a hidden history of misrecognition that has to be excavated and made public. Self-performance is dependent upon particular techniques that are always framed by the organization of power through knowledge, such as redemption narratives through religion, or expressions of interiority through psychological discourse, and we now need to add to these the formation of televisual spectacle in the interests of the media's own power.

Adam Phillips and Barbara Taylor (2009) argue that Freudianism and its variants exist as a kind of meta-narrative of intimacy. As it develops, psycho-analysis underpins what has become *the* story about what makes people, what brings people together and what breaks them apart (a process we repeatedly watch on reality television), providing a 'modern' framework for understanding intimacy, offering models of organization for family, sexual and selfhood that are morally loaded with ideas about what constitutes good and proper relationships.

Illouz (1997a) details how this process develops. The connection between speaking the self, romantic love narratives and expectations in the early 1900s became channelled through popular culture enabling women to think of men as routes to happiness. This was particularly visible in women's magazines of the period and converted into psychological discourse by the 1940s, especially through promot-ing the 'talking through' of emotions as a way of revealing a true self and solving conflicts. This became part of the repertoire of women's responsibilities and emotional management. Later in the 1970s, partially helped by feminism and also by the ideology of individualism, emotional fulfilment became figured as a 'right', a means for 'smuggling the middle class liberal and utilitarian language of rights and bargaining into the bedroom and the kitchen' (Illouz 1997b: 49). Communication thus became central to ideas of relationship equality and forms of emotional management to the extent that it is taken to be common sense, pro-moted as a 'truth', rather than a technique. Good communication is a dominant trait in Western values of self-improvement (Cameron 1995) and is often figured across reality television, particularly in family intervention programmes like *Supernanny* and *Family Contract*, which we discuss at more length in the next chapter.

Typically, but not surprisingly if we think of language as a form of capital, the extension of communication techniques fed into and intensified class differences.

In an empirical and narrative analysis of romantic love, Illouz (1997b) found significant class differences in the expectations associated with intimacy where her middle class interviewees replaced the classic Hollywood romance ideal (itself developed from the novels described by Thompson earlier in his 'models for mating') for a more dispassionate model of love based on compatibility, friendship and most importantly, *communication*. She illustrates how the emotional work involved in this form of communicative love resonated with their wider middle class identities where 'self-fashioning' was something to be wilfully constructed in a repeated narrative of improvement and advancement. Using Bourdieu's ideas of capital, Illouz argues that the ability to distance oneself from one's immediate emotional experience is the prerogative of those who have a readily available range of emotional options, who are not overwhelmed by emotional necessity and intensity, and who can approach their own self with the same detached mode that comes from accumulated competence. The reflexivity implied in this practice of communication demands a certain 'methodological linguistic capital' that enables one to feel at ease with the practice of solving problems through language. Others such as Diane Reay (1998) and Helene Nowotny (1981) have demonstrated how this linguistic competence is a form of emotional capital that can be dispersed into others (children, partners), and accumulated and experimented with by the middle class self.

Illouz identifies what she calls a 'therapeutic habitus' or what Benjamin and Sullivan (1996) define in their research on intimate relationships as the 'open marital conversation'. In this habitus the self is viewed as containing 'inner' thoughts and feelings, as having a uniqueness waiting to be revealed and shared with others through verbal performance. This 'uniqueness' is shaped by normative narratives. Ultimately it is a habitus that is not available to all. For as we have seen, it was historically developed through particular class politics, in which one group extends its claims to legitimation through colonizing the idea of interiority and reflexivity and particular standards and techniques of communication. However, as the influence of psychology extends, the imperative to display and tell the self as a source of value becomes a wider social prerogative that everybody is expected to perform: an imperative upon which reality television fully capitalizes. Yet historically, only some had access to the competencies and capacities for this type of performance, but as these forms extend across media the demand for the display of psychological competences increases. The rise of first person documentary series on female working class celebrities – *What Katie Did Next, Jade's Story, Living with Kerry Katona* – where they perform and account for their own lives makes spectacular their relationships to the historical legacy of the 'recuperable fallen woman', in which their communication reveals their distance from the 'proper' (Tyler and Bennett 2010).

As Lauren Berlant (2008) notes, expressions of sentimentality are the rhetorical means by which suffering is advanced as the true core of personhood and citizenship in the US in which the imperative to tell and reveal oneself has become a moral national American virtue. She notes how the telling of dramatic trauma and revealing of suffering has become a middle class performance of virtue, key to what makes the 'true subject' of America, what she calls 'intimate citizenship'. As a result, everyday suffering experienced by those who live bare life at the margins is eclipsed whilst spectacular stories of dramatic trauma are mediated and take centre stage. This singular spectacularization is initially made most evident on talk shows like *Oprah* which, as Illouz and Wilf (2008) argue, develops a form of 'moral person fetishism' in which the material conditions of people's lives become divorced from the techniques and narratives of the dramatic/traumatic self on display. People's attachments to the social and material conditions of their own labour, the conditions which have brought them to this place, are hidden from view to intensify the focus on their individual performance now in the present.

These arguments chime with the discussions in Chapter 1 about a documentary shift from the considerations of the social to the personal. Talk show structures of telling, like the repetition of the moral rules for relationships over time, enable the narrative and performative elements of trauma to appear as if they are induced from an individual's psyche. The performance of psychic misery is both spectacular: *did they really say that? do that?* and normative: the style of narrative and performance is constantly reiterated. The continual attachment of stories of individual experience to narratives that explain and organize intimacy is central to understanding how reality television is just one of many elements of women's culture to control and structure behaviour within the normative spaces of the family, couple[6] and heterosexuality. Performances are always framed by the performative, by the constantly iterated regulations that distribute value.

Performance and control

Intimacy is opened out on 'reality television' though the techniques for person performance that we have identified, relying on non-actors to amplify their daily experiences supposedly in their own self-interests, which dovetails neatly into the interests of television. Techniques such as long-held close ups, observational footage, and to-camera talking heads, enable bodies and gestures to come under close forensic scrutiny. John McKenzie (2001) claims performance will be to the twenty-first centuries what Foucault's disciplinary techniques were to the eighteenth and nineteenth centuries. In *Discipline and Punish* Foucault (1977) demonstrates how the power regime of eighteenth- and nineteenth-century Western Europe was modelled on a particular arrangement of statements and visibilities. He showed how discipline was an onto-historical formation of power, an episteme based on the juxtaposition of two forms of knowledge: legal statements and panoptic surveillance that extended into every domain. Extending the statements and visibility into an imperative to perform, McKenzie maintains that performance is a new onto-historical formation of power. He notes how as early as the mid-1950s Marcuse (1964) drew attention to the centrality of the 'performance principle' by which social relations are stratified according to the competitive economic performances of its members who act out pre-established functions. We can see reality television as an attempt to enshrine the performance principle through performance incitement, management and measurement. Just like the performance management to which we are subject at work it is an invitation to subscribe to certain criteria as normative standards that produce rewards.

Just as Thompson's (1996) eighteenth-century model of value describes the establishment of expectations in the formations of the spheres of affect and economy, McKenzie charts the contemporary development of performance measures across a range of sites which provide numeric calculations of workplace activity, including the codification of affect into psychological dispositions such as motivation, tardiness, innovation and the ability to establish and meet goals. Affect and economy enmesh more and more tightly. He points to the potent combination of old scientific management techniques developed via Taylorism – measurement – and the new 'ars poetica of organisational practice' (p.7), in which stage, 'show' business, play, art and creativity combine microeconomic practices and the psychological dispositions of workers in the name of operational efficiency. Alongside McKenzie, Nigel Thrift (2004) also notes how performing arts techniques have been imported into business practice and service culture, aimed at maximizing creativity to produce continual innovation, a response to increased competitiveness. And Lury (2004) in a study of branding products, suggests that it is performance knowledge that generates the value in the product as opposed to straightforward symbolic attribution. She calls this performance knowledge 'exhibition value', in which the value of labour is in the *response* that can be generated from branding, production and promotion creativity. All of these analyses underscore the opening out of a person's capacity to find new ways of increasing value and which also make the self responsible for its own performance. For Thrift, this is a bio-political process in which our perceptions are becoming increasingly instrumentalized:

> The half-second interval is being trained up. The dark side of this process is patently clear. Our room to play and dream is being cut down. There is a more and more habitual look to precocity. Our anticipation is being anticipated.
>
> (p.161)

As we have discussed in Chapter 1, reality television's heavy reliance on melodrama makes it easy to see how this capacity for micro-management performance techniques and measures play out, especially Lury's point about generating value through response. On reality television the more outrageous (sensational) the programme the more media coverage, the likely increase in audience figures, increased advertising revenue, and the success of producers and companies, as intimate performances are converted into economic capital. Participants may also see their performances on television as labour (Jost 2011), since labour itself has ultimately become about performance. Alison Hearn (2010) discusses the 'person-characters' on *The Hills* – a reality show about young wealthy Californian socialites – as a clear embodiment of the interplay between performance and labour whereby 'their work/lives are, apparently one seamless flow of value generation. Here "being" *is* labour and produces financial value, both for the individual person-characters, and for their producers, and for the MTV network' (pp.61–2). It is evidence of the capital/labour relationship acted out, but not in the ways we know it, a new form of performance-fuelled bio-politics.

Other researchers have also pointed out that the imperative to perform is built into other sites of the social. Janet Finch (2007), for instance, draws atten- tion to the obligation to display one's family relations across most social sites, an obligation which can quite clearly be connected back to Steedman's imperative to tell oneself as a source of moral value. Finch maintains that families are now expected to represent a *quality* rather than a thing with the emphasis being placed on *relationships* not structures. As family organization grows ever more complex people feel *compelled to demonstrate* that they are part of a family. Their display enables them to claim legitimacy for membership by attaching them- selves to the narrative fantasy of the family: 'families need to be "displayed" as well as "done"' (p.66). Performances combine acts of telling and doing in the display of responsibility. As Laura Kipnis (2003) notes, the collapse of the dis- tinction between public and private in 1990's public culture made for 'a stran- gely theatrical decade in American politics, one in which our elected representatives … transformed themselves into a massive public theatre project, impelled for reasons unknown to perform their marital dramas and dilemmas on the national proscenium' (p.158). Berlant (2000a) argues that we can see intimacy emerging from mobile processes of attachment and asks:

> What kinds of (collective, personal) future can be imagined if, for example sexuality is no longer bound to its narrative, does not lead to stabilizing *something*, something institutional (like patriarchal families or other kinds of reproduction that prop up the future of persons and nations); if citizens and works are no longer created by families and institutions of loco parentis, namely, schools and religions; if (because of AIDS, globally high mortality rates among national minorities, environmental toxins, virulent transnational exploitation, ongoing military and starvation genocides, and other ongoing sources of destruction) a generation is no longer defined by procreational chronology, but marked by trauma and death?
>
> (Berlant 2000b:7)

Performing one's intimate attachments has thus become an important route to legitimation, for value and authority: performing 'properly' is not only central to the distribution of value, but also to governance more generally.[7]

Thrift (2004) shows how everyday emotional saturation by the media has had the effect of enshrining the performative at the heart of modern Euro-American societies. He shows how political presentation works metonymically, increasingly focusing on small differences on the body to make them stand for the whole, a trait mirrored in reality television (a point we develop in Chapter 3 through the idea of 'metonymic morality'). The techniques across political and entertainment spheres are identical: for instance, televisual coverage of responses to 9/11 and 7/7 focused in on faces to see if they were emoting appropriately; thus, making the performance of emotion an index of credibility. The close attention given to George W Bush when he first heard the news of 9/11 made viewers think that he was not fully cognizant and hence judged to be morally faulty. Emotions are as much about what *others* feel in response to what *we* feel: we understand the emotion because we feel its affects. Therefore we need to think about how reality television participants' performances are replete with gesture in which different emotional performances (anger, sadness, care) come together to produce what we see as the whole person. It is, we argue, in the performance that a number of elements amalgamate to code value. These elements of behaviour and aesthetics are already part of a symbolic template of value, by which they can be understood in their constituent parts as well as a whole.

Andrejevic (2010) also demonstrates how a reality television programme partakes in escalating the significance of gesture via the logic of security violation since politics now works through gesture. He details how the *World Series of Poker* provides tutorials in the management of risk through reading the gestures and bodies of others who are attempting to deceive you. This leads him to argue that tournament poker serves as a metaphor for the universalization of suspicion. This is just like the use of 'lie detection' equipment in talk shows and in family intervention reality shows like *My Teen's a Nightmare*, where experts teach viewers how to recognize somatic symptoms. Andrejevic connects this to the general social increase in risk calculation and people-monitoring. Risk is in part a function of the reconfiguration of the discourse of competition in which everybody is pitted against each other so that no one can be trusted. Reality television therefore becomes not just a means of displaying the moral value of the self though performance, but also a pedagogy in self-promotion, self-protection and social suspicion. Reality television is just one space and medium by which the attribution of value through performance is achieved. Our social life is saturated with the demand to perform, be it through communication in relationships or at work, or in revealing suffering to claim propriety or belonging.

Performative critiques

When Judith Butler (1993) suggests that discursive performa*tives* and embodied perform*ances* are both modes of citationality she opens up the 'demand to perform'. Performatives are unconscious iterated enactments that produce and sustain the normative, whilst performances are conscious actions. All performances, spoken or enacted, are real only because they 'reel off and on' from a general matrix of citationality (McKenzie 2001). Performances are for McKenzie the territorialization of flows and unformed matters into sensible bodies, whilst performatives are encodings of these bodies into governable, articulable subjects and objects. What we often see on reality television that recruits those in need of transformation is ungovernable bodies, embodied performances that cannot be controlled by the demands that have called them into effect. The performance is not coded into the normative performative: instead we see failed relationships of every kind, of unhappy marriages in which behaviour is not stabilized through its association with narratives of happy families. We watch failure to tell or narrate oneself appropriately, and we observe all the elements that produce proper performance gone awry. The call to performance is a saturation of many different effects and affects that cannot be controlled. On reality television we see the failure of the Foucauldian 'conduct of conduct', the governmental requirement for self-disciplining and care of the self. Reality television makes visible the excess that cannot be captured or condensed by performative citationality: women 'do' gender but excessively, and sometimes improperly. Their size, noise, ingestion, aesthetics and language have not been restrained by the normative iteration of gendered norms. This is where class relations are constitutive and disruptive of gender, destabilizing the performative element of governmentality.[8] The performance element works to both provide entertainment through making spectacular forensic detailing (usually bodies behaving badly), and promote an intense form of governmentality – participants must learn to control themselves. As we will proceed to detail, the performance may also carry with it a critique of the required standards. The intense attention given by reality television to the performative, where repetitive habit is broken down into its minute elements, is displayed in the encounter between both the participants *and* the audience who are both positioned by normative performativity. Attempts to put back behavioural elements after breaking them down (through the trope of self-transformation) enable us as audiences to see how utterly incoherent, contradictory and unstable the production is of subjectivity and normativity and thus the impossibility of the governmentality project. If people did self-govern as is suggested they would not need the constant call to perform properly. If (unconscious) performativity worked we would not see it constantly made conscious in front of our eyes, and if the normative narratives that are supposed to hold performativity and governmentality operated successfully we would not see so many tales of failure, unhappiness and despair. Governmentality and performativity are theories for understanding bourgeois behaviour – for those that do unconsciously perform the proper person.

Reality television gives audiences time to evaluate people's reactions and responses, making explicit and visible that which is habituated and iterated. It enables us to enter different temporal and spatial coordinates revealing the class relations that underpin the normative 'standards' of gender, class and race as they are spectacularly performed. But it also enables us to see ourselves as part of a wider sociality, where other people are subject to similar 'proper performance demands'. We do not just watch television as individuals but as social beings that interact with the television in a variety of different ways. For instance, Wood's (2009) research demonstrates how women 'talk back' to the television, engaging with it as if in conversation with others, speaking from specific positions on issues of concern, and passionately engaging with talk show hosts and contestants. It is this social engagement, to the entanglements of participants, viewers and researchers to which we now turn.

Social affect and reality television

We want to stress how the recent emphasis on (neo-liberal reflexive) selves has deflected our attention away from the social relations by which personhood is produced. Recent 'turns' in social theory – to affect and ontology – have pointed to the irredeemable sociality of any form of self-behaviour. The self can only perform in the conditions established by the relationships in which it is located. If we turn to social understandings of affect (as opposed to the biological, neurological or psychological),[9] to those which understand affect as produced through the social encounter, we can proceed to analyse television as an affect-producing technology that is fully immersed in what it means to be social. We take our cue from Deleuze's reading of Spinoza, who used affects to explore the workings of power exercised by sixteenth-century priests (Deleuze and Deleuze 1978). Spinoza's theory of affect is premised upon what he calls 'the force of existing' which is in continuous variation in social encounters. He maintains that when we come across somebody positive, if they make us joyful, they increase our capacity/ability to act, whereas if we encounter sadness our capacity to act is diminished. Spinoza was concerned to understand how people with power use sadness as an affect to increase their power and decrease the power of others. This continual variation in feeling is experienced through social encounters: increase–diminution–increase–diminution. Skeggs' (1997b) previous ethnographic research identified how when working class women entered a social encounter with an awareness of the possibilities for denigration, possibilities learnt from birth and onwards, a defensive response to the potential negative evaluation was prepared. We thus learn from an early age how to anticipate social encounters with certain people who will decrease our capacity to experience social space with positive feelings and thus protect ourselves from their negative affects. We also learn that some encounters will produce positive affects that make us feel good about ourselves.

Spinoza notes how the continuous variation in the force of existing is understood by the ideas one gives to the affects we experience. So if we feel diminished we may look for an idea to explain our feelings, so affect works not just by producing feeling but also by attaching the feeling to an idea, an interpretation of affect. Some argue that it is the idea-attachment that generates what we recognize and know to be emotion, when affects are codified into feelings such as disgust, fear, joy. Feelings become the mechanisms that enable the connections to be made; affect is the means by which the feeling is brought into effect.

Theresa Brennan (2004) notes, 'the things that one feels are affects. The things that one feels with are feelings' (p.23). The definition between affect and emotion is that the latter codifies the former through ideas and discursive frameworks. This takes us back into the realm of the social, because not all people who occupy different social positions will attach the same ideas to the feelings experienced. As we have been discussing, access to narratives and frameworks for interpreting affects are differentially distributed: religion and psychoanalysis, for instance, are not equally available to all as forms of interpretation, and as others have noted (Hochschild 1983; Nowotny 1981; Reay 2004) emotion can operate as a form of capital.

Much analysis of the social and the media remains caught between an impersonal and deterministic model on the one hand, and first-person narratives of meaning, identity and intention on the other. Yet most social life is trans-individual, it is a 'socius', not indexed to the solitary subject, but is enmeshed in dynamics of communication that cannot be reduced to symbols, representations or propositions.[10] We are dialogical beings that come into effect through our relations with others. We continually negotiate what Lisa Blackman (2008) calls being 'one yet many'. Although we may have come to inhabit bodies as if we are self-enclosed, separate, autonomous units: what Teresa Brennan (2004) has termed, affective self-containment, and Ed Cohen (2010) calls 'biopolitical individualization'. All the efforts (made by the psy-sciences in their classed project – as we saw earlier) that go into persuading us that we are singular subjects do not capture the thoroughly singular-plural beings that we are (Nancy 2000).

For as Haraway (1991) and Strathern (1992) have argued for some time, to identify as 'one' can only be done through recognition of the social 'many', since it is impossible not to be social beings. Strathern, for instance, refers to the 'dividual' rather than the individual: we are not insular containments, our behaviour and dispositions are shaped by the social relations we inhabit. We cannot know who we are expected to be without the dialogical responses of others. We learn to recognize ourselves through others, potentially adopting the gaze of others, sensing what others think about us and how they judge and position us. Strathern developed her concept of dividual from her anthropological research in Melanesia where she shows how those who do not apply the Western perspective of the individual as an integrated solid whole, perceive each other to be made up of the parts of others, continually connecting and disconnecting (a process we will see occurring in our respondents, connections to television participants in Chapters 5, 6 and 7). Melanesian personhood is made up of a generalized sociality, not a psychologized individuality. As Joanna Latimer (2009) has noted this social perspective by which selves are made up of parts (in division but always connecting and always in extension) is an anathema to Western ideas of singularity because it embraces ambivalence. Yet as we will later explore through our empirical work, a huge amount of effort goes into closing down the ambivalence experienced by our respondents. This dividual perspective directs us away from a contained singular self towards co-extensivity, to the milieus or settings within which subjectivities are co-enacted, co-constituted, co-produced. This co-extension is made particularly evident through performances that contain affect which helps connect us to others and which is mediated through television.

Vikki Bell (2007) develops some of these 'new' relational ways of thinking about subjectivity to understand culture and performance. Bell criticizes Foucault's genealogical work, with its legacies and descendants (cited above) for its focus on historical discontinuities that obscure affective, corporeal and felt connections to others. She argues that studies of governmentality and performativity have tended to focus on the circulation, regulation and reproduction of norms, rather than on embodied relations and dispositions of connectivity. It is almost odd that a good deal of research on the quintessential medium of connectivity (in particular reality television) uses the singular self as its focus (often with the emphasis upon individualization or the self-governing thesis). We think about reality television as a technology devoted to producing sensation and intimacy which enables us to rethink how performativity, the speech acts and iterations that bring people and practices into effect, are routed through others in an expanded dialogical connection.

Because television is a medium of presence (Morse 1998, also see Chapter 1) it enables us to understand the co-extensive nature of relationships of proximity and distance. For instance, initial ideas about performative rootedness (through others and through time and space) came from Paul Gilroy's (1993) analysis of the Atlantic diaspora where dispositions inherited from the experience of slavery and traversed across the transatlantic were felt and routed through the diasporic experience of both proximity and distance. Thus the connections we feel to others are part of the *historical and present* production of which we are a part – race, gender and class relations that emerge – and hence why television is just one (technical) entry into the routes between people. When we speak back to the television it is as Wood (2009) shows 'as if' we are having conversations with others, with those whom we are sharing things or disagreeing vehemently. When we are prompted by the television to feel disgust, to be affectively moved by the television, it is as if we are there in the drama of the moment – this is reality television's ultimate promise and ultimate tension. As Mary Douglas (1988) has noted for some time, disgust is about the production of social consensus and normativity, generating understandings that we are part of a much larger 'socius of feeling'. In a similar way Peter Stallybrass and Allon White (1986) note how the constitution of the abject always defines the norm; these constitutive 'outsides' are incredibly revealing of what can be allowed inside and are hence central in setting social boundaries.

This is why Sara Ahmed (2004a) speaks of an affective economy: feelings are distributed, but not in disparate ways, they are organized socially. She maintains that in affective economies, affects *do things*, importantly (for us) they align persons with communities, or bodily space with social space, through the very intensity of their attachments. In particular, affects work, she argues, by sticking figures together (adherence). Sticking creates the very effect of a collective (coherence) and works to bind subjects together. In later chapters we discuss how our audiences convert feelings into responses, which allow symbolic alignment with others in fairly complex, but nonetheless socially located ways. For instance, Michael Herzfeld (2009) identifies cultural intimacy as the way gesture creates intimate communication whilst under the public gaze, whereby the members of a given society recognize more or less the same modalities creating a special kind of competence. He insists that this is not just about familiarity with a culture but recognition based on flaws and foibles: a 'fellowship of the flawed' (p.133), a recognition of something or someone at a distance from the normative or the proper. In daily life we often see these resonances and connections through the shared glances that acknowledge the presence and shared experience with others. Or the stares that reveal the opposite: the shock of the difference, the lack of proximity to practices with which we are familiar. In Skeggs' (1997a, 2004a, 2011) previous empirical research projects with working class women and men, the glance to other friends with lowered eyes revealed what was a clear sign of simultaneously acknowledging the presence of the judgemental middle class gaze in a shared recognition that also betrayed some level of resistance (even if it was quietly). In these moments (not often noticed as significant in research and everyday social encounters) a whole history of class and gender relations is expressed. Simon Charlesworth (2000) describes such moments as the phenomenology of class relations, the moments when the unsaid and unspoken passes between people in knowing silences and appropriate gestures. Or in this research project we see it through raised eyebrows, glances through the utterances the 'urghs' and 'ahs', the gasps and tuts, which became evident when we started paying close attention to how and when people were drawn into a connection with a TV programme (as detailed in Chapters 4 and 5).

Thus following Kirstyn Gorton (2009) and Misha Kavka (2008) as outlined in Chapter 1, we think it is through an attention to affect that we can more accurately stitch reality television's appeal to the social conjuncture. We want to think of television as a technology of the social that works through encouraging intensity, intimacy and belonging, in which the screen is generative of affect, providing an interface for connection. As Chapter 4 demonstrates some of our respondents even demand to be affectively drawn into the programme, to be absorbed, whilst others feared the addictive nature of the technology (see also Skeggs and Wood 2011). However, unlike other theorists, we do not believe that affect entirely de-stabilizes, makes queer or disrupts the social (Kavka 2008a); rather, we argue it intensifies and makes social divisions sensate (Skeggs 2012).[11] Clare Hemmings (2005) has warned about the take-up and over use of the idea of affect, where it is seen to replace any form of political or social reproduction, offering the new challenge to ideology and power as a new route to 'liberation'. Here we show how affect resides in rather than vacates histories and social positions. We locate affect as a 'new' way for understanding connectivity with our eye firmly on how it operates as an economy that disrupts, circulates and reproduces inequality in new more intensive ways.

Our research suggests that judgement is always key to the conversion of affect into an idea when making a connection, and that judgement is historically predictable (some people are more likely to be judged than others), for instance as Ahmed (2004b) shows in relation to racism, the mobilization of hate and disgust are predictable deployments of affect, it is their intensification and attachment to groups that becomes significant. However, we do want to draw attention to the ambivalence contained in a great deal of affect. As Purnima Mankekar (1999) noted in her ethnography of television viewers in India responses can be both emotional and critical, one does not exclude the other. The key is then interrelationality, sociality and connection, rather than the self. The intimate has become political through connectivity, what Kavka calls a 'socius of feeling'.

Conclusion

In the extension of self–performance as a staple of reality television specific performance measures are established based on historically developed models for calculation and evaluation that weaves the spheres of economy and affect together. The person is called upon to display their own value, not in conditions of their own choosing, but by relying upon institutionalized techniques that have been developed over time, such as telling and showing. These methods have been developed historically in relation to particular class, gender and raced interests. The conceptualization and revelation of interiority in particular was a means by which the middle class legitimated its authority and superiority. Likewise, techniques of psychoanalysis became promoted as universal understandings of social relationships generally and of intimacy in particular, eclipsing the very specific classed nature of their production.

As the universality of psychology was promoted and its many variants and techniques expanded, the imperative to display interiority as a measure of a person's value was extended to the working class. But the working class did not have access to the right kinds of communicative techniques or the 'therapeutic habitus' necessary for revealing interiority and negotiating power in the same way. This is primarily because the very ideas of the self-contained singular insular self were premised upon its constitutive limit, the 'mass', the working class. Exclusion was necessary to the constitution and recognition of the proper. For definitions of normativity to work they must have a corresponding constitutive outside through which the norm can be defined. Norms and limits are therefore established through relationships of distance. Thus, when the working class are recruited to television and asked to perform the techniques for the display of interiority and intimacy on a public stage they cannot but display their distance from the norm, and ultimately their historical and social positioning. But because all reference to their positioning and circumstances is eradicated and the focus is on the individual divorced from the circumstances of their making, they appear as if they are making 'bad choices' by behaving as they do. As Rose (1989) notes, psychology has been effective at firmly implanting the idea of choice as located within the individual, dislocated from the social conditions available for that choice to be made.

Television's reliance on performance, rather than just a theatre for normative performativity, makes it the perfect stage for demonstrating the breakdown of elements in participants' behaviours encompassing all the senses, the affects and embodiments that are contained in the contours of the self. Performance contains more than just statements and symbols. It combines speech, movement, aesthetics and gestures into an affective scene with which we as audiences are incited to make connections. We may 'feel' the discomfort of the performance, laugh at the ridiculousness of bodies and celebrate the endurance of participants. We may also feel things happening to participants that we have also felt, for we too are located in affective relations produced and consolidated over time in the social encounter. Codifications of the performative that enable governmentality to proceed through the unacknowledged repetition of the normative are ripped apart as the excessive are asked to perform their excess to demonstrate their need for transformation. The performance aspects of the performative are made explicit: through bodies, feelings and affects that cannot be fully contained.

This is why we need to move beyond understandings of the singular self into understandings of the unremitting social connectivity of television. As reality television opens out intimacy on the screen it opens out our locations and understandings in intimate relations and it enters into the realm of the sensory socius, in which we are located. It produces a form of connectivity that cannot be known and contained solely by cognition and speech. It offers us another way to think about how the media works on us and how we work with it as it encroaches further into the territory of feelings. The rest of the book unpacks this seepage and connects it to ways of understanding co-enactment and co-extensivity by which media 'affects' as well as 'effects'. Therefore, we want to think about how reality television is involved in the 'making' of the social and we begin this analysis in Chapter 3 with a mapping of the different incitements to perform one's value offered through self-transformation reality television programmes.

Notes

1 Developing an architecture of the self that was first used by Adam Smith (1757) which brought together the idea of an internal consciousness from religion to work in the interests of capitalism, the self-interested self.

2 Femininity can be a form of cultural capital if is symbolically legitimate (historically a particular version of middle-class moral femininity). But femininity poses particular problems for Bourdieu's analysis because although it is symbolically ubiquitous, it is not symbolically dominant in the same way as masculinity. Femininity is a form of regulation rather than domination. Yet it is embodied, and operates as a local cultural resource and can be used in local and relational rather than nationally symbolic forms

of exchange. And unlike traditional forms of capital its value can only decrease with time, for it is a youth-specific inscription. The *conversion* into the symbolic is central to understanding power and inequality; that is, what is realizable and propertizable as a resource can be made legitimate, attributed with dominant value and converted into the symbolic (Skeggs 2004b).

3 The history of the nuclear family is very much associated with the emergent middle-classes desire for increased wealth and consumption, thereby limiting the number of children to conserve costs.

4 In an interesting twist Paul Gilroy (2000) estimates that the promotion of marriage and domestic values among America's Black slave population did a good deal to promote the development of the concept of the 'free' self that was to play such an important role in anti-slavery campaigns.

5 This is exemplified in the research on dating agencies and advertisements, where users can be seen as 'rational consumers engaged in a process of constructing the self and the wanted partner as products in the dating market place' (Jagger 1998; Tyler 2004).

6 We include the couple as previous research demonstrated how being part of a couple was central to feelings of oppression and exclusion and the display of respectability (Skeggs 1997a).

7 A '*fit and proper person*' as a category of law was first invoked in England in a case against a slave trader – Lascelles – by the State who were trying to get him to pay taxes. The proper was first articulated in the seventeenth-century political discourse of the possessive individual and institutionalized in the social contract. The possessive individual is a category from which the working class have always been excluded (Skeggs 2004a). As Davies (1998) notes it is the law which creates property and confers certain characteristics on objects rather than simply recognizing them as already proper. Property is not a thing, a relationship between a person and a thing, or a network of relationships between persons with respect to 'things'. Property is not even a bundle of rights. It is a metaphor for an array of concepts centred on hierarchy, purity and limitedness: exclusivity, property, sovereignty, self-identity, law, territory, boundaries, title, limits, unity (Moran *et al.* 2004).

8 See Mariam Fraser (1999), who details how class and race break down the normative performative which is dependent upon visualization and does not take into account the valuation of visualization.

9 See Ruth Leys (2007), for a critique of the over-reliance of feminist analysis of affect on biological understandings.

10 From an introduction to a seminar series on affect, held in the Sociology Department of Goldsmiths, University of London 2008–9, organized by Mariam Fraser.

11 The sensationalism produced by using working class women's bodies and practices as objects in need of transformation does not work in the same way as does the expansion of gay markets; the logic is radically different. The latter is a market opportunity, an opening out, a new line of flight for capital to develop; the former is a symbolic figure of the constitutive limit.

References

Adkins, L. 2002 'Reflexivity and the Politics of Qualitative Research: Who Speaks for Whom, Why, How and When?', in T. May (ed.) *Companion to Qualitative Research*, London: Sage.

Adkins, L. and Lury, C. 1999 'The Labour of Identity: Performing Identities, Performing Economies', *Economy and Society* 28(4 November): 598–614.

Aguiar, J. 2011 'The aestheticization of Everyday Life and the De-classicization of Western Working-classes', *Sociological Review* 59(3): 616–33.

Ahmed, S. 2004a 'Affective Economies', *Social Text* 22(2): 117–39.

——2004b *The Cultural Politics of Emotion*, Edinburgh: Edinburgh University Press.

Andrejevic, M. 2010 'Reading the Surface: Body Language and Surveillance' *Culture Unbound: Journal of Current Cultural Research*, Vol. 2, Linkoping: Linkoping University Electronic Press.

Armstrong, N. 1987 *Desire and Domestic Fiction; A Political History of the Novel*, New York and Oxford: Oxford University Press.

Beck, U. 1992 *Risk Society: Towards a New Modernity*, London: Sage.

Bell, V. 2007 *Culture and Performance: The Challenge of Ethics, Politics and Feminist Theory*, Oxford: Berg.

Benjamin, O. and Sullivan, O. 1996 'The Importance of Difference: Conceptualising Increased Flexibility in Gender Relations at Home', *Sociological Review* 44(2): 225–51.

Berlant, L. (ed.) 2000a *Intimacy*, Chicago and London: University of Chicago Press.

——2000b 'Intimacy: A Special Issue', in L. Berlant (ed.) *Intimacy*, Chicago and London: University of Chicago Press.

——2008 *The Female Complaint: The Unfinished Business of Sentimentality in American Culture*, London and Durham: Duke University Press.

Blackman, L. 2007 'Reinventing Psychological Matters: The Importance of the Suggestive Realm of Tarde's Ontology', *Economy and Society* 36(4): 574–96.

——2008 'Affect, Relationality and the Problem of Personality', *Theory, Culture and Society* 25(1): 27–51.

Bourdieu, P. 1984 [1979] *Distinction: A Social Critique of the Judgement of Taste*, London and New York: Routledge and Kegan Paul.

——1987 'What Makes a Social Class? On the Theoretical and Practical Existence of Groups', *Berkeley Journal of Sociology*: 1–17.

——1988 *Homo Academicus*, Cambridge: Polity Press.

——1989 'Social Space and Symbolic Power', *Sociological Theory* 7: 14–25.

——1990 [1965] *Photography A Middle-brow Art*, Stanford, California: Stanford University Press.

——1996 *The State Nobility: Elite Schools in the Field of Power*, Cambridge: Polity Press.

——2000 *Pascalian Meditations*, Cambridge: Polity.

Brennan, T. 2004 *The Transmission of Affect*, Ithaca: Cornell University Press.

Briggs, M. 2009 'BBC Children's Television, Parentcraft and Pedagogy: Towards the "Ethicalization of Existence"', *Media, Culture, Society* 31(1): 23–39.

Buckingham, D. and Scanlon, M. 2003 *Education, Entertainment and Learning in the Home*, Buckingham: Open University Press.

Butler, J. 1993 *Bodies That Matter: On the Discursive Limits of 'Sex'*, London: Routledge.

Cameron, D. 1995 *Verbal Hygeine*, London and New York: Routledge.

Charlesworth, S. 2000 *A Phenomenology of Working Class Experience*, Cambridge: Cambridge University Press.

Cohen, E. 2010 *A Body Worth Defending: Immunity, Bio-Politics and the Apotheosis of the Modern Body*, Durham: Duke University Press.

Couldry, N. 2006 *Listening Beyond the Echoes: Media, Ethics and Agency in an Uncertain World*, Boulder, Colorado: Paradigm Publishers.

Davies, M. 1998 'The Proper: Discourses of Purity', *Law and Critique* ix(2): 147–73.

Deleuze, E. and Deleuze, J. 1978 'Giles Deleuze: Lecture Transcripts on Spinoza's Concept of *Affect*', Vol. 2006: http://www.webdeleuze.com/php/sommaire.html.

Douglas, M. 1988 *Purity and Danger: An Analysis of the Concepts of Pollution and Taboo*, New York: Ark Paperbacks.

Dovey, J. 2000 *Freakshow: First Person Media and Factual Television*, London: Pluto.

du Gay, P. 1996 *Consumption and Identity at Work*, London: Sage.

du Gay, P. and Salaman, G. 1992 'The Cult[ure] of the Customer', *Journal of Management Studies* 29(5): 615–33.

Eagleton, T. 1989 'The Ideology of the Aesthetic', in P. Hernadi (ed.) *The Rhetoric of Interpretation and the Interpretation of Rhetoric*, Durham and London: Duke University Press.

Featherstone, M. 1991 *Consumer Culture and Postmodernism*, London: Sage.

Feher, M. 2009 'Self-Appreciation; or, The Aspirations of Human Capital', *Public Culture* 21(1): 21–41.

Finch, J. 2007 'Displaying Families', *Sociology* 41(1): 65–81.

Fine, B. 2001 *Social Capital versus Social Theory: Political Economy and Social Science at the Turn of the Millenium*, London: Routledge.

Foucault, M. 1977 *Discipline and Punish: The Birth of the Prison*, London: Allen Lane/Penguin.

——1979 *The History of Sexuality: Volume One, an Introduction*, London: Penguin.

Fraser, M. 1999 'Classing Queer: Politics in Competition', *Theory, Culture and Scociety* 16(2): 107–31.

Giddens, A. 1991 *Modernity and Self-Identity; Self and Society in the Late Modern Age*, Cambridge: Polity.

Gilroy, P. 1993 *The Black Atlantic: Modernity and Double Consciousness*, Cambridge, Mass.: Harvard University Press.

——2000 *Between Camps: Nations, Cultures and the Allure of Race*, London: Penguin.

Gorton, K. 2009 *Media Audiences: Television, Meaning and Emotion*, Edinburgh: Edinburgh University Press.

Haraway, D. 1991 *Simians, Cyborgs, and Women: The Reinvention of Nature*, London: Free Association Books.

Hartigan, J. J. 2005 *Odd Tribes: Towards a Cultural Analysis of White People*, Durham: Duke University Press.

Hartley, J. 2004 '"Kiss Me Kat": Shakespeare, *Big Brother* and the Taming of the Shrew', in L. Oullette and S. Murray (eds) *Reality TV: Remaking Television Culture*, New York and London: New York University Press.

Hawkes, G. 1996 *A Sociology of Sex and Sexuality*, Buckingham: Open University Press.

Haylett, C. 2001 'Illegitimate Subjects? Abject Whites, Neoliberal Modernisation and Middle Class Multiculturalism', *Environment and Planning D: Society and Space* 19: 351–70.

Hearn, A. 2008 'Insecure: Narratives and Economies of the Branded Self in Transformation Television', *Continuum: Journal of Media and Cultural Studies* 22(4): 495–505.

——2010 'Reality Television and the Limits of Immaterial Labour', *Triple C* 8(1): 60–76.

Heath, S. 1982 *The Sexual Fix*, London: Macmillan.

Heelas, P. 2002 'Work Ethics, Soft Capitalism and the "Turn to Life"', in P. Du Gay and M. Pryke (eds) *Cultural Economy*, London: Sage.

Heller, D. (ed.) 2006 *The Great American Makeover: Television, History, Nation*, New York: Palgrave.

Hemmings, C. 2005 'Invoking Affect: Cultural Theory and the Ontological Turn', *Cultural Studies* 19(5): 548–67.

Herzfeld, M. 2009 'The Cultural Politics of Gesture: Reflections on the Embodiment of Ethnographic Practice', *Ethnography* 10(2): 131–52.

Hey, V. and Bradford, S. 2006 'Re-engineering Motherhood? Sure Start in the Community', *Contemporary Issues in Early Childhood* 7(1): 53–67.

Hochschild, A. 1983 *The Managed Heart: Commercialisation of Human Feeling*, Berkeley, CA: University of California Press.

Illouz, E. 1997a 'Who will Care for the Caretaker's Daughter? Towards a Sociology of Happiness in the Era of Reflexive Modernity', *Theory, Culture and Society* 14(4): 31–66.

——1997b *Consuming the Romantic Utopia: Love and the Cultural Contradictions of Capitalism*, Berkeley and Los Angeles: University of California Press.

Illouz, E. and Wilf, E. 2008 'Oprah Winfrey and the Co-production of Market and Morality', *Women and Performance: A Journal of Feminist Theory* 18(1): 1–7.

Jackson, S. and Scott, S. 2004 'Sexual Antinomies in Late Modernity', *Sexualities* 7(2): 233–48.

Jackson-Lears, T. J. 1981 *No Place of Grace: Antimodernism and the Transformation of American Culture 1880–1920*, New York: Pantheon.

Jagger, E. 1998 'Marketing the Self, Buying an Other: Dating in a Post-Modern, Consumer Society', *Sociology* 34(4): 795–814.

Jost, F. 2011 'When Reality TV is a job', in M. M. Kraidy and K. Sender (eds) *The Politics of Reality Television: Global Perspectives*, London and New York: Routledge.

Kasson, J. 1990 *Rudeness and Civility: Manners in Nineteenth Century Urban America*, New York: Hill and Wang.

Kavka, M. 2008 *Reality Television, Affect and Intimacy: Reality Matters*, London: Palgrave Macmillan.

Kipnis, L. 2003 *Against Love: A Polemic*, New York: Vintage Books.

Kroker, A. 1992 *The Possessed Individual: Technology and the French Postmodern*, New York: St Martin's Press.

Latimer, J. 2009 'Unsettling Bodies: Frida Kahlo's Self-Portraits and Dividuality', in J. Latimer and M. Schillmeier (eds) *Unknown Bodies*, Oxford: Blackwell.

Lawler, S. 2000 *Mothering the Self: Mothers, Daughters, Subjects*, London: Routledge.

Lewis, T. 2008 *Smart Living: Lifestyle Media and Popular Expertise*, New York: Peter Lang.

Leys, R. 2007 *From Guilt to Shame: Auschwitz and After*, Princeton: Princeton University Press.

Lubin, D. M. 1997 'Modern Psychological Selfhood in the Art of Thomas Eakins' *Inventing the Psychological: Towards a Cultural History of Emotional Life in America*, New Haven and London: Yale University Press.

Lury, C. 1998 *Prosthetic Culture: Photography, Memory and Identity*, London: Routledge.

——2004 *Brands: The Logos of the Global Economy*, London: Routledge.

Mankekar, P. 1999 *Screening Culture, Viewing Politics: An Ethnography of Television, Womanhood, and Nation in Postcolonial India*, Durham and London: Duke University Press.

Marcuse, H. 1955 *Eros and Civilisation*, Boston, MA: Beacon.

——1964 *One Dimensional Man: The Ideology of Industrial Society*, London: Sphere Books.

McKenzie, J. 2001 *Perform or Else; From Discipline to Performance*, New York and London: Routledge.

McRobbie, A. 1996 'More! New Sexualitities in Girls' and Womens' Magazines', in J. Curran (ed.) *Cultural Studies and Communications*, London: Arnold.

Moran, L., Skeggs, B., Tyrer, P. and Corteen, K. 2004 *Sexuality and the Politics of Violence and Safety*, London: Routledge.

Morse, M. 1998 *Virtualities: Television, Media Art, and Cyberculture*, Indianapolis, IN: Indiana University Press.

Moseley, R. 2000 'Makeover Takeover on British Television', *Screen* 41(3): 299–314.

Munro, R. 1996 'The Consumption View of Self: Extension, Exchange and Identity', in S. Edgell, K. Hetherington and A. Warde (eds) *Consumption Matters*, Cambridge: Blackwell.

Nancy, J.-L. 2000 *Being Singular-Plural*, Stanford, CA: Stanford Univeristy Press.

Nowotny, H. 1981 'Women in Public Life in Austria', in C. Fuchs Epstein and R. Laub Coser (eds) *Access to Power: Cross National Studies of Women and Elites*, London: George Allen and Unwin.

Ouellette, L. and Hay, J. 2008 *Better Living through Television*, Oxford Blackwell.

Peters, T. 1999 *The Brand You*, New York: Random House.

Pfister, J. 1997 'On Conceptualising the Cultural History of Emotional and Psychological Life in America', in J. Pfister and N. Schnog (eds) *Inventing the Psychological: Towards a Cultural History of Emotional Life in America*, New Haven and London: Yale University Press.

Pfister, J. and Schnog, N. 1997 'Inventing the Psychological: Towards a Cultural History of Emotional Life in America', New Haven and London: Yale University Press.

Phillips, A. and Taylor, B. 2009 *On Kindness*, London: Penguin.

Pitt, K. 2002 'Being a New Capitalist Mother', *Discourse and Society* 13(2): 251–67.

Reay, D. 1998 *Class Work: Mother's Involvement in their Children's Primary Schooling*, London: UCL Press.

——2004 'Gendering Bourdieu's Concept of Capitals? Emotional Capital, Women and Social Class', in L. Adkins and B. Skeggs (eds) *Feminism After Bourdieu*, Oxford: Blackwell.

Reiger, K. 1984 *The Disenchantment of the Home: Modernising the Australian Family 1880–1914*, Melbourne: Oxford University Press.

Rieff, P. 1966 *The Triumph of the Therapeutic: Uses of Faith After Freud*, New York: Harper Row.

Rose, N. 1989 *Governing the Soul: The Shaping of the Private Self*, London: Routledge.

Savage, M. 2003 'A New Class Paradigm? Review Article', *British Journal of Sociology of Education* 24(4): 535–41.

Skeggs, B. 1997a *Formations of Class and Gender: Becoming Respectable*, London: Sage.

——1997b 'Introduction: Processes, Frameworks and Motivations', in B. Skeggs (ed.) *Formations of Class and Gender: Becoming Respectable*, London: Sage.

——2002 'Techniques for Telling the Reflexive Self', in T. May (ed.) *Qualitative Research in Action*, London: Sage.

——2004a *Class, Self, Culture*, London: Routledge.

——2004b 'Introducing Pierre Bourdieu's Analysis of Class, Gender and Sexuality', in L. Adkins and B. Skeggs (eds) *Feminism After Bourdieu*, Oxford: Blackwell.

——2004c 'Exchange Value and Affect: Bourdieu and the Self', in L. Adkins and B. Skeggs (eds) *Feminism After Bourdieu*, Oxford: Blackwell.

——2011 'Imagining personhood differently: person value and autonomist working class value practices', *Sociological Review* 59(3): 579–94.

——2012a 'Feeling Class: Affect and Culture in the Making of Class Relations', in G. Ritzer (ed.) *The Wiley-Blackwell Companion to Sociology*, Oxford: Blackwell.

——2012b 'Struggles for Value: Value Practices, Injustice and Affect' *Sociology* March.

Skeggs, B. and Wood, H. 2011 'Turning it on is a Class Act: Immediate Object Relations with the Television', *Media, Culture and Society* 33(6): 941–53.

Smith, A. 1757 *Theory of the Moral Sentiments*, London: Liberty Press.

Stallybrass, P. and White, A. 1986 *The Politics and Poetics of Transgression*, London: Methuen.

Steedman, C. 1990 *Childhod, Culture and Class in Britain*, New Brunswick, New Jersey: Rutgers University Press.

——2000 'Enforced Narratives: Stories of Another Self', in T. Cosslett, C. Lury and P. Summerfield (eds) *Feminism and Autobiography: Texts, Theories, Methods*, London: Routledge.

Strathern, M. 1992 *After Nature: English Kinship in the Late Twentieth Century*, Cambridge: Cambridge University Press.

Thompson, J. 1996 *Models of Value: Eighteenth Century Political Economy and the Novel*, Durham, NC: Duke University Press.

Thrift, N. 2004 'Intensities of Feeling: Towards a Spatial Politics of Affect', *Geografiska Annaler* 86B(1): 57–78.

Tolson, A. 2011 '"I'm Common and My Talking is Quite Abrupt" (Jade Goody): Language and Class in Celebrity Big Brother', in H. Wood and B. Skeggs (eds) *Reality Television and Class*, London: BFI/Palgrave.

Tyler, I. and Bennett, B. 2010 'Celebrity Chav: Fame, Femininity and Social Class', *European Journal of Cultural Studies* 13(3): 375–93.

Tyler, M. 2004 'Managing Between the Sheets: Lifestyle Magazines and the Management of Sexuality in Everyday Life', *Sexualities* 7(1): 81–106.

Urry, J. 2000 *Societies Beyond the Social: Mobilities for the Twenty First Century*, London: Routledge.

Vincent, D. 1981 *Bread, Knowledge and Freedom: A Study of Working-Class Nineteenth Century Autobiography*, London: Europa Publications.

Walkerdine, V. and Lucey, H. 1989 *Democracy in the Kitchen: Regulating Mothers and Socialising Daughters*, London: Virago.

Weber, B. 2009 *Makeover TV: Selfhood, Citizenship and Celebrity*, Durham, NC: Duke University Press.

Wood, H. 2001 '"No, YOU Rioted!": The Pursuit of Conflict in the Management of Expert and Lay Discourses on Kilroy', in A. Tolson (ed.) *Television Talk Shows: Discourse, Performance, Spectacle*, Lawrence Erlbaum: New Jersey.

——2009 *Talking with Television: Women, Talk Shows and Modern Self-Reflexivity*, Illinois: Illinois University Press.

Zelizer, V. A. 2005 *The Purchase of Intimacy*, Princeton: Princeton University Press.

Chapter 3

Textual intimacies

This chapter analyses the explosion of reality television in relation to theories of the mediation and performance of personhood outlined in the previous two chapters. We have argued for a particular blend of sociological and media analysis in order to capture the specificity of reality television as simultaneously representation *and* intervention. This requires us to work through, not just how the form is constructed as a textual/aesthetic entity, but also how it calls non-actors to engage in public performances. We reiterate Richard Johnson's (1997) observations that the textual/social split in cultural research is inherently 'phoney' and that preserving such a distinction is ultimately disabling. Instead he argues for a position (informed by Stuart Hall and Michel Foucault) in which the textual is a broad category and just one way of looking at social practice as such, as a way that is preoccupied by looking at meanings, feelings, knowledges, subjectivities, etc. Following in the tradition of early television analysis (e.g. Lenox Lohr 1940) we agree that television's essential properties are immediacy and intimacy, making reality television a prime example of the medium and the television image a performance *in* the present. Television is, as Jane Feuer (1983) notes, a process, in which every television frame is always in a state of becoming, a composition of the constantly changing present living off the instantaneous and uncertainty of the moment, mirroring the temporal everyday. This opens up ways for us to understand how audiences and images are located within the same social relationships, circuits of value, discourses and narratives. Like Philip Auslander (1999) we argue that all performance, including the performance of personhood is mediatized, hence our interests in how this mediatization works through people, performances, practices and texts.

Our intent to capture a relatively broad range of the self-transformation reality television phenomenon suggests a reach which necessarily prevents us from the kind of closer textual analysis that pays attention to more subtle shifts in genre. Jason Mittell (2004) argues for a move away from a homogeneous notion of reality television 'noting the crucial cultural, political, and ethical differences between formats' (p.200). Much excellent work of this type already exists which largely focuses on one programme and defines its textual characteristics in relation to other televisual legacies and the particular hybridization of genres (see the now numerous collections on reality television). Others have pointed to the continued use of the term 'reality TV' by academics, the industry, critics and audiences, but the confusion arises as it is also surrounded by a host of other nuanced descriptions: formatted documentary, fly-on-the-wall series, gamedocs, lifestyle, make-over, transformation TV, etc. This points to the impossibility of offering any definition of reality television as a coherent genre, but as Holmes (2008) points out, in any case it is the *processes* of genre construction that are more interesting than the pursuit of certain categories.

We hold on to 'reality television' as a useful term – recalling Nick Couldry's (2003) discussion of its suggestiveness about the myth of the mediated centre: 'presenting itself as the privileged "frame" through which we access the reality that *matters to us as social beings*' (p.58, our emphasis). Thus we would argue that it is the notion of an alternative 'framing' – the exposition of self and self-interrogation as a powerful and potent trend in contemporary society – that drives us to hold the conceptual features of the form together under the umbrella term. The presence of websites such as 'Reality TV World' http://www.realitytvworld.com/, covering the latest news from a variety of styles of show, attests to the term's continued salience in the interplay between audiences and producers in the ongoing discursive negotiation of the genre.

In this light our analysis in this chapter works in two ways. First, we map a specific period in British television in the years 2004–5 and produce a descriptive taxonomy of reality television which captures the mediated 'opening out of intimacy' across our screens. Second, we choose four clusters of programmes from that map which we identify as indicative of reality television's reach into particular intimate fields, and offer textual analyses in relation to the economy of person production outlined in Chapter 2. There we argued that the extension of performance as an act of 'value' is how reality television participates in the wider political economy of personhood. We also consider these programmes in relation to the traditions of melodrama and documentary outlined in Chapter 1 which points to the repetition of elements that code the moral value of participants. This further enables us to discuss how the visibility of self-performance is embroiled in contemporary politics of class and gender. The first section of this chapter shows how the format allows for the 'opening out of intimacy' across our screens, whilst the textual analysis in the second section demonstrates how the politics of performance also closes down the possibilities that the representation of intimate relations may take.

Opening out intimacy through the drive of the format

As we described in the introduction to the book, our initial research proposal was to empirically investigate ideas of individualization and self-reflexivity as televised phenomena. We were interested in how people on reality television were called to perform transformation and hence publicly display their value. We did however draw some boundaries around our textual analyses, deciding to discount so-called 'event' television, for example *Big Brother, Pop Idol, I'm a Celeb-rity*, etc., because the notion of event seemed to provide a too powerful structure over our analysis of self-transformation, as well as the fact that numerous studies were already underway on these phenomena. Nonetheless it was impossible to remove these programmes from the equation during our research, where respondents continually referred to them and their famous participants (provid-ing further evidence for retaining reality television as a viable generic term). Guided by the literature on changing notions of the performance of self (see Chapters 1 and 2) we made the potential of 'self-transformation' the defining characteristic for selection when we looked across the schedules for reality tele-vision formats, although of course this is still a rather broad and uncontainable brief.

In the period 2004–5[1] we counted 42 programme series – not including potential one-off programmes – across the UK terrestrial schedule (which con-sists of five channels BBC1, BBC2, ITV, Channel 4 and Channel 5) that we felt subscribed to an emphasis upon self-transformation outside of the more promi-nent 'event' programmes – see Table 3.1.

However, it quickly became apparent that the number of programmes broadly defined as reality television was massively growing, further hampering our ability to draw a clear perimeter around our programme sample. To get some sense of the scale of this growth we then counted again. This time we included *all* programmes that could be described as reality television available in just one week of November 2005 from 'Freeview' (free digital television service in the UK), discounting those available across the numerous channels available through other subscription television services. In that one week alone we counted 92 different programmes (see Table 3.2).

This list includes a wide range of programmes: from those more broadly defined as belonging to the police-doc sub-genre (which some argue was the genesis of reality television, such as *World's Wildest Police Videos*), whilst others clearly belong to the 'event' sub-genre (such as the talent quest *X-Factor* or celebrity *Strictly Come Dancing*). What is noticeable however are the numerous sites in which 'ordinary' people, non-actors are recorded (work, home, public spaces) as well as the numerous areas of personal life that are under investigation (dress, gardens, relationships, sex, etc.). Most of these programmes do not make the news headlines like *Big Brother*, but instead offer more 'ordinary' fodder: programmes like *Who Rules the Roost, Wanted: New Mum and Dad* and *My Teen's a Nightmare*. This more mundane stream of investigation of the every-day with emphasis on self-performance in familiar settings emerged as our primary focus. Hill's (2007) study also details different formats and hybrids of programmes in this field, her priorities over the relationship of these forms to documentary led her to work with four categories of programming: news, cur-rent affairs and investigations, documentary and popular factual. However, our focus was with the 'popular factual' end of these categories and with the numerous ways in which personal and 'private' lives are constituted and

Table 3.1 List of 42 UK terrestrial programmes which focus on self-transformation as described in programme guides.

Programme	Key for programme title	Production company, channel, year
The Apprentice	A	Talk back Thames, BBC, 2005
Bad Lads Army	BLA	Twenty, Twenty Television, ITV, 2004–5
Bank of Mum and Dad	BMD	BBC, 2004–9
Beyond Boundaries	BB	Diverse, BBC, 2005–6
Brat Camp	BC	Shapiro/Grodner Productions, Channel 4, 2005–6
Bricking It	BI	IWC Media, Channel 4, 2004
Club Reps	CR	Scottish Media Group, ITV, 2002–4
Date My Daughter	DMD	Lion Television Production, ITV1, 2005
Desperately Seeking Sheila	DSS	Carlton UK Productions, ITV, 2005
Dream Home Abroad	DHA	RDF, Channel 5, 2005
Driving Mum and Dad Mad	DMDM	Granada, ITV, 2005
Faking It	FI	RDF, Channel 4, 2000–6
Family Contract	FC	BBC1, 2004–5
Fool Around with …	FAW	Endemol, Channel 4, 2004–5
… my girlfriend		
… my boyfriend		
… my mum		
Get a New Life	GNL	Brighter Pictures, BBC2/3, 2003–5 BBC2, 2005
Grown Up Gappers	GUG	RDF, ITV, 2003–9
Holiday Showdown	HS	World of Wonder, Channel 5, 2005
House Busters	HB	BBC3/UKTV, 2005–
House of Tiny Tearaways	HTT	BBC3, 2005–7
Honey We're Killing The Kids	HKK	Talk Back Productions, Channel 4, 2003– London Weekend Television, Sky 1/C4 1997–2004
How Clean Is Your House	HCH	RDF, ITV, 2005–
Ibiza Uncovered	IU	Talk back Thames, BBC, 2005
Ladette to Lady	LL	RDF, 2005–
Little Angels	LA	BBC, 2004–6
Made For Each Other	MEO	Talkback Productions, Channel 4, 2003–4
Make Me a Million	MMM	RDF, Channel 4, 2005
My Fair Kerry	MFK	Granada, ITV, 2005
Nanny 911	N9	Granada Entertainment USA, ITV 2, 2004–
Nigel's Place in France	NPF	Tiger Aspect, Channel 4, 2005
Playing It Straight	PIS	20th Century Television, Fox/Channel 4, 2004
Risking It All	RIA	Ricochet South, Channel 4, 2004–5
Supernanny	SN	Richochet, Channel 4, 2004–6
Sex Inspectors	SEX	Talk Back Productions, Channel 4, 2004–6
Straight Dates for Gay Mates	SDGM	Prospect Pictures, ITV, 2003–
Ten Years Younger	TYY	Maverick Television, Channel 4 – 2004–2010
Too Posh to Wash	TPW	Talkback Thames, Channel 4, 2004–2006
The Unteachables	U	Talkback Thames, Channel 4, 2005
What Not to Wear	WNT	BBC, 2001–2006
What the Butler Saw	WBS	Endemol, Channel 4, 2004
Wife Swap	WS	RDF, Channel 4, 2003–2009
Who Rules the Roost	WRR	Ricochet, BBC, 2002–6
You Are What You Eat	YWE	Celador, Channel 4, 2004–7

Table 3.2 List of reality programmes from one week in 2005, available on Freeview.

30 Days	Parish In The Sun
60 Minute Makeover	Playing It Straight (USA)
A House in Florida	Property Ladder (incl. spin-offs)
Airline (and spin-offs)	Property People Shorts
Antiques Ghost Show	Redcoats
Arresting Design	Restored to Glory
Beyond Boundaries	Risking It All
Body Hits	Road Rage School
Brat Camp (and spin offs)	Rock School
Bricking It	Scream Team
Britain's Best Back Gardens	Seaside Rescue
Britain's Worst …	Seven Year Makeover
Car Booty	Shops Robbers and Videotape
Cash In The Attic	Spendaholics
Chalet Slaves	Spending Other People's Money
Commando VIP uncut	Straight Dates By Gay Mates
Date My Daughter	Streets Ahead
Design ER	Strictly Come Dancing (and spin offs)
Desperate Midwives	Switched
Double The Fist	Tales From The Green Valley
Dream Business	The Brothel
Flog It	The Coach Trip
Fool around with …	The Market
Frontline	The Next Joe Millionaire
Garden Invaders	The Osbournes
Garden Rivals	The Queens Cavalry
Grand Designs (and spin offs)	The Simple Life: Interns
Homes Under the Hammer	The Unteachables
Honey We're Killing The Kids	Trading Spouses
Hotel On Sea	Trading Up
House Detectives	Trauma (and spin offs)
House of Tiny Tearaways	Tudor Times
How Not to Decorate	Turf Wars
How to Rescue a House	Uncharted Territory
I'm Moving Out	Video Vigilantes
Little Angels	Wanted: New Mum and Dad
Love to Shop	War at the Door
Make Me a Million	Weed It and Reap
Mind Your Own Business	Welcome to Fatland
Model Gardens	What Not To Wear
Most Haunted	Who Rules The Roost
My Teens a Nightmare	Wife Swap
Natural Born Racers	Wildlife SOS
Office Monkey	World's Wildest Police Videos
Our Home	X Factor (and spin-offs)
Our House	Your Life In Their Hands

interrogated in these spaces. Since we conducted this survey the genre has mutated even further with forays into more 'scripted' versions of reality television such as *The Hills* and *The Only Way is Essex*, but we want to build a picture of the programmes that were screened when we were talking to our audiences since we are concerned to think about the relay between performances and audiences.

We also collected a range of intertextual material that surrounded the programmes, including internet sites, TV listings magazines, women's magazines, newspapers and the television programmes that feed from reality television. There were key moments such as the 'Jade Goody' race incident on *Big Brother* where Jade sparked a huge row over race relations when she was accused of bullying Bollywood actress Shilpa Shetty in the house[2] and the 'Queen incident' where RDF re-edited the Queen's procession producing a national scandal and supposedly bringing the genre into disrepute. We were continually vigilant about the mutation of genre as it morphed into different forms and spin-offs such as accompanying books and even board games.

The commercial ecology of the contemporary television landscape is often cited as the explanation behind the exponential rise in the number of reality television programmes across our screens (Magder 2004; Raphael 2004). But what is the relationship between this economic imperative and the intervention into areas of personal life? Albert Moran (2000) locates the rise and globalization of the make-over within the television market's reliance on the format. Keane and Moran (2008) are keen to point to the difference between the notion of 'genre' as often applied via a literary set of classifications, and 'format' which is the industry's commodification of textual items so that they can be included in licensing agreements. They are critical of the often easy conflation of 'genre' with 'format' in academic critique (see Mittell 2004 above) and they describe elements of the format as 'engines' which drive the explosion and internationalization of certain types of programme. They argue that the television format industry is a calculated response to globalization and to the contemporary television environment of increased interactivity and audience involvement in programme production: 'as more and more people contribute to the making of content, there is a concomitant increase in the amount of appropriation of existing content through sampling, synthesizing, mixing, cloning and formatting' (p.167). In a form of evolutionary struggle 'engines' such as particular devices like 'in-built conflict' in the case of *Wife Swap*, or renovation (transformation of the self or property), or exotic locations, or talent competitions, can be combined and hybridized to continually find new shape:

> You hybridise by taking something that's familiar, say in an information show like renovation, then you add a challenge, and then you get a bunch of people together to create conflict. That way you move beyond information, beyond information challenge, into a new form.
>
> (Franken cited in Keane and Moran 2008:167)

Rather than being concerned to delineate the various sub-genres of reality television clearly, which appeared to be impossible, our concern therefore was to produce some kind of taxonomy of reality television in order to help order what kind of social practices operate as interventions in various arenas of personal life. Therefore, we would add to the notion of 'engines' as particular textual devices, the intimate fields of personal life that they interrogate, by which the form can continually take new shape. We began with our list of 42 programmes and then used two indices in order to produce a cross-tabulation: the format 'engine' that helps to structure the programme, and the intimate field that it interrogates. We provide a visual mapping of the relationship between the economic drive of the format and the opening out of intimacy across our television screens – see Table 3.3.

Taxonomies tend to be used to produce hierarchies, but instead we map out the intimate arenas of personal life that seemed to have become most prominent across the reality television provision in the period. We can clearly see that there is a clustering of programme which use expert observation to intervene in areas of personal life around families, relationships, appearances, etc. Thus we can see that the economic structures which support the augmentation of these programmes help constitute the seemingly endless opening out of the ways in which television intervenes in personal life. Intimate fields such as bodily hygiene, finances, familial relations, manners, food and health are therefore commodified into forms which can be explored and tested through a range of technical devices (engines) to produce a televisual narrative: these include life overhauls, swaps, tests of passing, challenges, make-overs and expert interventions. The various elements of the 'self' within this model are therefore also potentially economic units, ones that can be exchanged and combined in the endless pursuit of the lucrative format. Therefore, the commercial drive of the format fuels the endless opening out and intensification of intimacy as part of the broader drive towards the commodification of self-performance in the interests of capital accumulation.[3]

In previous chapters we have discussed the ways in which the project of the self and the ways in which it should be performed have come to shape social relations. Reality television can be seen as a barometer of this procession of selfhood as it is increasingly made visible across cultural fields. Jon Dovey (2000) suggests that reality television represents 'spectacular subjectivity' as interiorities are increasingly externalized (and commodified). However there is a problem inherent in this process of visualization. In media debates around the Habermasian notion of the public sphere, the potential for a liberatory politics resides in access – in bringing the lifeworld to system. This analysis has led to the re-evaluation of the talk show genre as it offered space, particularly for women and often women of colour, to articulate (if not always to politicize) the personal and particular in a public realm (Smith-Shomade 2008; and see Chapters 1 and 2). Similar reasoning has occasionally been used in analyses of reality television. For instance, Peter Lunt and Tania Lewis (2008) argue that in lifestyle

Table 3.3 Formats indexed by intimate fields.

			Format 'engines'					
	Abject	Swaps	Passing/ Disguise	Challenges	Competition	Physical make-over	Expert observation	Life overhaul
Work	CR		FI	MMM, BI, BLA	A		BLA	RIA, BLA GNL
Money				GNL, MMM		BMD		
Holidays/Travel	IU	HS		BB				GUG
Homes				DHA		HB		NPF
Intimate field — Food & Health							YWE HKK	
Hygiene						TPW	HCH	
Families/ Relationships		HS WS		DSS, BC, DMD, FAW	DMD, FAW SDGM	WRR, BMD	SN, FC, DMDM MEO, BC LA N9, U, HTT	BC
Sex				FAW	FAW		SEX	
Appearance			FI, PIS	FI, FAW	PIS, FAW	TYY EM WNT		
Manners		HS	FI, PIS	FI	PIS WBS	WBS		
Explicit class mobility			WBS MFK	FI			LL	

television one should also be aware that alternative subjectivities are made available, maintaining that a make-over programme like *What Not to Wear* must also be thought about in terms of this politics of (public) recognition, where particularly older women's bodies take centre stage in a culture which has tended to marginalize them, thereby highlighting 'the potentially positive role of popular media forms and modes of expertise in recognizing and rendering visible certain modes of social otherness' (p.22). As with the arguments about increasing access to television representing the democratization of the media away from elites, this neo-Habermasian argument posits visibility as inherently progressive. This chimes with other arguments in Chapter 6, which suggest that by making visible women's labour a programme like *Wife Swap* offers some ambiguous feminist credentials (Holmes and Jermyn 2007). Yet as critics of the politics of recognition have shown, it is not visibility but value that is crucial to how women are evaluated through public recognition; their bodies may be made visible but in so doing denigrated (Fraser 1999; Skeggs 2001). As Peggy Phelan (1993) notes, young naked white women are highly visible in Western media but this does not correlate with power or value. Likewise Sara Ahmed (1998) points to the problematic of assuming visibility to be a good thing; she notes for Black people who have no choice but to be repeatedly made visible through the scopic regime of racism, invisibility may offer a much more radical politics.[4]

Moreover in her book *Against Recognition*, Lois McNay (2008) argues that the insights of recognition theorists are undercut by their reliance on an inadequate account of power that overlooks the complex ways in which the person is connected to social structures. Guy Redden (2008) also suggests that although couched in relatively governmental social norms, lifestyle choices availed on reality television offer some source of agency in their 'depictions of ordinary people imbued with desire to fashion successful lives by manipulating elements within their spheres of control' (p.53). But we would argue that inequality is *worked through* the contours of the economy outside of what the market promises as 'a better life'. Here we argue for a more sustained analysis of the patterning of the visibility (who and how) through the conventions of reality television, in terms of how television invites performances from subjects already visibly symbolically inscribed as in need of transformation. The supposed need for transformation is a visible lack of value by which participants are marked. Their willingness to be potentially transformed temporarily enhances their value as they are shown performing their adjustment to the required transformation, meaning that they must leave behind that which marked them as lacking value as in the first place.

Textually shaping personhood

In order to capture the range of intimate relations and formats, we focus on four clusters of programming taken from our sampling in the following textual analysis.

1. Life overhauls: *Nigel's Place in France, Grown Up Gappers, No Going Back.*
2. Domestic interventions in family and relationships: *Wife Swap, Supernanny, Family Contract, Honey We're Killing the Kids.*
3. Appearance and health transformations: *What Not to Wear, 10 Years Younger, You Are What You Eat.*
4. Explicit experiments in class mobility: *What the Butler Saw, Faking It, Ladette to Lady.*

The particular episodes that we discuss here are also ones that we watched with our audiences, in order to enable a more visible relay between text and audience that is central to our overall analysis. When we began our study of a particular period in British reality television, we noticed a difference in style between some programmes which involved a more obvious conceit, 'format engine', and those that were closer to documentary conventions. In terms of documentary analysis discussed in Chapter 1 we described a distinction between those programmes which engineered a 'new' reality and those that followed a reality which may have taken place outside of the television production. In programmes such as *Wife Swap, Faking It, Supernanny, Nanny 911*, etc., situations are engineered either by the swapping format, the passing format, or the appearance of an expert in one's home, and are hence spatially familiar and limited in time (usually edited to 30 minutes or an hour). In other programmes like *Nigel's Place in France, Grown Up Gappers* and *No Going Back* (which we call life overhauls), personal journeys are observed *over* time without an obvious conceit or intervention, and each of these latter examples involves an expansion of space and usually a journey abroad in pursuit of self-discovery. Why does it matter that two very different style of 'reality' are broadcast during the same time period? It is obvious that they represent very different sub-genres of reality television and whilst the latter are closer to traditional documentary conventions, they are nonetheless stories of personal narratives of toil, rather than offering any direct socio-political commentary remaining 'spectacles of particularity' in Nichols' (1991) terms.

In Helen Piper's (2004) analysis of *Wife Swap* she argues that it is perhaps a mistake to ally *Wife Swap* with documentary, better instead to see it as 'improvised drama' closer to a 'fictive boundary', since the staging of the format invites participants to improvise the drama of their circumstances. We thus attempted to plot programmes on a scale from the fictive boundary to those closer to conventional documentary – see Table 3.4.

There is a certain cluster of programmes of self-discovery that are mostly populated by the middle classes (closer to documentary), whilst another cluster of programmes that involved a more obvious narrative intervention, are more often populated by the working class. In terms of how we see performances of personhood these two clusters offer us a way of seeing how class is made through the specific time/space organization of the format. Yet all of our programmes can be said to incite the 'reflexive self' and/or the prosthetic self (the

Table 3.4 Between improvised drama and documentary.

Programme	Structuring relations	Selfhood	
Wife Swap	To 'other' wife	Better mothers, better wives	Fictive Boundary
Ladette to Lady	To finishing school mistresses	Better behaved and feminized selves	
Family Contract	To higher authority (psychologists)	Behaved selves	
What the Butler Saw	To absent higher class authority	Culturally failed selves	
What Not To Wear	To material goods (clothes) and style advisors	Tasteful self	
Supernanny	To child	Better parent/ mother	
Faking It	To mentor	An alter 'self'	
10 Years Younger	To beauty coach	Beautiful self	
You Are What You Eat	To dietician/life coach	Healthier self	
Grown Up Gappers	To a range of transient individuals and place	Deepening of self	
No Going Back	Potential self	Alter self	Documentary
Nigel's Place in France	Absent	Deepening of self	

quintessential models that rely on middle class cultural resources as described in Chapter 2). At the bottom of the table, the programmes that are closer to documentary formats emphasize a long psychological journey with time spent on participants telling their experience in detail. For instance, *Grown Up Gappers* is a series which explores mostly middle-aged professionals, taking a year out of their lives to pursue an alternative life abroad. In one episode (first broadcast on 24 March 2005) Paul Edmonson, an airport manager, travels to Africa to 're-connect to the world' where we hear him regularly speak directly to camera about his own self-development. He reflexively tells us how he used to be cowardly, shirked emotional responsibility and was in a 'bad mind-set' but through the physical journey he has made a psychological transformation towards becoming more responsible. The hour-long documentary gives him considerable time and space to tell this narrative in a variety of ways. He talks about how Africa has made him reflect on his previous life and how he is going to change and direct what he has learnt into a better life in the future.

No Going Back is a series about couples leaving the 'rat race' to move abroad to pursue their dream. In one episode of the series (first broadcast in 2003 and repeated on 5 November 2004), Miranda and William Taxis buy a Tuscan farmhouse in need of renovation. Over the one-hour documentary we see two years of their lives operating across both private and public spheres: their struggles and financial hardship, their children going to a new school and their community relationships with locals. Over and again we watch them reflexively talking directly to camera expressing moments of exasperation, despair and joy. We see them working in different environments, making their case at Italian Planning courts and even challenging the local mayor over a proposed airport. We see where they have come from, the routes they take, and where they plan for the future in a narrative of transformation, which involves time and reflection, movement through space and considerable economic and personal investment. We finally learn that the struggle and investment in themselves and their properties pays off and by looking at the Channel 4 website we can browse their extensive complex of Tuscan holiday properties where they 'live the dream' and which we can rent.

Similarly in *Nigel's Place in France* the whole series is devoted to his journey to set up a guest house in the Ardeche in France. Each programme dwells on the telling of his story where he reflects on his various decisions, both directly to camera but also in the conversations with others. In one episode (first broadcast on 29 April 2005), whilst looking for day trips for his guests we see Nigel and his two business partners go horse riding in the mountains, go flying over the region and attend a bull fight in Avignon. These programmes all provide examples of 'mobile reflexive selves' (Urry 2000), where different landscapes and geography provide the aesthetic backdrop to the adventure of the cosmopolitan self (Africa, Tuscany, the Ardeche). The programmes are geographically and socially expansive, not based upon cramped containment by the domestic verisimilitude of the kitchen, bedroom or home. Yet there is still little comment on what these narratives of escape might say about cultural or economic conditions: white flight from British urban environments, perhaps? Or masculinity without domestic responsibility? Or the power of property markets (before the crash) as a variant of colonial relations? The important point here is the *time* and *space* given to these subjects for the reflexive articulation and visualization of their personhood.

In the opening to the same episode of *Nigel's Place in France* we see him ask himself, 'The question is do we want to spend the rest of our days looking after B&B guests?' Later we see Nigel begin to get 'bogged down' by the daily repetitiveness of running the business. Over an edited sequence of visits to the shops, driving the van, making beds and ironing, the voice over says, 'Sally-Ann and Nigel find themselves on a treadmill of chores. For Nigel it's all a bit of a shock.' Then to camera he says:

> Well it's great, you know it's everything I thought it would be, it's just a bit relentless, that's the only thing you know. Up every morning making bloody eggs and bacon and the other thing that I hadn't really thought too much about was that by 12 o'clock the day's really finished and there's nothing really to do which to start with was great and now isn't so great.

Nigel here is reflecting on his daily routine, but he can also demonstrate the ability to escape that routine. The voice over tells us he has a call 'that calls his new life in France into question'. He then arranges to go to Marseille to visit a friend and we see him in a marina talking about a yachting trip to Corsica. Nigel then soon looks at a boat for sale and begins to think about sailing around the world. When asked by a faceless member of the production crew about the B&B, he replies to camera:

> Yeh but this is something that I've always wanted to do; I've not always wanted to run a B&B, that was just a means to an end to like stay in France. You know but this I can see myself doing, I really can, I'd love to do it.

Programmes of this sub-genre follow the central participants demonstrating control over their circumstances, able to reflexively account for where they are as ultimately self-determining, able to invest in a future self and able to move across national spaces. Nigel gets bored with the responsibility of the bed and breakfast and yachts off to Corsica.

On the other hand reality television programmes which involve a more obvious conceit or 'engine' visualize very different conditions for the performance of personhood. They are more intensely engineered around a closely defined set of relationships or 'structuring relations' towards a very particular interrogation of self defined *by* that relationship and are often confined to a limited number of settings. Consider *Wife Swap* which takes place over two weeks and is portrayed in 50 minutes in which we enter the drama immediately as the swapped wives are called to account for how they feel about the ensuing set up. Their visibility is for the show and not despite it. They are cast for their conflict potential, be it religion, aspiration, discipline or sexuality and so on, which usually also amplifies class differences. Participants are also cast for their symbolic excess: the *Wife Swap* website advertised for some time for 'another Lizzie Bardsley'. Lizzie was a mother of eight, who smoked, had asthma, had never worked, swore and 'lived off benefits', thus offering great dramatic potential when swapped with a very aspirational wife. These programme formats are not a commentary on their 'everyday life' in which they can show that they are periodically in control, but instead they are premised upon the drama of the immediate moment and immediate reaction.

For instance, in an episode of *Wife Swap* first broadcast in January 2003[5] Tracy swaps with Kate: both are working class mothers but their difference is generated through Tracy's aspiration to social and material mobility. They are called to perform those differences from looking around each other's homes from the outset and testing out the other's life. Closer to the fictive boundary, the improvised drama that ensues is very much 'in the moment': their to-camera accounts are direct reactions to immediate situations that arise in the home – emphasizing reaction rather than reflection. Tracy is dedicated to a career and a nice home, whilst Kate, a stay-at-home mum, dedicates herself to her six children.

How the women have come to these positions is not part of the narrative: their differences speak only about immediacy of the drama and not to the evolution of a longer or more developed version of their circumstances.

The 'reality' is generated through the verisimilitude of the locations, the kitchen, the dining room, etc., where 'everyday life' is confined to the local and the immediate. The numerous shows which work with other 'engines', particularly expert observations of family life such as *Family Contract, Supernanny*, etc., confirm a repetition across the genre of this more immediate reactive intervention in the domestic arena. In *Honey We're Killing Kids* time is stretched visually by morphing images of the children into images of themselves in 40 years time only to confirm the problems in the present.

If we refer back to the current demand (mapped in Chapter 2) to display one's value and prove oneself as a proper person by performing the 'self-work' ethic, we can see that the time compression in the format sets opportunities and limitations for different groups of people. Those who are called to perform reaction have no mechanisms for displaying to the audience their extended labour on the self, whereas a family such as the Taxis' deliberate reflexively over their investments in their selves (in the past, present and for the future). Reaction cuts down the time available to show one's investments in the self, as it is only in the moments of accountability that people are given a space to justify their actions. The emphasis upon reaction establishes for some the impossibility of displaying their investment in the self-work ethic, and thus the impossibility of appearing as a morally good citizen/subject/person.

These very different performances of personhood by participants across British reality television makes the structural conditions of possibility for their lives, such as access to resources, appear as if they are individual dispositions reduced to their own making. In Tony Bennett's (2003) analysis of the literatures on everyday life he talks about the emergence of two very different 'architectures of the self':

> On the one hand there are those who are said to live spontaneously at the level of everyday life, reproducing its habitual routines through forms of consciousness and behaviour that remain resolutely single-leveled – the bearers of Marcuse's (1964) 'one dimensional consciousness' for example. On the other hand, the critique of everyday life is also concerned to identify those whose social position, in vouchsafing them an ability to acquire a double-leveled consciousness enables them to pierce the flat surface of the everyday by introducing another dimension (the extraordinary in the ordinary) which, by warding off the prospect of the endless repetition, re-animates the movement of history.
>
> (2003:22)

He notes how such a conceptualization of subjectivity emerges as part of the demise of the sovereign state in a move towards forms of liberal government in

the nineteenth century (Poovey 1998) where the double-levelled self was attributed to the middle classes whilst strategies of liberal government led to a 'spec-
ular morality' in which other individuals learned how to govern themselves. The
working classes were seen as unable to lift themselves out of the immediacy of
the everyday or to view their behaviour reflexively, conceptualized, as we saw in
Chapter 2 as not having an interiority, and by European social theory as susceptible and lacking in self-discipline and control (Blackman 2007). We see this
moral value coding of personhood visually reproduced across the different formats of reality television as the working classes are over-represented in the programmes for which, not only are they recruited as in need of transformation, but
they are revealed as requiring reform as they dramatize themselves in the
moment. The single-levelled self according to Bennett is often allied to the mass
and to the working class, whose perceived lack of depth generated the claim for
a different form of control:

> Where there is a layered structure to the self within which the self can act
> on itself so as to become self-regulating, liberal forms of indirect governance
> are possible. Where the self is denied an interior space within which such a
> reforming activity of self-on-self can be fashioned, more direct forms of rule
> are called for.
>
> (2003:22)

Thus the 'format' tells us who is deemed to have a more complete architecture
of the self and who is not, who needs to transform and who does not. Whilst we do
not claim this as a blanket statement about all forms of reality television, this is
certainly a pattern we found across the genre in which architectures of selfhood
are espoused through different narrative and filmic conventions. Visibility here is
not enough of an explanation – it is the *mode* and structuring of visibility that
requires closer scrutiny.

Melodramatic moments

The emphasis upon the immediate, fictive and the dramatic in reality television
is further complicated by the use of melodrama to frame the relationship
between the personal and the social. The melodrama 'of the moment' also offers
another technique for producing evocative responses. In melodrama participants
react to circumstances beyond their control, becoming experiments in social
living by showing us how they respond to unexpected circumstances (as discussed
in Chapter 1). Programmes such as *What Not to Wear* and those which rely on the
make-over format tend to hone in closely on the reaction of the participant to
evaluations, observations and ultimately to their own transformation (recall
Moseley 2000 in Chaper 1). Here we want to focus on the consequences of an
emphasis upon reaction, rather than action.

Traditions of literature and theatre have tended to position realism in opposition to melodrama (Gledhill 1987a). Peter Brooks (1976/1995) poses

melodrama's relationship to realism as a response to the psychic consequences of the bourgeois social order in which the social *is* expressed as moral and personal. For Brooks the drive of realism is to understand the world by explaining it, whilst on the other hand melodrama forces meaning from the personal situations where language is inadequate and bodily gestures and somatic responses become the means by which the self is revealed. Melodrama privileges a 'language of presence and immediacy' (p.67) thereby making 'large but unsubstantial claims on meaning' (p.199) which work not so much at the level of 'Yes, but' than of 'So what!' (Gledhill 1987a:33). As Pullen (2004) argues, and as we discuss in Chapter 1, reality television relies on the unknowable through which surprises and the potential for critique may emerge outside of the intent of the director, a point we develop through a reading of how affect shapes the unknowable in Chapter 5, and how viewer challenges are incited through participants' non-verbal reactive gestures in Chapters 4 and 6.

Unpredictability also resonated in the production of family melodrama of the 1950s as discussed by Thomas Elsaesser (1972). For him family melodrama relies on moments of 'happenstance' to drive the narrative, rather than the hero-protagonist determining the action. In programmes like *Nigel's Place in France* the central character, Nigel, provides a narrative of continuous movement explaining why he is doing things with an elaborated reflexive articulation of reasons, whilst the participants in formatted reality programmes like *Wife Swap*, *Supernanny* and *Faking It* are instead acted upon, constantly forced to react and rely on their cultural and emotional resources, and ultimately unable to 'change the stifling social milieu' (p.55). The root of domestic melodrama's realism is that we are all governed by forces of happenstance even in the most familiar and mundane of settings. This has at least two consequences in reality television. First, in the element of uncertainty we can discern moments of rebellion in the gestures of participants – in the reluctant make-over participant whose pulled face registers her dislike of the expert, in the ladette in *Ladette to Lady* who sticks her fingers up to the finishing school mistress, in the wife in *Wife Swap* who turns her back on the other husband who is deemed to be too controlling. It is these bodily gestures of melodramatic reaction, which defy linguistic referents, which make the drama so compelling.

Second, reality television relies not only on the power of gesture in the drama of the moment, but also on documentary techniques which require the participant to report direct to camera. It is this blending of melodrama with documentary that structures how participants are called to account for actions that are ultimately beyond their control. These moments – which we call judgement shots – also prove to be significant for engaging audiences into talking back to the television (which we discuss in later chapters). In *Wife Swap* for example the participant is detached from her history, moved into an unknown context and bound to the other family, not as part of a longer life narrative but revealed as a situational response to being placed in another home. Thus participants often find themselves in a position of impossibility in which they have no resources

upon which to draw to understand what is happening (such as why other people's children are behaving so badly) and often they break down emotionally, as
the moment resists reason and language. In the episode of *Wife Swap* discussed
above, when Tracy fails to control the six children that she is not used to looking
after, she retreats to the kitchen and talks to camera as if it is the conduit to the
public witnessing of her fate: *Bollocks to them it's not fair that they should play me up like
this. I'm here to look after them.* ... [voice breaks and she begins to cry].

There are moments in *Wife Swap*, as Holmes and Jermyn (2007) note, where it
seems that emotional responses offer critical commentary on the mundane
experiences that constrain women. In one episode (first broadcast on 14 January
2003), Barry and Michelle swap with Carole and Paul. Michelle does every bit
of housework, works a 60-hour week and is clearly not loved by Barry. This
episode emerged as memorable for our audiences and we discuss their reactions
to it in Chapter 7. Michelle who does everything for her husband enters the
swapped home where the gender relations are more equal, which makes her
uncomfortable. When she speaks to the camera she gets very emotional:

> I feel really guilty now today because I've got these thoughts going round
> my head that I don't want to live my life next week now. That's why I feel
> guilty because it is my life and I should – what's wrong with my life?

But ultimately Michelle's reflexivity cannot show that she has enough control
over the situation to change it – it simply *is* her life. Whatever might really
happen at home the structure to the format is in the confrontation of the two
wives – not within the existing relationships. Michelle's only route to gain control
and claim access to moral authority is to blame the other wife: 'You've actually
failed at being a housewife and for a woman to fail at being a housewife is
absolutely ridiculous.' Despite the programme focusing on the revelation that
Barry has never made Michelle a cup of tea, the antagonism set up towards the
other wife, leads Michelle to conclude to camera: 'It's actually made me think
that the way me and Barry are is actually alright and the grass isn't greener on
the other side.' In this kind of format the performance of personhood can only
develop in relation to the structure of the programme, only able to react rather
than to act; reflexivity is contained through both time and space.

Similarly in *Supernanny*, mothers are asked to explain their child's or their own
bad behaviour after a dramatic situation that is 'out of control' and for which
they are often at a loss. This replays Berlant's (2000b) observations about how
contemporary culture constantly forces us to give intimacy a narrative in order
to control and stabilize the emotions which it threatens to disrupt. But as Lea
Jacobs (1993) notes, at the heart of melodrama is the element of 'situation',
defined as a striking and exciting incident that momentarily arrests the narrative
action whilst the character encounters powerful new circumstances, which generates heightened tension. Reality television both generates *and* disrupts the
narrative attachment that can contain and explain the emotions. And whilst this

potential detachment from traditional narratives may offer momentary radical potential, it also reveals the politics of the containment of intimacy. Geoffrey Nowell-Smith (1977) suggests that melodrama contains a 'conversion hysteria' which ferments the psychic energies and emotions that the narrative seeks to repress. Because emotions usually cannot be contained within the narrative they find an outlet through other forms of expression, especially in the mis-en-scène and the music.

On reality television time and space containment is emphasized by music and ironic commentary but it also remains connected to the participant's performance. The dramatic moment is impossible to define in terms of an articulate telling of the self – it is revealed as an affective reaction to the immediate situation in which participants find themselves. Stanley Cavell (1996) maintains that doubt is the motor of melodrama which leads to unrealistic demands for access to other people's thoughts, emotions and explanations. Out of desperation for not being understood, or not being able to understand the demands of accountability, the participant when forced to constantly explain and justify acts that they do not understand, can only remain totally silent. This appears as sullenness and is often located by experts as stupidity by the refrain of 'Don't you understand?', 'Why did you do that?', 'Why did you let him do that?'. *Supernanny* is replete with instances of the camera held on the face of a non-responsive mother as she struggles to understand the structure of the action of which she is a part. This production and structuring of intensity condenses social relations and places them in conditions of dramatic spectacle in which the melodrama operates, as Brooks suggests, drawing out moral positions on good and bad conduct and ultimately contributing to a moral economy of personhood.

Communication and 'how' knowledge

The conceits of the programmes and the compression of time and space therefore generate constraints around performances of personhood. As we have argued in Chapter 2 telling itself has been historically prescribed as an important cultural resource for the display of one's value. This is carried into the lessons of governance that we see expounded across reality television. 'Good communication' appears again and again as a trope to be learned and deployed across all relationships. The rules and advice from *Supernanny* are often about how to communicate with children, to explain, to elaborate, to educate, to remain calm, and certainly not to shout. When mother Claire in *Supernanny* (first broadcast 29 June 2005) loses her temper with her son who throws a tantrum over wearing his shoes, she is told by Supernanny Jo:

> I feel like I'm watching two eight year-olds in a playground and I'm begging for you to take control of the situation and be the parent. Instead of coming together clashing heads, what you can do is step back and choose your battles, so present it in another way. He's strong willed and doesn't want to

wear his shoes, so give him an option; make it seem like an option, rather than 'no' you've got to wear them.

Jo attempts to incite an elaborated speech code of the kind discussed by sociologist Basil Bernstein (1971) to explain how the education system advantages the middle class. Bernstein demonstrates how the middle class use a linguistic elaborate code which relies on explanation, reasoning and complex articulation, whereas the working class use a more direct, command-based language structure. Many years have been spent debating, challenging and confirming Bernstein's analysis for its problematic association with pathologizing the working class. It has more recently resurfaced in debates about reality television by David Morley (2010) and Andrew Tolson (2011) in an attempt to account for some of the registers of communication like 'incivility' that are now made spectacular on television. Eva Illouz (1997) considers the elaborated speech code to be a form of linguistic capital – it enables one to feel at ease with the practice of solving problems through language. Using Bourdieu, she argues that the ability to distance oneself from one's immediate emotional experience is the prerogative of those who have a readily available range of emotional options, who are not overwhelmed by emotional necessity and intensity, and who can therefore approach their own self and emotions with the same detached mode that comes from accumulated emotional competence. Deborah Cameron (2000) has extensively detailed how communication has become a central imperative to many areas of social life, including the workplace, in which the self is expected to develop itself through linguistic competence. Likewise, Andrew Wernick (1991) discusses how linguistic aptitude is a key means to enterprising the self, or enhancing emotional capital (Reay 1998, 2004).

Emotional inarticulacy is represented as a problem on reality television produced through bad parenting and even the wrong taste culture. For instance in *Honey We're Killing the Kids* the Bucks family are forced to open up their dining room, which had previously been saved for 'best' in the interests of the family sitting together to eat and talk. We see the mother's despair as one of the new rules is that her 'fancy' dining room should now be subject to regular use by the family. The dining room table is a matter of pride and symbol of her (working class) respectability: 'Its absolutely gorgeous and when we actually bought it I thought there's no way we can afford anything like this in the house'. Both parents are reluctant, but are presented with a moral dilemma by the psychologist: 'If it's a choice between giving kids the social skills, of having the family time and living together, and protecting the table? … ' They are told that good social skills improve career opportunities and eventually concede, with Jimmy Buck relenting: 'I want my children to be more successful than I've been.' Even more spectacularly, in *Family Forensics* domestic appliances that are seen to be blockages to communication – the plasma television set and the PlayStation – are typically cordoned off with crime scene tape in order to force family members into more direct forms of communication because they are presented as lacking the skills to articulate their differences when they shout and argue. The moral primacy of emotional literacy in order to calm and order lives that were previously seen to be out of control, and to enable a more productive future self, serves to psychologize forms of linguistic classed cultural capital. Kathy Pitt (2002) documents the amount of UK government attention now given to the 'pedagogic discourse of family literacy'. She examines the government-funded Basic Skills Agency's agreement with the BBC to develop programmes on family literacy directed at the socially excluded. In these programmes speaking is an item to be assessed, with its own 'Communication Skills Certificate' (see also Chapter 1). Ouellette and Hay (2008) go a stage further and describe programmes like *Honey We're Killing The Kids* as examples of 'the neo-liberalization of social work through television' (p.89).

It is not just parents who are encouraged to address their communication skills, most relationships are exposed as in need of advice in this area. *What Not to Wear* constantly references the communication of 'women's needs': they propose that wearing the right clothes would generate the right confidence to communicate needs to partners and sometimes bosses, hence solving relationship and workplace problems. This formula was developed extensively in their later programme, *Trinny and Susannah Undress,* made for ITV, where fashion experts take on the role of therapists in the tradition of 'tele-advising' identified by Mimi White (1992). Francis Bonner (2008) discusses how this move by Trinny and Susannah signalled a shift to greater intimacy and emphasis upon interpersonal and even sexual relations, where a broader range of affective reactions of both participants and presenters are brought into play. Benjamin and Sullivan (1996) comment on the stress placed on relationship management across popular culture, such as magazines, self-help books, novels, television and film. They note the promotion of an 'open marital conversation' as *the* sign of a good relationship in which women are aware of their needs, verbalize them, ask for change, and are able to negotiate with their partners the terms of that change, whereby power is secured through bargaining and negotiation. There is a repetition of the trope of the 'therapeutic habitus' in all this popular material whereby the self is viewed as containing 'inner' thoughts and feelings, as having a uniqueness waiting to be revealed and expressed and shared with others through verbal performance. Illouz notes:

> Perhaps the single most striking cultural feature of the ethos of communication is its basic moral proposition that one's own and others' interests can be simultaneously served by using adequate speech patterns ... If there is one single message that the therapeutic communicative world-view incessantly conveys, it is the fact that bonds are formed, maintained or destroyed through partners' ability to express verbally their needs, emotions and goals and through the ability to negotiate these needs with another through *language*.
>
> (1997:50 emphasis in original)

Communication is extensively promoted across reality television as the key to psychological problem solving: but communication is also a class issue, a form of linguistic capital, which exists alongside emotional capital. It can be used, as in the Bucks' family example, as a form of symbolic violence. The guilt produced in the present in order to open the possibility of a better future means that the family is forced to let go of their own cultural resources – of the respectability associated with a 'fancy' dining room. Some reality programmes directly promote this detachment as part of their format 'engine'.

Ladette to Lady, *Faking It* and *What the Butler Saw* use class mobility as the programme structure, engendering competition and teaching participants to learn new rules, new skills, manners and dispositions. When we are introduced to the ladettes in *Ladette to Lady* they are symbolically inscribed as working class. They are loud, uncompromising women that are excessive in many ways: drinking, sexually aggressive, shouting, swearing and smoking. They are fashioned into 'ladies' through aristocratic etiquette teachers at a finishing school who are constantly shocked by the ladettes' behaviour. *What the Butler Saw* takes a working class family to live in an aristocratic manor to compete against each other by performing as a Lord or Lady for a £50,000 prize. *Faking It* takes participants out of their own environment and 'tests' them in another milieu – factory worker to fashion designer, fast food worker to chef – and so on. (Only occasionally is the classed transformation directed the other way when a classically trained musician is groomed to become a DJ – a position with some considerable degree of cultural value). Of course much humour is derived from the mistakes participants make due to their lack of understanding of the new environment – repeating the narrative trope evident in films like *Pretty Woman* where the pleasure for the audience is in 'catching out' those who attempt to become socially mobile (Tasker 1998).

What is also visible in these programmes is that just learning skills is not enough. In Bourdieu's (1977) explication of tacit knowledge he demonstrates how people do not just need to know 'that' but also need to know 'how', 'which exists in a practical state in an agent's practice and not in their consciousness' (p.27). The how knowledge relies on an episteme that underpins the practice: it is not just learning about which knife and fork to use. So skills are not enough since one also needs to be able to embody the right dispositions to perform the skills in order to act appropriately. In the social mobility programmes a great deal of the drama is in the detailed visualization of the lack of correct performance. In *What the Butler Saw* judges, disguised as the servants, sneer at the lack of manners, language use, appearance and the futile attempts made at performing correct deportment: they laugh uncontrollably at one participant who reveals her knee-high socks (we learn that apparently aristocrats would never reveal undergarments or wear knee highs): 'you can't make a silk purse out of a sow's ear' they conclude, revealing how much hidden episteme lies behind upper-class performances.

When Mick the factory worker in *Faking It* attempts to pass as a fashion designer it is not his skills that let him down – his design and sewing convince some of the judges. When he comes to the finale of the show – the 'interview' with the actual fashion experts – he must show his ability to both 'be' and 'do' a fashion designer. Yet no matter how much time is spent learning his lines, he is still unable to be comfortably confident, and perform and inhabit the correct manners and dispositions. In the following sequence Mick is questioned by the fashion judges and his responses are inter-cut with the close ups of disappointed reactions and winced sighs of his mentors, who are observing him on video from another room:

JUDGE: Which other designers do you admire most?
MICK: Erm [sigh exhale of breath].
MENTORS: Oh no [hand on head].
MICK: I suppose the designers that I admire most I like Marc Jacobs and I like D&G as well.
MENTORS: Oh my God [hands over mouth].
JUDGE: What would you like to achieve with your fashion career?
MICK: Well obviously I'd like to have my name in lights but erm, erm …
MENTORS: He's stumbling, oh God …
MENTORS TO CAMERA: That didn't go off as well as it should have done at all you know [shaking head].

Mick can *do* the skills required by a fashion designer but it is much harder to *perform* being a fashion designer, to exude the bodily dispositions and corporeal affects such as confidence and entitlement, or to articulate a narrative of future investment when questioned about class passing. Whilst many reality programmes show the rules of self-narration and self-control, what they also show is just how difficult it is to operationalize those rules without the history of experience, the right capitals and more importantly without the 'how' knowledge. Failure always appears as if it is a psychological disposition of the participants, their personal inadequacy. The dramatic intensity of the programme is enshrined in the 'will they or won't they' be able to modify their behaviour. The command to perform reveals their lack of capitals, but the concentration on *self*-performance turns our attention away from social circumstances to the solitary self, illuminating the way in which class is currently psychologized in contemporary culture.

Metonymic morality

The presentation of self across reality television is therefore determined by the intensity of the melodrama and the calls to tell, communicate and perform oneself as access to future potential. These set in motion powerful demarcations of the value of people and the display of their cultural resources. As we have described in Chapter 1 melodrama offers a major force of moral reasoning about the state of persons and the state of the nation (Gledhill 1987b; Williams 2001). It is the continued enactment of the struggle between forces of good and evil at the level of the moral that cues us into the relations between the textual and the social. As the moral resides on the body they are displayed through parts and practices that are attributed with good and bad value in a metonymic process: where the parts come to stand in for the whole. For Williams (2001) melodrama operates as *the mode* for American culture rather than as a genre, where representations from Uncle Tom to O. J. Simpson are representative of how the US 'talked to itself' in a moral code about race. In this talking process moral values of the good and bad people of the nation are established. This is taken one step further on reality television: every aspect of behaviour is subject to scrutiny and evaluation, in order that the (good/bad) part comes to stand in for the whole person (metonymy). We detail the way in which reality television can be seen to offer a moral conversation on contemporary class relations.

As we have seen, in melodrama the narrative is not so much about the role of the protagonist to challenge the world, but rather about a struggle for clear moral identifications of all protagonists that is finally resolved by public recognition of where good and bad values (guilt and innocence) really lie (Gledhill 1987a). Domestic melodrama draws upon traditions whereby women have been made the bearers of the moral good of the nation through a focus on the home and biological reproduction. Recall the discussion in Chapter 1 about the relation between lifestyle and reality television and early etiquette manuals which espouse bourgeois standards through 'rules' of behaviour as women's responsibility (Davidoff and Hall 1987). But the 'rules' of morality on offer in any particular epoch must be contextual and this is worked out on reality television in relation to contemporary conditions of possibility for the performance of personhood by which specific practices are loaded semiotically as 'visual emblems' of morality (Gledhill 1987a). We now turn to these emblems, examining the 'grammar of conduct' (Foucault 1977) available through reality television.

One of the most obvious ways in which behaviour is interrogated on many transformational styles of reality television is through questions of taste. In programmes like *What Not to Wear, 10 Years Younger, You Are What You Eat*, participants are taught by lifestyle experts in matters of 'correct consumption' in order to attain a better life. Others have already commented on how these aesthetic forms of lifestyle intervention reinvent taste, style and design and sometimes etiquette, in relation to traditions of bourgeois culture (Biressi and Nunn 2005; Lewis 2004; McRobbie 2004; Palmer 2004; Taylor 2005). We do not want to repeat that discussion here but in *What Not to Wear* the transformation of the self is complete only if the subjects conform to the right kind of bourgeois femininity. The focus is on parts of the body, clothes and elements of bad taste to indicate the moral failings of the person who has not invested correctly in the project of the self. For instance in one episode (first broadcast 11 September 2004) experts Trinny and Susannah make over 'harassed mothers'. The presenters talk of 'summoning the main offenders for closer inspection', where Trinny declares, 'Why do they all look so dirty?' When commentating on one woman's video, Michalena, the presenters even 'scream' with horror and then declare: 'She scares me as a woman!' The camera focuses on her bright brash clothing, droopy breasts, garish jewellery and heavy make-up as she is placed in the 360-degree mirror to highlight and intensify the bodily elements of failure. The experts peer into the mirror as their reactions to each faux pas are recorded and dramatized. When wearing her favourite outfit reflected in the mirror Michalena says: 'Overall I think that's quite classy.' But the presenters snigger and ask: 'What's classy about it?' Trinny, peering from behind her hands, eventually screams: 'It's hideous – you scare me as a woman in that outfit!' We see Michalena's discomfort as she says 'That's a bit harsh' as Trinny and Susannah draw attention to her waist, her bottom and the various areas that she should or should not emphasize. Music and voice-over also offer critical comment, whilst the unflattering lighting emphasizes the breaking down of bodies and style into its errant parts. Shaming the participant for her previous lack of care of self, visualized on her body is central to the programme's requirement to identify the need for transformation.

The lifestyling project must first de-value working class culture and taste before it offers suggestions for improvement. A more complete life therefore is deemed to be accessible through relationships with material goods and style where middle class taste is universalized as good taste. This echoes contemporary cultural trends in which Mike Savage (2003) argues, the middle class have become *the* normative, the 'particular universal class' … ' in which an increasing range of practices are regarded as universally 'normal', 'good' and 'appropriate' (p.536), or in which the nation is made beige and all excess is cleared away. Like Weber's (2005) argument about make-over programmes espousing an 'economy of sameness', we argue these programmes are exercises in the paradoxical production of a 'normative uniqueness' in which the person will become unique – true only to themselves, *if* they follow the expert advice to be normative, but also universal – measuring up to certain historically established class standards in order to engage more fully in the world. As we have discussed earlier commentators on the make-over discuss the 'shame' invoked for the transformation to take place (Doyle and Karl 2007; McRobbie 2004; Walkerdine 2011). Others argue how this involves the embodiment of ideas about surveillance where participants also perform 'being looked at' (Weber 2009). And for us this involves the incorporation of the dialogic judgemental gaze that the working classes live with on a daily basis (Skeggs 1997). We have also discussed how the particular emphasis upon women involves them enjoining in espousing pseudo-feminist empowerment strategies in keeping with post-feminist culture (McRobbie 2009). But we maintain that elements of gender shaming and surveillance have longer classed histories in which we are located in uneven ways.

We also want to focus here on how the dramatic focus on bodily parts and the production of shame transcends elements of style and interrogates life practices based upon investments in prior, present and imagined future temporalities. In *10 Years Younger* smoking, sun-worshipping and unhealthy eating are blamed for a lack of investment in a body which now displays wrinkled skin, cellulite and bad teeth – features that are held in close-up. Parts then become specific spectacles of shame operating metonymically in which the intense focus, coupled with appropriate music, and often voice-over, invite a moral response. In *Honey We're Killing the Kids* working class parents stand in a white room in front of a large screen where images of their children appear as they are now and are then aged by computer graphics to the age of 40. The visual images of children metamorphose into those of their parents whilst the music dramatizes horror as we see the parents physically shocked and distressed when they are told by a psychologist: 'The lifestyle you are giving them is killing them.' They are presented with themselves as the problem in the present and in the melodramatic excess of the moment can only react, break down and often cry. This reification of the parents' social location and their cultural capital is condensed onto the image of the child – of the receding hair line, the wrinkled skin, the puffed face, which stand in for the poor diet, lack of exercise, and lack of investment by parents in their children. As Julie a participant in *Honey We're Killing Kids* (first broadcast on 29 March 2005) says to camera: 'The image of the children like this doesn't actually go out of my head. It's with me all the time. I think that's why we're carrying on doing what we're doing. This gives me the determination.' Participants are revealed to be morally inadequate in the past and present and must therefore make a promise to improve for future redemption. The future is here imagined not as an expanded social space but a space for present damage to be rectified, again revealing very different time/space vectors in the making of class. But also, we argue, demonstrates the programme's ideological dimensions: gaining consent from participants in the present in order to regulate themselves and their family in the future.

Similarly, in *You Are What You Eat* the close-up is extended from face to faeces as a symbolic representation of a badly managed life. Quantities of food are splayed across dining room tables, or even in one episode across a car, in order to visualize how food is emblematic of the failure of excess, the dramatic and spectacular failure of the person who cannot exercise self-discipline, who does not care about their future or the costs of ill health to the nation. Bodily fat is subject to the cameras' intense attention, metonymically used to signify not just immorality but also the cost that other members of society must pay for their lack of care of their selves. The surface 'emblems' of life used to rhetorically dramatize moral codes and bad conduct are not just visualized but also affective, electrified through evocation in a circuit of reaction as the participants' reactions of shame are met by the experts' reaction – shock – in order to set in motion a process of transformation, self-determinism and redemption, but also to promote reaction in audiences.

Weber (2009) points out that such elements in controlling the 'real' physical body are metaphorically transposed as ways to better regulate the social body: clutter, disorganization and dirt come to stand in for participants' place in the social body. For us this intervention in the social body carries with it the legacies of class and gender from earlier regimes. In the condensation of problems, the lack of a more complete architecture of the person is made apparent by presenting the television participant as a series of parts and practices that require modification and work. Achieving proper person value is made available through following rules and advice through which one can recapture legitimacy through normativity. Those that have not already invested time developing one's person value – the working class – must now be given lessons in self-government, just as Poovey (1995) detailed in relation to the rise of the liberal self of the nineteenth century. A great deal of reality television relies on a mixture of behaviour modification – strict rules and discipline and psycho-lite, a banal version of psychoanalysis premised upon revealing an inner self in order to improve the outer self (*Wife Swap*, *Grown up Gappers*), or in the case of *What Not to Wear*, improving an outer self in order to find an inner self. In *Honey We're Killing the Kids*, psychologist Kris Murrin produces her list of golden rules: healthy food, daily routine, one-on-one time, no smoking, 'you' time, give children responsibilities, family activities, children's learning, adult learning, challenge yourself and your kids, get kids motivated. *Supernanny* is replete with rules for shaping and containing behaviour. Jo the expert nanny uses 'the naughty step', 'the stay-in-bed technique', 'voice training technique', 'same page training technique' and the 'good eating technique'. These techniques produce better, more wholesome families, enabling you to 'get your life back' and 'to live a more fulfilling life'. Similarly in *What Not to Wear* there are style rules for each body shape whose take up is realized through a therapeutic register. Rules enable a psychological transformation in which participants espouse the ability to have 'found themselves' to have revealed the 'real me'. This often translates into a greater entitlement to social and physical space: 'now she has confidence to enter the world', 'to hold her head up high at work', etc. Only when the subject accepts the advice can she become more mobile and be ready to accrue person value.

The emphasis on constant self-work, rules and revelation are continuations of the attempts since the nineteenth century (Donzelot 1979) to modify the behaviour of the working classes and women, particularly mothers. The therapeutic state (Reiff 1966) with its emphasis on suffering (Boltanski 1999) and trauma are brought into legitimacy through the extension of intimacy (Berlant 2000a). The emphasis on moral pedagogy, on advice, self-help and psychology enables attention to be deflected away from the socio-economic conditions that shape people's lives onto their own self-production. As Francis Bonner (2008) points out the 'person not in need of a make-over is a person who has paid attention to the passage of time' (p.116). In many of these shows it is a concentration on the moment of the present that occludes history and the passage of time from entering into the narrative. Thus we are not made aware of how participants come to be how or who they are since they are not required to tell but rather *to react*. This is also how programmes are able to flatten out inequalities as everybody is subject to the evaluation of self-performance that is reified. They rely on what Celia Lury (1998) in her analysis of the prosthetic self calls 'out-contextualization' – we use this to explain the process by which the participant is increasingly asked to lay claim to features of the context or environment *as if* they were the outcome of the testing of his or her personal capacities.

The process of metonymic morality is intensified further by the emphasis that is placed upon the face in the performance of the self. Whereas body parts and practices come to stand in for an immoral history, the face becomes the site where the truth of personhood is told. In relation to film, Mary Ann Doane (2003) has pointed to the significance of the close-up as an enhancement which is added to the object in the process of its subjection to visualization, but which is also often considered to be bound up with an ethics (the enhancement of moral character by filmic reproduction). The close-up is often a privileged site for this moral enhancement in which the face becomes a geographical map that reveals the propriety of the expression, or for Walter Benjamin (1959) the close-up of the face was one of the significant entry points to the optical unconscious, making visible what in daily life went unseen. For a participants' performance to be recognized as morally good they must emote properly: reactions through gestures and speech acts must be matched to the appropriate emotion for the scene. For Deleuze (1986) the close-up embodies the pure fact of presentation, of manifestation, of showing. Thus the face brings together a relation of semiotic authenticity – what can be read against what is supposed. On reality television attempts are made to attach ideas and narratives to the gestures of the face. In the scene above with Michalena in the mirror we move between the horror on the faces of the presenters to the dismay on the face of Michalena, which was also a key moment with our audiences as it heightens the interplay between adjudicator and judged. This is an affective exchange which is powerful and which opens up a space for alternatives. Doane (2003) maintains that the close-up offers us a moment to relate to a character and to bring narrative judgement to bear upon the reading of type. So it is not surprising that the close-up engaged our audiences and nearly always led to the expression of, or defence against, moral judgement.

As Kavka (2008) argues, television, like film, is a technology of intimacy. Reality television offers us the opportunity to dwell on people's reaction, to see crisis evoked, to anticipate responses, to ask ourselves what we would do, how we would behave. For instance, as Hill (2005) has previously noted, audiences take pleasure in the identification of authenticity. It is in the mis-match between words and deeds, the gap between speech and emotion, read off or experienced through the gesture of the performance, that moral judgement is incited.

Christian Metz (1974) maintains that the close-up offers an index of actualization, of presence, of being-there, 'It carries with it a kind of here' (p.67) that enables our audience respondents to evoke prior temporal and spatial events which they have experienced, to locate themselves within the experience of the participant, an argument we develop through the idea of constitutive actualization (Sobchack 1999) in Chapter 4. Paradoxically the liveness of the performance invites viewers to evoke and connect their experiences to the participant on television in what Kavka (2008) identifies as a 'zone of immediacy' (p.17) in which participants are out-contextualized and their circumstances reified. We propose it is this immanent present that relies on melodramatic and metonymic techniques which invites moral judgement through connection to the issue, crisis or situation that has to be performed.

Conclusion

In this chapter we have shown how the pursuit of profit has driven the opening out of intimacy as producers look for new ways to attract viewers and hence advertisers. That opening out has involved a focusing in on different aspects of personal life that require investigation as formats evolve via various conceits which provide the 'engines', cementing the ways in which personhood can be broken down into its elements. Through the different organization of time and space a distinction is drawn between those that are allowed a more 'complete' narrative of the self and those that are subject to format intervention. In that space melodrama allows for moments of subversion, but in the drama of the moment some can only respond at the level of reaction, rather than direct the action, unable to display control and self-determinism, even unable to understand and speak. And as we demonstrated in Chapter 2 self-determination is the explicit moral code of contemporary culture where other forms of authority have receded. Thus those that are considered to be failing are reduced to their inadequate parts having not invested properly in the bourgeois project of the self. Ultimately this process eclipses the economic and social structures of inequality and relocates them as psychological dispositions where morality becomes a matter of the grammar of performance. As theorists of melodrama have long noted, melodrama is a historically specific mode of expression that can tell us about the state of social relationships, often becoming central at moments of social upheaval and crisis (Karlsson 2002).

Thus we argue that the compressed time and space of melodrama, deployed to generate reaction in the immediacy of reality television, works politically to bolster social inequality at the level of both representation and intervention. But that immediacy also positions viewers to locate themselves and their experiences within the drama/narrative, offering the position of judgement over the behaviours which reality television lays bare, in which they too are located. If Williams (2001) argues that melodrama is the format that race relations take in the US, and Gledhill (1987a) maintains that melodrama enables us to understand gender and the structure of heterosexuality, we propose that melodrama has a new social variant. Class is repeatedly 'made' through demands for the televised performance of personhood, by displaying relationships in all their relational and corporeal elements, but by divorcing them from the circumstances of their production.

Kavka (2008) argues that the simulated settings of reality television stimulate feeling, in part *because of* the removal of participants from their history, stripping them down to the space of performance and the affects of social encounters. The participants, given the structure of the shows, cannot but perform intimacy, which creates feeling: 'the performance of reality generates reality effects, just as the performance of intimacy generates intimacy effects' (p.25). We agree, but affect is always understood through the ideas to which it is attached, hence the performance of intimacy becomes a site for moral judgement, for intimacy operates with narratives of 'proper' relationships. If reality television is another form of media that provides an aesthetic characterized by the priority of feeling over fact, we can see how it operates as a pedagogic intervention that (in some forms) attempts to incite people to enact ethical discourse. The participants' self-performances involve the display of ethical acts, which Lilie Chouliaraki (2008) argues, is how television mediates ethics: morality becomes performative and moral acts have to be continually repeated to display the sustained value in the person. Yet as we proceed to show through our audience research, there is not always agreement over what constitutes ethical acts. Motherhood in particular is a site of substantial contestation.

This makes us ask, how does reality television intervene in social relations if it calls us into new forms of moral surveillance, and on what level does it invite us to engage in evaluations of ourselves and others? In the next chapter we turn to our audience methodology and how we developed a range of methods in order to further unpick how this theatre for the performance of personhood enters into the social relations of viewers.

Notes

1 Before the official start of our funded project which began in April 2005 and ended February 2008.
2 Jade Goody was accused of being racist on *Big Brother*, provoking a national scandal (Tolson 2011).
3 Our list of 42 programmes made for public service terrestrial television are made by 17 production companies (not including in-house production) and dominated by RDF and Talk Back Thames productions. RDF floated in May 2005 and reported profits of £5.3 million with a turnover of £59.5 million helped by the number of BBC commissions (*Broadcast* 23 May, 2006). Talkback Thames is the UK production arm of Freemantle Media, which reported revenue of €947 million in 2005 according to the RTL Group annual report (http://www.rtlgroup.com/www/assets/file_asset/AR2005_RTLGroup_FREEMANTLEMEDIA.pdf accessed 28 July, 2009).
4 Skeggs' ethnography noted how young white women considered recognition as working class to be a misrecognition of their value, because it always came with an assumption and attachment of pathology (Skeggs 1997).
5 In our mapping exercise we picked up repeated viewing programmes, as we were interested in audience responses we made these available for our viewing sessions if they were broadcast during our research period.

References

Ahmed, S. 1998 'Tanning the Body: Skin Colour and Gender', *New Formations* 34: 27–43.
Auslander, P. 1999 *Liveness: Performance in a Mediatized Culture*, London: Routledge.

Benjamin, O. and Sullivan, O. 1996 'The Importance of Difference: Conceptualising Increased Flexibility in Gender Relations at Home', *Sociological Review* 44(2): 225–51.

Benjamin, W. 1959 *Theses on the Philosophy of History, Illuminations*, New York: Schocken.

Bennett, T. 2003 'The Invention of the Modern Cultural Fact: Toward a Critique of the Critique of Everyday Life', in E. B. Silva and T. Bennett (eds) *Contemporary Culture and Everyday Life*, Durham: Sociology Press.

Berlant, L. (ed.) 2000a *Intimacy*, Chicago and London: University of Chicago Press.

——2000b 'The Subject of True Feeling: Pain, Privacy, Politics', in S. Ahmed, J. Kilby, C. Lury, M. McNeil and B. Skeggs (eds) *Transformations: Thinking Through Feminism*, London: Routledge.

Bernstein, B. 1971 *Class, Codes and Control*, London: Routledge and Kegan Paul.

Biressi, A. and Nunn, H. 2005 *Reality TV: Realism and Revelation*, London: Wallflower Press.

Blackman, L. 2007 'Reinventing Psychological Matters: The Importance of the Suggestive Realm of Tarde's Ontology', *Economy and Society* 36(4): 574–96.

Boltanski, L. 1999 *Distant Suffering: Morality, Media and Politics*, Cambridge: Cambridge University Press.

Bonner, F. 2008 'Fixing Relationships in 2-4-1 Transformations', *Continuum: Journal of Media and Cultural Studies* 22(4): 547–57.

Bourdieu, P. 1977 *Outline of a Theory of Practice*, Cambridge: Cambridge University Press.

Brooks, P. 1976/1995 *The Melodramatic Imagination: Balzac, Henry James, Melodrama and the Mode of Excess*, New Haven and London: Yale University Press.

Cameron, D. 2000 *Good to Talk? Living and Working in a Communication Culture*, London: Sage.

Cavell, S. 1996 *Contesting Tears: The Hollywood Melodrama of the Unknown Woman*, Chicago and London: Chicago University Press.

Chouliaraki, L. 2008 'The Media as Moral Education: Mediation and Action', *Media, Culture and Society* 30(6): 831–52.

Couldry, N. 2003 *Media Rituals: A Critical Approach*, London: Routledge.

Davidoff, L. and Hall, C. 1987 *Family Fortunes*, London: Hutchinson.

Deleuze, G. 1986 *Cinema 1: The Movement Image*, Minneapolis: University of Minnesota Press.

Doane, M. A. 2003 'The Close Up: Scale and Detail in the Cinema', *Differences: A Journal of Feminist Cultural Studies* 14(3): 89–111.

Donzelot, J. 1979 *The Policing of Families: Welfare versus the State*, London: Hutchinson.

Dovey, J. 2000 *Freakshow: First Person Media and Factual Television*, London: Pluto.

Doyle, J. and Karl, I. 2007 '"Shame on You": Discourses of Health, Class and Gender in the Promotion of Cosmetic Surgery on Television' *The Big Reveal Conference*, Salford, UK.

Elsaesser, T. 1972 'Tales of Sound and Fury: Observations on the Family Melodrama', in C. Gledhill (ed.) *Home is Where the Heart Is*, London: Routeldge.

Feuer, J. 1983 'The Concept of Live Television: Ontology as Ideology', in E. A. Kaplan (ed.) *Regarding Television: Critical Approaches – An Anthology*, Los Angeles: American Film Institute.

Foucault, M. 1977 *Discipline and Punish: The Birth of the Prison*, London: Allen Lane/Penguin.

Fraser, M. 1999 'Classing Queer: Politics in Competition', *Theory, Culture and Scociety* 16(2): 107–31.

Gledhill, C. 1987a *Home is Where the Heart Is: Studies in Melodrama and Women's Film*, London: Routledge.

——1987b 'The Melogramatic Field: An Investigation', in C. Gledhill (ed.) *Home is Where the Heart is: Studies in Melodrama and the Women's Film*, London: BFI Books.

Hill, A. 2005 *Reality TV: Audiences and Popular Factual Television*, London: Routledge.

——2007 *Restyling Factual TV: Audiences and News, Documentary and Reality Genres*, London: Routledge.

Holmes, S. 2008 '"A Term Rather too General to be Helpful": Struggling with Genre in Reality TV', in L. Geraghty and M. Jancovich (eds) *The Shifting Definitions of Genre: Generic Cannons*, Jefferson, NC: McFarland.

Holmes, S. and Jermyn, D. (eds) 2004 *Understanding Reality Television*, London: Routledge.

——2007 '"Ask the Fastidious Woman from Serbiton to Handwash the Underpants of Aging Oldham Skinhead ... " Why not *Wife Swap*?', in T. Austin and W. de Jog (eds) *Rethinking Documentary: A Documentary Reader*, Buckingham: Open University Press.

Illouz, E. 1997 'Who will Care for the Caretaker's Daughter? Towards a Sociology of Happiness in the Era of Reflexive Modernity', *Theory, Culture and Society* 14(4): 31–66.

Jacobs, L. 1993 'The Women's Picture and the Poetics of Melodrama', *Camera Obscura* 31: 121–47.

Johnson, R. 1997 'Reinventing Cultural Studies: Remembering for the best version', in E. Long (ed.) *From Sociology to Cultural Studies: New Perspectives*, Oxford: Blackwell Press.

Karlsson, M. 2002 *Kanslans Rost: Det Melodramatiska i Selma Lagerlofs Romankonst*, Stockholm: Brutus Ostlings Bokforlag Symposium.

Kavka, M. 2008 *Reality Television, Affect and Intimacy: Reality Matters*, London: Palgrave Macmillan.

Keane, M. and Moran, A. 2008 'Television's New Engines', *Television and New Media* 8(2): 155–69.

Lewis, J. 2004 'The Meaning of Real Life', in L. Ouellette and S. Murray (eds) *Reality TV: Remaking Television Culture*, New York and London: New York Univesity Press.

Lohr, L. 1940 'Television Broadcasting', New York: McGraw Hill.

Lunt, P. and Lewis, T. 2008 'Oprah.com: Lifestyle Expertise and the Politics of Recognition', *Women and Performance: A Journal of Feminist Theory* 18(1): 9–24.

Lury, C. 1998 *Prosthetic Culture: Photography, Memory and Identity*, London: Routledge.

Magder, T. 2004 'The End of TV 101: Reality Programmes, Formats, and the New Business of Television', in S. Murray and L. Ouellette (eds) *Reality TV: Remaking Television Culture*, New York and London: New York Univesity Press.

Marcuse, H. 1964 *One Dimensional Man: The Ideology of Industrial Society*, London: Sphere Books.

McNay, L. 2008 *Against Recognition*, Cambridge: Polity.

McRobbie, A. 2004 'Notes on "What not to Wear" and Post-Feminist Symbolic Violence', in L. Adkins and B. Skeggs (eds) *Feminism after Bourdieu*, Oxford: Blackwell.

——2009 *In the Aftermath of Feminism: Gender, Culture and Social Change*, London: Sage.

Metz, C. 1974 *Film Language: A Semiotics of the Cinema*, Oxford: Oxford University Press.

Mittell, J. 2004 *Genre and Television: From Cop Shows to Cartoons*, London: BFI.

Moran, L. 2000 'Homophobic Violence: The Hidden Injuries of Class', in S. Munt (ed.) *Cultural Studies and the Working Class: Subject to Change*, London: Cassell.

Morley, D. 2010 'Mediated Class-ifications: Representations of Class and Culture in Contemporary British Television', *European Journal of Cultural Studies* 12(4): 487–508.

Moseley, R. 2000 'Makeover Takeover on British Television', *Screen* 41(3): 299–314.

Nichols, B. 1991 *Representing Reality: Issues and Concepts of Documentary*, Bloomington and Indianapolis: Indiana University Press.

Nowell-Smith, G. 1977 'Minnelli and Melodrama', *Screen* 18(2): 113–18.

Ouellette, L. and Hay, J. 2008 'Makeover Television, Governmentality and the Good Citizen', *Continuum: Journal of Media and Cultural Studies* 22(4): 471–85.

Palmer, G. 2004 '"The New You": Class and Transformation in Lifestyle Television', in S. Holmes and D. Jermyn (eds) *Understanding Reality Television*, London: Routledge.

Phelan, P. 1993 *Unmarked: The Politics of Performance*, London: Routledge.

Piper, H. 2004 'Reality TV, Wife Swap and the Drama of Banality', *Screen:* 45(4): 273–86.

Pitt, K. 2002 'Being a New Capitalist Mother', *Discourse and Society* 13: 251–67.

Poovey, M. 1995 *Making a Social Body: British Cultural Formation 1830–1864*, Chicago: Chicago University Press.

——1998 *A History of the Modern Fact*, Chicago: University of Chicago Press.

Pullen, C. 2004 'The Household, the Basement, and The Real World: Gay Identity in the Constructed Reality Environment', in S. Holmes and D. Jermyn (eds) *Understanding Reality Television*, London: Routledge.

Raphael, C. 2004 'The Politcal Economic Origins of Reali-TV', in L. Oullette and S. Murray (eds) *Reality TV: Remaking Television Culture*, New York: New York University Press.

Reay, D. 1998 *Class Work: Mother's Involvement in their Children's Primary Schooling*, London: UCL Press.

——2004 'Gendering Bourdieu's Concept of Capitals? Emotional Capital, Women and Social Class', in L. Adkins and B. Skeggs (eds) *Feminism After Bourdieu*, Oxford: Blackwell.

Redden, G. 2008 'Economy and Reflexivity in Makeover Television', *Continuum: Journal of Media and Cultural Studies* 22(4): 485–95.

Reiff, P. 1966 *The Triumph of the Therapeutic: Uses of Faith after Freud*, New York: Harper Row.

Savage, M. 2003 'A New Class Paradigm? Review Article', *British Journal of Sociology of Education* 24(4): 535–41.

Skeggs, B. 1997 *Formations of Class and Gender: Becoming Respectable*, London: Sage.

——2001 'The Toilet Paper: Femininity, Class and Mis-recognition', *Women's Studies International Forum*, 24(3–4): 295–307.

Smith-Shomade, B. E. 2008 '"You'd Better Recognise": Oprah the Iconic and Television Talk', in C. Brunsdon and L. Spigel (eds) *Feminist Television Criticism: A Reader*, Berkshire: OU/McGraw Hill.

Sobchack, V. 1999 'Towards a Phenomenology of Nonfictional Film Experience', in J. Gaines and M. Renow (eds) *Collecting Visible Evidence*, Minneapolis, Minnesota: Minnesota University Press.

Tasker, Y. 1998 *Working Girls: Gender and Sexuality in Popular Culture*, London: Routledge.

Taylor, L. 2005 '"It was Beautiful Before you Changed it all": Class, Taste and the Tranformative Aesthetics of the Garden Lifestyle Media', in D. Bell and J. Hollows (eds) *Ordinary Lifestyles: Popular Media, Consumption and Taste*, Maidenhead: Open University Press.

Tolson, A. 2011 '"I'm Common and My Talking is Quite Abrupt" (Jade Goody): Language and Class in Celebrity Big Brother', in H. Wood and B. Skeggs (eds) *Reality Television and Class*, London: BFI/Palgrave.

Urry, J. 2000 *Societies Beyond the Social: Mobilities for the Twenty First Century*, London: Routledge.

Walkerdine, V. 2011 'Shame on You! Intergenerational Trauma and Working-class Femininity on Reality Television', in H. Wood and B. Skeggs (eds) *Reality Television and Class*, London: BFI/Palgrave.

Weber, B. 2005 'Beauty, Desire, Anxiety: The Economy of Sameness in ABC's Extreme Makeover', *Genders* 41.

——2009 *Makeover TV: Selfhood, Citizenship and Celebrity*, Durham, NC: Duke University Press.

Wernick, A. 1991 *Promotional Culture: Advertising, Ideology and Symbolic Expression*, London and Newbury Park, CA: Sage.

White, M. 1992 *Tele-Advising: Therapeutic Discourse In American Television*, Chapel Hill and London: University of North Carolina Press.

Williams, L. 2001 *Playing the Race Card: Melodramas of Black and White from Uncle Tom to O. J. Simpson*, Princeton: Princeton University Press.

Chapter 4

Reacting to reality television
Methodology

In this chapter we set out the methodology of the project. We outline how the theoretical imperatives underpinning this research, explained in previous chapters, informs our understanding of the research process, experience and encounters, describing the key elements of the empirical design to demonstrate how our methods 'make' class and gender through the research process. Allied to this description is the way in which the television as an object emerges as a site through which classed positions are articulated. The research respondents' accounts of their varying modes of attention to television clue us into the affective dimensions of television viewing. By examining these reactions we unpack the methodological implications of the shift away from only thinking about representation to also understanding the immanence and intimacy of relationships with reality television. Our methods therefore allow us to explore the affective and cognitive reactions of viewers through interviews, 'text-in-action' viewing sessions and focus groups.

Previous scholars have posited, through observations on reality television texts, that the genre re-organizes the traditional boundaries between text and audience that we have become accustomed to in media research. Chapter 1 described reality television as more about intervention than representation: a mode of television in which viewers' own lives are dramatically at stake in the mediation of everyday interpersonal drama. The affective traditions of melodrama, combined with the observational modes of documentary as discussed in Chapter 3, generate a focus on the economy of personhood in which viewers are always implicated. The domestic and relationship emphasis of most of our sample of reality television shows also makes these programmes sites with particular gendered appeal, reinforced by Hill's (2007) survey which supports an overall assumption about the feminization of the genre.

In Chapter 2, we also made connections between reality television's expansion of intimacy and wider social and cultural theories of the rise of bio-politics. Reality television's forensic detailing of the performance of bodies, behaviours and practices enables new types of exploitation to extend into the realm of that previously designated 'private': in this way some persons can be shown to be value*able*, whilst others, value*less* depending upon their dispositions towards working on themselves, others and sometimes for employers. Therefore, the *performance* of personhood has become central to both capitalism and governance. Our analyses of various reality television texts in Chapter 3 showed how the immediacy of the text allows some television participants to demonstrate their investment in the self-work ethic through self-determinism and self-management, whilst others must only 'react' to the conditions with which they are faced. We argued that the reactive behaviours and bodies of television participants are subject to a process of 'metonymic morality', which forensically focuses on their body parts and practices to evidence their failure to perform as a 'proper' person. This process enables us to see how value is distributed, revealing an economy of personhood. We also demonstrated how in this metonymic evaluation social circumstances are reduced to faulty psychology, an individualized inability to behave appropriately, rather than a product of structural inequality.

Our methodology is therefore designed to examine these theoretical positions with female audiences of reality television. It is not a broad survey on the meanings that can be taken from 'reality television' per se: good substantive work in that vein is to be found elsewhere (Hill 2005, 2007). The parameters we drew around particular genres to focus on questions of intimacy and to enable some point of manageable 'capture' for our method also set some limitations on what we can say about particular sub-genres. The focus of this audience research project is to bring into view a detailed account of *how* television intervenes in social life through connections and disconnections, drawing a sharper focus on television's entry into intimate and social relationships through the textual mediations of proximity and distance. Therefore, we ask, in what ways are viewers involved in reality television drama? Does the genre encourage particular kinds of affective relations and if so, how do we capture that mediation of affect? How do the political distinctions in the performances of personhood, suggested in Chapters 2 and 3, circulate amongst viewers and does this bear any relationship to the politics of social position and inequality? The design of our methodology is therefore underpinned by a desire to examine *these* questions, but of course the reach, scale and mutation of the genre since we began our research in 2005, means that there are inevitably a plethora of other questions that we leave unanswered.

Research design and social relations

Our research took place between October 2005 and February 2008, funded by the UK Economic and Social Research Council.[1] It deployed four different methods: textual analysis (as outlined in Chapter 3), interviews, 'text-in-action' viewing sessions, and focus groups. These took place with 40 women, middle and working class, white, black and South Asian, settled and recent residents, aged between 18 and 72, from four areas in South London: New Addington, Brockley, Clapham and Forest Hill. A key informant from each area introduced us to their social networks in a broad effort to approach the racial and classed mix of the social milieu of South London.

- **New Addington**: 10 white British working class, ages 18–72, 5 mothers. 5 work in the same nursery, 1 is training to be a nursery nurse, 1 works part time at a play group, 1 is retired, and 2 are full-time mothers. Connected by friendship or working in a local nursery which formed 2 sub-groups. New Addington is a ward of Croydon, an outer London Borough noted for its physical isolation. At the time of the 2001 census it had a population of 10,351. Nearly half of the accommodation in the area was social council rented housing. It was mostly white British (88%) with the majority of the population born in the UK.
- **Brockley:** 10 working class, 6 black British, 3 white British, 1 Maltese, ages 26–68. 9 mothers. Mostly public sector and service workers: 1 social worker, 1 small business owner, 1 judges clerk, 1 university administrator, 1 ex-legal secretary training to be a child worker, 1 shop manager, 1 trainee teaching assistant, 2 retired, 1 full-time mother. Friendship group. Brockley is a ward of Lewisham, in inner London. At the time of the 2001 census it had a population of 13,697. 37% of housing was owner-occupied and 26% social council rented. Brockley had a lower percentage of British residents (48.8%) than the London average (59.8%), nearly 30% identify as black or black British.
- **Clapham**: Southern and British Asian, Asian, Pakistani, Bengali, Bangladeshi, settled and recently arrived, complicated trans-national class differences, ages 18–45. 7 mothers. 2 full-time students, 1 part-time student and mother, 1 special needs worker, 1 receptionist/restaurant worker/part-time student, 1 teaching assistant, 4 full-time mothers. Friendship group. Clapham is a ward of Lambeth, in inner London. At the time of the 2001 census it had a population of 13,332. Most accommodation was apartment blocks, approximately 35% owner occupied, 63% rented with 30% rented from the council. Clapham is known to be a diverse area in terms of affluence. 38% of the population are from 'ethnic minorities'.
- **Forest Hill**: 10 middle class, 7 white, 3 self-defined as mixed race, ages 30–57. 5 mothers, 1 mum-to-be. 4 theatre/arts education, 1 actor, 1 writer, 2 special needs teaching assistants, 1 solicitor, 1 arts therapist. Friendship group. Forest Hill is a ward of Lewisham, an inner London Borough. At the time of the 2001 census it had a population of 14,000. Over half the accommodation in the area was owner occupied (Victorian housing), approximately 23% was council housing. Over 70% of its population were born in the UK.[2]

We began our research with in-depth individual interviews where we asked about employment, education, housing, living arrangements, social position, leisure activities, domestic and cultural habits and taste to gain a sense of the capitals to which the women in our study had access and the different social fields they occupied. We asked about biographies in order to understand what Bourdieu calls (1977) 'how' knowledge – the episteme that underpins how capital is used and performed – namely the processes by which different capitals were acquired and converted.

From the outset class and race framed the process and direction of the research. For instance, recruitment was a massive problem. Whilst our Forest Hill group came together rather easily, largely through our researcher Nancy Thumim's connections, finding willing working class participants took over six months and was finally only achieved through the help of colleagues making available their families and friendship groups. This was accompanied by the offer of payment in vouchers for participation, an offer which some of our middle class participants thought unnecessary and 'immoral'. We realized that problems with recruiting working class participants may well be related to the increase in the micro-management of the working classes in the UK, and reinforced through the New Labour government's Respect Agenda.[3]

Recruitment to the South Asian group from Clapham raised even more unanticipated issues. When Nancy arrived to interview Saj, she discovered that Saj did not have enough English for the interview, but Saj (and her husband who insisted on being present) were keen to take part in the project and so the interview continued. The interview was uncomfortable for both parties because it became clear that Saj viewed Nancy as a representative of the state, offering her bank statements as if to prove her legitimacy. Therefore there are powerful contexts at work here around class and race surveillance which worked to *frame* the politics and performance in the research encounter.

Partly due to the conditions we outlined above, some of our interviews, particularly with our working class participants, were often uncomfortable and generated some awkward silences and defensive responses. We made some difficult decisions about our class identities as researchers in terms of who was best placed to go into which homes and interview whom. Just as previous research has identified on class dis/identification there was a disinclination by our working class groups to directly answer questions about class.[4] We got responses particularly from younger participants such as: 'I'm just average', 'I don't think of myself as of a class' or 'having more money doesn't make you a better person', which directly links a type of moral evaluation to class position. When we added the question 'Do you think you get a fair deal in life?', discussion more easily focused on class issues, but this points to the difficulty of lay explanations of classifications (Payne and Grew 2005). We were not at all surprised, for in the UK, following concerted political attempts to eradicate the word from the political lexicon over the last 30 years, the public discourse for identifying positively as working class has diminished although the negative symbolic value attached to the term has increased (e.g. the use of the term 'chav' as a euphemism for class).

However, unlike other research which proposes that the middle class in the UK are often too embarrassed to admit they are middle class (Savage *et al.* 2001;

Sayer 2005), some of our Forest Hill group directly answered the questions about class using empirical evidence of cultural capital to substantiate their answers, with some suggesting that they were born working class but their education, occupation and interests now made them middle class. The South Asian group often identified themselves as middle class because they, or their parents worked, but they frequently blocked further questions we asked by stating we would not understand because of cultural difference (as all white researchers). Clearly hierarchies of status and caste opened up a more complicated set of issues that were not easily translated to the UK via the range of different migrant experiences of these women.

The most radical differences that emerged from the interviews were around leisure and social activities. Time spent in museums and art gallery cafes was a regular activity for our middle class group, whilst our South Asian group's social activities were nearly all focused on families and in the home. Family activities with 'treats' such as shopping with friends, pub meals and bars were more usual for our black and white working class participants. Differences around culture and sociality emerged with phenomenal regularity and are intricately connected to how reality television is experienced, as we elaborate later. But these social relationships amongst the groups also influenced the research design as we allowed participants some control over how they experienced the research methods. Most interviews took place in homes, but when that was considered inappropriate (for instance some of the Clapham women shared accommodation) some took place in a local community centre and library. Most viewing sessions also took place in homes, but we allowed some who were friends to take part in viewing sessions together, whilst others watched alone with the researcher. This decision was made to make the research environment less pressured and more comfortable, but it also means that some text-in-action sessions are influenced by the effect of a group, whilst others are a product of a different dynamic between television, sole participant and interviewer.

The third and final stage of the research involved drawing the women together for focus groups and again these took very different forms. The South Asian group used the focus group to have a party with their children, each bringing different food, using the legitimate excuse of the research to carve out time with their friends. The two researchers were encouraged to join the party afterwards and the research became a pretext for a more social occasion. The black working class group literally organized themselves into performing a version of an *Oprah* programme with one woman designating herself as Oprah, some consciously performing a debate, whilst the white working class group used it to discuss family issues and problems amongst themselves, splitting into two groups so that they could be with their closest friends. The middle class group performed as if in a university seminar and answered questions politically and abstractly, with substantial critical insight and cultural knowledge.

Each research encounter therefore offered a particular mode of articulation that relates as much to available cultural resources, contexts and social relations as they do to the actual 'findings' on reality television. Whilst we conducted interviews with the same interview schedule and focus groups with a similar set of prompts, the differences that emerged from social contexts of the research suggest that we are not comparing 'like with like' 'data' and raises the usual questions of validity and reliability. As we have argued elsewhere some of these issues can only be made explicit by the reflexive practices of the researcher which allows the reader the ability to see how the data is 'made' through the explication of the politics and values that shaped the methodology and research practice (Skeggs 2002; Wood 2009b). Nevertheless, we were interested in *enabling* different forms of participation in our research in order to understand different types of responses to television, such as teasing out affective phenomena that are not easily 'told', or being alert to the differentially distributed discursive resources, aware as we are from Chapter 2 that people are already constrained by the modes of telling afforded by their social position. We would argue that any research encounter encourages a mode of self-performance, the conditions for which need to be made explicit as an integral part of validity about 'findings'. Form (method, encounter) and content (speech, affect), history and social relations are therefore intricately entwined in any research output (see Skeggs *et al.* 2008).

Television and articulation

The relationship between the *form* of performance and the *content* of our interview transcripts is demonstrated by the way in which our participants articulated their relationship to the television itself. Here we want to draw out some important contextual issues related to talking about television. Roger Silverstone (1994) points to the usefulness of object-relations theory to give us a grip on 'the space television occupies in culture and in the individual psyche' (p.8). Research has pointed to the relationship of the object of television to forms of conspicuous consumption: on the TV aerial as a sign of modernity (O'Sullivan 1991); on the satellite dish as a symbol of class taste and status (Brunsdon 1997; Moores 1991); on class differences in the adornment and concealment of the set (Leal 1990); and on how the placement of the set in the home helps materialize family relationships (Ureta 2008). In the current conjuncture in the UK large plasma wide-screen televisions usually evoke a set of moral classed value judgements, ironically these also appear within the realm of make-over and reality television advice programmes where the television is considered to be a visible sign of bad taste and blockage to good communication in family relationships.

In the interviews we asked our participants questions about how many televisions they owned, their location, how often they watched and which other media platforms they used. On the whole our working class groups describe television as a fairly benign object with a constant presence, always on '24/7', and which needed to 'grab' their attention, without any guilty attachments to television viewing. The group from Clapham made similar responses about the amount of viewing time and having it 'always on' even if they were not viewing, but these responses were also related to their use of a range of satellite channels used to connect back to conversations with family and make comparisons with British culture.

Asking the same questions to our middle class respondents generated more lengthy and reflexive responses about their relationship to the object, echoing the findings of other researchers about middle class discussions of the debased object of television as presented to the university researcher (Gray 1992; Seiter 1990). This group reported television as a 'guilty pleasure' and under-estimated their television viewing in the interviews. Their detailed descriptions of numerous television programmes revealed that they all watched much more than they were prepared to admit. But they also describe wanting to control their television use, setting themselves rules, one even physically hiding the set, often concerned about its 'hypnotic' ability to 'pull them in' and 'waste time'. They maintained that their time was much better spent on other activities and television was a 'waste'. Talking about television was connected to how they told us as researchers about their value; how they pursued alternative activities such as visiting galleries, theatre and watching art films. They ensured that time was spent productively reflecting discussions of the modern 'enterprising self' (du Gay 1986) and 'prosthetic self' (Lury 1998) of Chapter 2. This also echoes Roy Lembo's (2000) findings on TV viewing in the US where 'discrete viewing' was part of a broader presentation of the 'productive individual'.

Yet the other groups talk about the value of television in different terms. Lembo's (2000) research also describes a working class 'distracted sociality', but that term does not fully fit the working class women in our study, who also use television viewing to perform a variety of purposeful social functions. Some of the women describe watching particular programmes so they can text their friends throughout, or talk about it at work the next day, whilst the Clapham group had a range of uses related to babysitting, overcoming isolation and language training. Whilst the middle class women speak of activities related to accruing person-value through personal development, the working class women were more likely to speak of their leisure time as related to *who* they would spend time with, usually friends and family rather than events or places. This also corresponds to Leroux *et al.*'s (2008) research which suggests the middle class are more orientated to educational/cultural activities, whilst the working class spend less specifically directed time 'just being' with their families.

Thus the working class groups were more interested in connecting the details of programmes to their own lives and personal dilemmas as part of the fabric of their social networks. These differences reflect different spatial and temporal value forms: for the working class this is localized social capital with present use-value to themselves and friends, and for the middle class this is symbolic convertible cultural capital that enables self exchange-value to be enhanced, structured through time and invested for future reward. Thus class relations are performed through the human-technology interface: staying in, turning on the television or giving it attention are class acts that generate very different forms of sociality and subjectivity (for a more detailed discussion of these findings see Skeggs and Wood 2011).

Findings about television use are also findings about the *articulation* of personhood. Talking about the television reveals classed modes of performing one's value and this was further exacerbated when discussing a devalued cultural form like reality television. There were divisions in women's responses in relation to preferences for reality television. It is important to state however that members of *all* groups demonstrated high levels of literacy about televisual techniques and the constructed nature of the 'reality'. All groups discussed formulas, contrivances, narrative structures, the manipulation of crisis for drama and the significance of editing and casting 'crazy' freaks. However, the Forest Hill group used their televisual knowledge to distance themselves from the programmes, maintaining that because they knew the formula they would be bored. In contrast, formula knowledge only added to the pleasure of the Addington group (white working class) 'you know it's all a set up but it's good fun anyway: I like it when they argue', or 'it's all a set up, I hate it when they make them fight, but I always watch it'. But the Addington group also often stated how they hated 'being told what to do' and 'talked at', hence recognizing that some advice was directed towards them: Nicola (22, nursery nurse) describes her dislike of *Wife Swap*, for example, because it is 'taking the mick out of other people for the way they are'. The Forest Hill group thought reality television was generally exploitative and humiliating for the participants, but they also talked about the problem of 'kids who just want to be famous, you know it doesn't matter what I do but I want to be famous'. (Chapter 7 discusses the different values afforded to types of labour performances by our participants.)

These differences were also played out in response to the TV 'expert' advice on offer. Our middle class respondents did not believe that advice was directed to them, and our working class respondents selectively 'chose' the elements of advice that fitted into their aesthetic, social and domestic lives. Our Clapham group seemed most interested in 'tips' responding to what has been assumed to be the governmental address of much reality television (as discussed in Chapter 1, a good deal of Foucauldian textual analyses of reality television suggests that it incites people into disciplining themselves). As we go on to discuss in Chapter 5, this process is not straightforward in our findings: our working class respondents were rarely persuaded by experts, edits or narrative closures, challenging the attempts to put people in their place and often defending television participants. For instance when Nicola (Addington) is watching *Ladette to Lady* in a text-in-action session she says, 'I prefer the ones that get chucked out' and 'they are a lot like my friends, they have got opinions on things haven't they?'.

Admitting to and being intensely involved with programme content was only a problem for the Forest Hill group. That is not to say that these women did not watch and express taking pleasure from reality television, but when asked to discuss particular programmes they often did so by displaying their skill in holding the form at a distance. As the following exchange with Ann, a solicitor and mother of two, (who in the initial phone contact claimed not to watch reality television) illustrates:

ANN: Oh yes, oh my goodness, yes I love *Supernanny*, I even bought the book.
BEV: Really, I'll write this one down, book [laughs].
ANN: Oh goodness, I *am* watching reality TV.
BEV: So you would purposefully watch *Supernanny*?
ANN: Well I watched a bit of it and I did, I even did watch it purposefully, but I think its novelty would have worn off. I think I must have watched about three of them and the reason I watched them is that I have difficulty with my five-year-old and ... she's a wilful child and ... in the evening totally strung out over what, she's very ... really–
BEV: Right so *Supernanny* would be a?
ANN: But also I quite liked, I like the advice, I didn't, I mean I didn't like the reality aspect of it, I thought these poor families, they were so exposed, these couples with difficulties in their relationships, everything was just wide open for the whole world to see and I thought that was terrible. But in terms of, I did use tips yes and I bought the book and I read it in about two hours and it was very accessible 'cos a lot of things, parenting books are American, and *Supernanny* books ... by her writer under her name, is actually very, I thought it was very accessible ... and it was very English and that was good.

Ann expresses surprise when she realizes that a programme she watches counts as reality television for our research and proceeds to legitimate her interest in the programme and demonstrate a 'useful' educational reason for watching, whilst still being able to recognize the apparent flaws of the programme type – the reality aspect – and demonstrate a considered opinion on exploitation. She even notes the irony in her own position of being engaged in something that she has previously stressed has absolutely no value. Ann's surprise at her own viewing choice and its conversion into a cultural asset that is both told and performed (as reason and irony) enables Ann to use reflexivity as a form of cultural capital to maintain her critical distance and moral value position in relation to reality television. Ann therefore offers a post-hoc justification for her viewing that is a reflexive research performance. For these reasons we have discussed at length elsewhere the acute need for an understanding of the deployment of cultural resources in research encounters (see Skeggs *et al.* 2008).

Therefore, our findings on the ways in which women *articulate* their relationship to television as an object and reality television as a text are thus heavily influenced by the ways in which they approached the interview encounter and were able (or not) to mobilize certain capitals. More adept at handling interview questions and the techniques of reflexivity, we are left with the impression that the middle class group fear the consequences of reality television and want to understand how to control its influence over their lives, whilst the Addington

group were much more dismissive of the form as 'just funny' and 'only entertainment'. These positions could perhaps be corralled into the frame of understanding those with less capital as duped, the passive vessels of ideology, but this
barely tells us anything of what has been deemed *most* interesting about reality
television: about its immediacy and its pull on emotion and affect. Asking people
what they 'think' about programmes did not always give us insights into what
they 'feel'. Presented one way we could see a 'cool' picture of the middle class
educated viewer and an 'indifferent' image of the working class viewer which
does not really marry with our claims about the more sensational nature of
reality television and its affective appeal to immediacy.

Deleuze (2001) maintains that power works through differentiating the
affecting from the affected. This makes us ask if our working class respondents'
demand for entertainment, and the distraction displayed when it is not provided
displays a different relation to power than is often assumed via debates about the
influence of ideology or the positioning by or taking up of discourse. We suggest
that the organization of time and space generates very different classed, gendered and raced subjectivities produced through the giving of attention. If
attention is refused, interpellation cannot happen.

Researching affect

Other feminist work has asked us to take seriously the working of emotion in
understanding audience attachments to particular dramatic forms. Most well-
known is Ien Ang's (1985) discussion of 'emotional realism' where she describes
the viewers in her study of *Dallas* recognizing the truth of the emotion of the
character, rather than the truth of the narrative per se. Therefore we align
ourselves with other feminist writers who ask for a reappraisal of viewers' emotional attachments towards an understanding of how feeling registers issues of
considerable importance to viewers' personal lives, and thus their social and
political locations (Berlant 2008). In relation to television Elisabeth Bird (2003)
suggests that her fans of the drama *Doctor Quinn* 'make clear judgements about
the quality of different story lines in terms of their ability to evoke emotion
through moral debate' (p.137). Kristyn Gorton (2009) too, suggests that emotion
is the key to reasserting questions of quality in relation to television.

However, we are less interested in using these discussions to make judgements
on the aesthetic quality of texts, but rather in attempting to gain insights into
how the emotive process might be at work in terms of how media forms enter
and make sociality. In Purnima Mankekar's (1999) research on Indian television
viewing she describes the way in which emotions ultimately cannot be divorced
from critical readings. Reactions to the disrobing of Draupadi in the text the
Mahabharat suggested that:

> The semiotic excess surrounding the figure of Draupadi as she was disrobed
> in front of her family, the range of memories and emotions sparked by her

predicament, enabled the Hindu viewers I describe here to confront and theorize their own vulnerabilities as women.

(1999:256)

In the context of the violence of the Indian state and rising Hindu chauvinism, their responses are potent insights into the political relationship between text and context. Mankekar describes these emotional responses as a product of 'symbolic excess', something that has the ability to 'move' past the purely representational as personally evocative. Alerted by Kavka (2008) and others to reality television's constant appeal to emotional excess beyond the level of the semiotic, to reaction rather than to action, and to theories of affect as a new dimension for understanding the workings of politics (Ahmed 2004a, 2004b; Berlant 2000; Blackman 2008; Skeggs 2000), we pay closer attention to these moments at work as empirical phenomena.

Therefore we are interested in how the manipulation of affect invites responses from our audiences. In Chapter 1 we discussed Peter Brooks' (1976/1995) observations of how melodrama is premised upon the heightened performance of gesture, whereby actors are instructed to perform 'sorrow', 'anger', and 'disgust'. Laura Grindstaff (2002) demonstrates how talk show producers incite 'the money shot' – the outpouring of emotion or anguish as the ultimate televisual moment, just as Illouz (2003) notes how Oprah Winfrey milks misery to entice viewers. Likewise, Alice Leppert and Julie Wilson (2008) show how reality television producers select participants on the basis of their capacity to 'show motivation through faces and eyes'.[5] In the many melodramatic moments of reality television gesture is intensified and it exudes abundant information. Actors learn to intensify feelings through bodily gesture, whereas reality television participants are incited through context and event, consciously and unconsciously, to display their feelings bodily. Actors attempt to make the audience 'feel' through their performance: think of the raised eyebrow, the glance made whilst a speaker is talking, of smirking, sarcastic smiling, the tongue in the cheek, wincing, bristling, silent rage and the many other somatic gestures used to transmit feelings.[6] In 'acting out' the conditions of being watched (Kavka 2008) such gestures are also performed by non-trained television participants to full effect.

Gestures that encode ideas about feelings are always positional – our position in relation to another or an object. But there has been little attempt to directly capture the interplay between textual gesture and audience response as a type of interaction. Film scholars such as David Bordwell (2005) speculate on the affective responses on the bodies of the spectator and Linda Williams (2004) notes how a sensationalized on-screen body produces an almost involuntary mimicry of emotion or sensation in the bodies of spectators. Whilst we do not work with the notion of a 'spectator' (which implies a figurative textually inscribed subject) and want to think about the 'viewer' (who may or may not sit in front of the screen), the literature on reality television suggests that it too works with sensation that speaks directly to bodily reaction, potentially producing an involuntary mimicry of emotional response. However, most available television audience research addresses questions of emotion in retrospect, asking people to reflexively account for their affective responses to television, either through the interview encounter, or even in the case of Ang (1985), through letter writing. They all call for some reflexive account of emotion, and as we have established reflexive accounts draw on linguistic resources that rationalize behaviour.

Recall Chapter 2 where we discuss the difference between affect as bodily feeling, and emotion as the cognisized interpretation of feelings, which rely on access to the discursive frameworks through which feelings can be codified. How do we get to the 'moments' of excess that are not reflexively produced? They have often been lost to the researcher. Writers like Gorton (2009) even suggest that capturing such moments is impossible since the researcher's presence may break the affective charge. But as we argued in Chapter 2 what is important to us from the theorizations of affect is the way in which they must reference our relations to others, they implicate us in a 'socius' of feeling and so we have looked for a way to capture the reactive 'moments' of television as a route to understanding television's more immediate intervention in the making of sociality.

Part of the design of this research project follows on from Wood's (2005, 2007a, 2009a) previous audience work on talk shows and magazine shows which outlines the method 'text-in-action' (TIA). There we argue that some texts necessitate overcoming the text/reader binary distinction in order to engage with interactivity. That research moves us beyond an understanding of text and meaning as an entirely semiotic relationship where texts are 'read', assuming a literary equivalence. Rather, the emphasis is on a communicative framework, using the work of pragmatics to understand television viewing as established through performative and ritual *acts*. In Wood's research, capturing women talking back to the television displays how women viewers mutually construct the text's meaning through enacting a communicative relationship. That work concentrates on 'moments' of television in order to locate television as taking place dynamically 'in time', whereby a moment can also refer to a physical mechanical process 'a product of force from a line of action to a particular point' (2009a:106). This registers television's actuality as 'happening', in order to encourage us not only to think about television as texts and representations but also to think of their interactive potential (Wood 2007a, 2007b).

The emphasis in that work was on the possibility for some types of talk television to invoke the audience into language interaction, and findings are premised upon the establishment of a new form of 'mediated conversation floor' to explore television as a communicative event. Instead of focusing on the production of meaning from interactivity we now emphasize the affective *moments* of television away from post-hoc rationalizations to take us into the spatial and temporal 'now' of television's presence. To think of the affective *dimensions* of television (in space and time, in the here and now) is therefore to think about how one is 'moved' in time from one place to another as a *process*. Therefore, in keeping with those working on bodily affects we think of bodies as processes (Blackman and Venn 2010), and attempt to understand the role of television in the workings of bodies, their affective states in their alignments with and against others.

Kavka (2008) proposes that reality television participants do not act up for the camera so much as 'act out' the social conditions of always being watched by others, making reality television a public stage where surveillance and judgement becomes intensified and amplified. We noted, through the duration of our research, how television participants and research respondents became increasingly conversant with the sensational techniques used to produce responses of disgust and sympathy: 'she expects sympathy by crying, but she's not getting it from me' (Mel, Addington watching *Wife Swap*). Developing Deleuze's point about attention, Silvan Tomkins (1995) notes that affect can make us pay attention (disgust, abjection and screaming in particular) but it can only make things matter to us if we connect to them in some way. He maintains that affect amplifies not only its own activator, but also the responses to both that activator and to itself. The temporal nature of the affective response and how it triggers significant issues for the person draws lines between reaction and significance.

We wanted to find the alignments of the televised gesture, the long-held close up, the focus on parts and behaviours, etc. (Chapter 3) with the reactions of our viewers. Therefore, we also watched television with our research respondents and recorded their responses as they viewed. We then transcribed their responses, alongside a transcription of the television speech and a visual description of what is occurring on the programme. Our text-in-action method drew our attention to significant reactive moments. Whilst we capture connections through recording microphones and our own records of 'being there' we did not video record the events. We felt that this may be too great an intrusion, but this still leaves the emphasis in our data on the audible rather than the somatic. This is of course a limitation to any research working with affect since its inability to be captured by established available normative recording devices, makes it difficult to envisage. It is questionable whether video recording might better recall what we as researchers 'felt' from being there, since affect is, as Brennan (2004) discusses, contagious. But our intent was to understand the immediacy of reality television viewing, to see what reactions the television programmes induced, and in capturing the spatial temporality of the text we have moved some way beyond the cognitive retrospective reconstruction of viewing behaviours.

The text-in-action method produced both comfort and discomfort for our research participants, depending upon their cultural resources. In order to minimize this discomfort we decided to take with us a sample of programmes highlighted from our textual analysis and those indicated as favourites by the interviews. We asked the respondents to choose a programme that they felt happy to watch. As a result we conducted 23 text-in-action (TIAs) viewing sessions. Some women were highly suspicious of us: 'What, you want to watch us watching television and you're being paid for it!' (Michelle, Addington) and our middle class participants were keen to know the 'rules of engagement', sometimes even questioning the methodological design. Bev had spent a few viewing sessions with some members of our Addington group, with them watching alone, sharing the discomfort of the research respondents, who felt uncertain as to what to do and hence spoke very little unless encouraged. Helen advised listening very carefully to what appeared to be an almost empty tape. This requires close attention to all utterances, including minimal responses which do important work in interaction to signal involvement (Wood 2009a). When viewing in pairs or groups of friends, responses were more uninhibited, leading to reactions that were far removed from the 'cool' or 'indifferent' picture that might have been available only from the interviews, as we go on to detail later.

With repeated intense listening we immediately recognized that there was a clear patterning to minimal responses such as tuts, gasps, sighs, etc., as clues to affective responses. When we compared different viewing sessions to the same programmes we could see affective reactions occurring at exactly the same moment across groups in viewers' encounters with the text. For example in this extract below where 'make-over' expert Trinny asks a harsh question of the television participant:

Table 4.1

	Cue/Image	Television Text What Not To Wear	Viewer Comments Lucy (Forest Hill)
1	1.04	Trinny and Susannah amongst crowd of	
2	Opening	mums cut to	
3	montage scenes	Trinny talking to a mum	
4	with music	'So have you always looked such a mess?'	
5	interspersed		Aaargh (sharp intake of breath)
6	with dialogue		Ooh there's no need

Table 4.2

	Cue/Image	Television Text What Not To Wear	Viewer Comments Chabera (Clapham)
1	Opening	Trinny and Susannah amongst crowd of	
2	montage scenes	mums cut to	
3	with music	Trinny talking to a mum	
4	interspersed	'So have you always looked such a mess?'	
5	with dialogue		Heh, heh, laughter

Laughter and para-linguistic retorts as one might expect often occurred at the same moments when we compared the same episodes of texts, often in response to particular harsh questions asked by experts as above, or in response to particular juxtapositional edits, or the use of ironic voice-over. Another significant place that evoked viewer reactions came after reality participants were asked to explain themselves to camera. In Chapter 3, we discussed the use of the close-up held on the face as participants are often called to account for their actions, which we called the 'judgement shot'. This particular technique worked as an incitement to our viewers, provoking them to make judgements of the participants. Interestingly they always put themselves in the position of the camera directly facing the TV participant, as in the following examples from two different sets of viewers watching an episode of *Wife Swap*. The television participant Tracy talks to camera suggesting that she does not want to go to a 'posh' house in the swap. Her voice is then carried over as commentary edited into an overlapping visual sequence whereby her host family are cleaning out a very modest caravan for her stay. The editing of sequences like this is often ironic and comic, but seems to work like a goal-oriented 'turn' in interaction, eliciting judgement from our viewers.

Able to compare the same texts and episodes in different viewing sessions we realized that across all the programmes most responses came where the camera was held on the face, producing a particular invitation to judge. In the example above the voice-over and visual editing of the sequence passes comment on the television participant, Tracy, for mentioning a multi-million pound house against the image of the caravan. The impact of the edit is that these two different sets of viewers judge Tracy to be pretentious (and to see how this judgement develops see Chapter 6).

Quite often affective noises were translated into mediating statements such as, 'Oh my God', which were then converted into moral judgements like, 'how can they let their children behave like that' (in response to *Supernanny*) or 'how can they let themselves go' (in response to *What Not to Wear*). We began to refer to these instances as 'affective-textual encounters' (ATE) in which a powerful non-verbal response is made immanently in the television encounter. If we had asked later about their responses, it is likely that an apparatus of cognized (possibly) reflexive interpretation would have been accessed, displaying linguistic capital and discursive resources rather than immediate reaction. From this type of tracking between listening, transcript of viewer and television text, *and* response, we were able to identify the exact point where participants reacted which made us further investigate significant moments in the programmes: the trigger points that incited reactions across groups. Rarely does audience research involve such an integrated movement between text and audience analyses.

As discussed earlier, many of our working class participants described reality television as 'just funny', in keeping with their dismissive relationship with television, refusing a detailed reflexive account of their understanding of the genre, unlike the more detached critique that was so readily available to our middle class group. The text-in-action method therefore enabled some participants a different way to *perform* their relationship to reality television that did not rely on their cultural capital. For example, Saj (discussed earlier who was initially intimidated by the researcher's presence) became thoroughly engaged when watching an

Table 4.3

	Cue/Image	Television Text Wife Swap (Tracy and Kate)	Viewers' comments Sally, Sonia, Sally Mc (Brockley)
1	04:12	**Voice over:** It's the day of the swap and both wives are getting ready to leave.	
2	Tracy packing clothes		
3			
4		Because the Thomas house is so crammed full of kids Tracy will be staying in the fa:mily caravan.	
5	Cut to image of caravan in the		
6			
7	garden	**Tracy to camera:** I'm worried that I'm going to be going to a house (.)	
8			
9	Cut to Tracy with	totally above my level you know sort of multi million pound house or something	
10	Mark on sofa to		
11	camera	going into this big house with nannies and a guy who's you know (.) really (.) pompous	**Sonia:** You see what I mean, how does *she* kno:w?
12	Edited over		**Sally:** Laughter .hh hh
13	Trevor with		**Sonia:** you know because people have this thing about a legal secretary and she's nothing special (?) nothing special at a:ll
14	shovel.		
15	Kate in caravan	**Kate:** I hope she thinks this is nice	
16	getting it ready	**Trevor:** Well this is a five star hotel if she moans I'm goina 'av a:	
17			

Table 4.4

Cue/Image	Television Text Wife Swap (Tracy and Kate)	Viewers' comments Vicky and Mel (Addington)
	04:14	
1		
2	Tracy packing	**Voice over:** It's the day of the swap and	
3	clothes	both wives are getting ready to leave.	
4		Because the Thomas house is so: crammed	
5	Cut to image of	full of kids Tracy will be staying in the	
6	caravan in the	family caravan.	
7	garden	**Tracy to camera:** I'm worried that I'm	
8		going to be going to a house (.)	
9	Cut to Tracy with	totally above my level you know sort of	
10	Mark on sofa to	multi million pound house or something	
11	camera	going into this big house with nannies and	**Vicky:** Don't you think that's kind of
12	Edited over	a guy who's you know (.) really (.)	saying more about her?
13	Trevor with	pompous	**Mel:** The other one seems more (.)
14	shovel		normal
15	Kate in caravan	**Kate:** I hope she thinks this is nice	**Vicky:** yeh
16	getting it ready	**Trevor:** Well this is a five star hotel if she	
17		moans I'm goina 'av a	

episode of *Supernanny*. Here Saj did not have to self-consciously articulate her understanding of the programme; rather, she demonstrated how she experienced the programme through loud affective declarations of 'No!' Saj is a fan of *Supernanny* because of the way the nanny, Jo, imposes what Saj refers to as 'guidelines' on parents in crisis. Saj showed sympathy for the mother in the *Supernanny* episode but also a certain morality informs her response to the programme: her tutting utterances followed by 'No!' suggest the uptake of a moral position around mothering which is more revealing of her relationship to this reality television text than was available in the interview stage of the research. Therefore our methods produced stark differences between the groups in their dialogue *with*, responses *to*, as well as *about* 'reality' television. Being able to understand our respondents' different types of reactions – reflexive, immanent, moral, affective – offers us an invaluable lens through which to understand their responses.

Conclusion

We therefore want to argue that methods bring class relations into view, making visible the cultural resources required in order to take positions in relation to the object (television) and its content (reality television as a genre). This drew our attention to the significance of time and space in the different shaping of their lives, as our working class participants from different backgrounds were all more concerned with the local and familial social 'value' of reality television, whilst our middle class group were more concerned with value-accrual and future projection. Crucially this finding maps onto the ways in which our participants articulated *their* value, where the content of their explanation cannot be divorced from the *form* of its telling. Therefore in addition to the post-hoc rationalizations when researchers ask viewers to account for their viewing practices, we also decided to intervene directly in the viewing encounter.

The significance of attention and evaluation was revealed when we examined the affective responses that were made to the television content. Reality television programmes manipulate affect to gain attention, to move audiences, to make them connect, to feel and provoke a reaction. We realized that non-verbal actions, the bodies and gestures of television participants, produced reactions in our research participants. It was possible to map through the ATE the moments of affective response across groups to the incitement by programme edits and their use of 'judgement shots' which suggests that immediation is a central process to understanding viewer encounters with television.

But we could not anticipate what the production of affect would 'do', and we go on to detail this complicated picture in Chapter 5. As theories of affect suggest, it is only when affect is connected to an idea that it has significance. The significance was revealed through moral judgements that were spoken. Thus when affect moves our respondents to judgement, it is through bringing their own lives into play to make connections. They evoke how they have felt when placed in similar situations or similar relationships, positioning themselves both as the judge and judged as they locate themselves in similar circuits of value. Our research methods revealed that audiences are not simply cognitive rational viewers whose relationship to television is sedimented over time, but also immediate sensational subjects produced through gender, race and class. Here the judgemental gaze is a dialogic one, refracted through the recognition of similar emotional feelings and events to which they attach and defend themselves.

Judith Butler (in Butler *et al.* 2000) suggests that we need ideas about an 'affective sociality' in order to understand human connectedness and we want to suggest it is produced through different time and space vectors (present/future, home/public) and different modes of attention. Marshall McLuhan (1964) maintains that the media is a prosthesis of human experience, part of an extended social realm, and we think it is also incorporated into the same person values by which the viewer is located. The viewer therefore becomes a node, which may always be provisional and capable of being redistributed, but s/he is also a node that is part of the wider production of an economy of personhood. We explore this simultaneously *provisional* and yet *located* status of our viewers in the following chapters, where we explain the empirical findings of our research through ideas about governance, affect, judgement and labour.

Notes

1 ESRC project number 148-25-0040. Full details of the project can be found at http://www.identities.org.uk/. Nancy Thumim was research fellow on the project between 2005 and 2007 and we are grateful for her part in securing participants and conducting fieldwork. All members of the research team conducted fieldwork across the three empirical stages.

2 Area information compiled from the 2001 census: http://neighbourhood.statistics.gov.uk

3 The UK has seen a range of civil and criminal micro-management behavioural legislation: The Local Government Act of 1972 was used to introduce ASBO's, Anti-Social Behaviour Orders, IBO's, Individual Behaviour Orders, Parenting Orders, and 'Community Payback' as well as to bring injunctions against public nuisance. The New Labour government's Respect Agenda, in place between 2005 and 2008, criminalized modes of behaviour that were previously lawful, and over 3,000 changes were introduced to the Criminal Justices act which penalized public behaviour.

4 The ethnography of white working class women shows how disidentification is the likely gendered response to the classification working class, primarily because of the pathologizing and lack of value that identification would produce (Skeggs 1997).

5 They describe how Lauren Conrad, star of MTV's semi-scripted reality show *The Hills*, was cast precisely because of her facial agility in the use of gesture.

6 A theatre review asks: 'What makes Clare Higgins so strong an actress? Above all, the ability to show herself altering. On the spot. She seems to change the quality of her flesh, and to do so while remaining completely still. She thawed eyelash by eyelash, shifting from monster to matriarch simply by rearranging her weight' (Susannah Clapp, 'Shrink Rapt' *The Observer* 1 November 2009).

References

Ahmed, S. 2004a 'Affective Economies', *Social Text* 22(2): 117–39.
——2004b *The Cultural Politics of Emotion*, Edinburgh: Edinburgh University Press.
Ang, I. 1985 *Watching Dallas: Soap Opera and the Melodramatic Imagination*, London: Routledge.
Berlant, L. 2000 'The Subject of True Feeling: Pain, Privacy, Politics', in S. Ahmed, J. Kilby, C. Lury, M. McNeil and B. Skeggs (eds) *Transformations: Thinking Through Feminism*, London: Routledge.
——2008 *The Female Complaint: The Unfinished Business of Sentimentality in American Culture*, London and Durham: Duke University Press.
Bird, E. 2003 *The Audience in Everyday Life: Living in a Media World*, New York and London: Routledge.
Blackman, L. 2008 'Affect, Relationality and the Problem of Personality', *Theory, Culture and Society* 25(1): 27–51.
Blackman, L. and Venn, C. 2010 'Affect', *Body and Society* 16(1): 7–28.
Bordwell, D. 2005 *Figures Traced in Light: On Cinematic Staging*, Berkeley: University of California.
Bourdieu, P. 1977 *Outline of a Theory of Practice*, Cambridge: Cambridge University Press.
Brennan, T. 2004 *The Transmission of Affect*, Ithaca: Cornell University Press.
Brooks, P. 1976/1995 *The Melodramatic Imagination: Balzac, Henry James, Melodrama and the Mode of Excess*, New Haven and London: Yale University Press.
Brunsdon, C. 1997 *Screen Tastes: Soap Opera to Satellite Dishes*, London: Routledge.
Butler, J., Laclau, E. and Zizek, S. 2000 *Contingency, Hegemony, Universality: Contemporary Dialogues on the Left*, London: Verso.
Deleuze, G. 2001 *Pure Immanence: Essays on a Life*, New York: Zone Books.
du Gay, P. 1986 *Consumption and Identity at Work*, London: Sage.
Gorton, K. 2009 *Media Audiences: Television, Meaning and Emotion*, Edinburgh: Edinburgh University Press.
Gray, A. 1992 *Video Playtime*, London: Routledge.
Grindstaff, L. 2002 *The Money Shot: Trash, Class and the Making of TV Talk Shows*, Chicago: University of Chicago Press.
Hill, A. 2005 *Reality TV: Audiences and Popular Factual Television*, London: Routledge.
——2007 *Restyling Factual TV: Audiences and News, Documentary and Reality Genres*, London: Routledge.
Illouz, E. 2003 *Oprah Winfrey and the Glamour of Misery*, New York: Columbia University Press.
Kavka, M. 2008 *Reality Television, Affect and Intimacy: Reality Matters*, London: Palgrave Macmillan.
Leal, O. F. 1990 'Popular Taste and Erudite Repertoire: The Place and Space of Television in Brazil', *Cultural Studies* 4(1): 19–29.
Lembo, R. 2000 *Thinking Through Television*, Cambridge: Cambridge University Press.
Leppert, A. and Wilson, J. 2008 'Living *The Hills* Life: Lauren Conrad as Reality Star, Soap Opera Heroine, and Brand', *Genders Online Journal* 48.
Leroux, B., Rouanet, H., Savage, M. and Warde, A. 2008 'Culture and Class in Britain', *Sociology* 42(6): 1049–1071.
Lury, C. 1998 *Prosthetic Culture: Photography, Memory and Identity*, London: Routledge.
Mankekar, P. 1999 *Screening Culture, Viewing Politics: An Ethnography of Television, Womanhood, and Nation in Postcolonial India*, London and Durham: Duke University Press.

McLuhan, M. 1964 *The Medium is the Message*, London: Routledge and Kegan Paul Limited.

Moores, S. 1991 'Satellite TV as Cultural Sign: Consumption, Embedding and Articulation', *Media, Culture and Society* 15(4): 621–40.

O'Sullivan, T. 1991 'Television Memories and Cultures of Viewing 1950–60', in J. Corner (ed.) *Popular Television in Britain*, London: BFI.

Payne, G. and Grew, C. 2005 'Unpacking "Class Ambivalence" Some Conceptual and Methodological Issues in Accessing Class Cultures', *Sociology* 39(5): 893–910.

Savage, M., Bagnall, G. and Longhurst, R. 2001 'Ordinary, Ambivalent and Defensive: Class Identities in the Northwest of England', *Sociology* 35(4): 875–92.

Sayer, A. 2005 *The Moral Significance of Class*, Cambridge: Cambridge University Press.

Seiter, E. 1990 'Making Distinctions in TV Audience Research: a Case Study of a Troubling Interview', *Cultural Studies* 4(1): 61–85.

Skeggs, B. 1997 *Formations of Class and Gender: Becoming Respectable*, London: Sage.

——2000 'The Rhetorical Affects of Feminism', in S. Ahmed, J. Kilby, C. Lury, M. McNeil and B. Skeggs (eds) *Transformations: Thinking Through Feminism*, London: Routledge.

——2002 'Who Can Tell? Reflexivity in Feminist Research', in T. May (ed.) *Issues and Practices in Qualitative Research*, London: Sage.

Skeggs, B. and Wood, H. 2011 'Turning It On is a Class Act: Immediated Object Relations with the Television', *Media, Culture and Society* September 33(6): 941–53.

Skeggs, B., Wood, H. and Thumim, N. 2008 '"Oh Goodness I am Watching Reality TV": How Methodology Makes Class in Multi-Method Audience Research', *European Journal of Cultural Studies* 11(1): 5–24.

Silverstone, R. 1994 *Television and Everyday Life*, London and New York: Routledge.

Tomkins, S. 1995 'Shame-Humiliation and Contempt-Disgust', in E. K. Sedgwick and A. Frank (eds) *Shame and its Sisters: A Silvan Tomkins Reader*, Durham: Duke University Press.

Ureta, S. 2008 '"There is One in Every Home": Finding the Place of Television in New Homes Among a Low-Income Population in Santiago, Chile', *International Journal of Cultural Studies* 11(4): 477–97.

Williams, L. 2004 'Porn Studies: Proliferating Pornographies On/Scene: An Introduction', in L. Williams (ed.) *Porn Studies*, Durham: Duke University Press.

Wood, H. 2005 'Texting the Subject: Women, Television, and Modern Self-Reflexivity', *The Communication Review* 8(2): 115–35.

——2007a 'The Mediated Conversational Floor: An Interactive Approach to Reception Analysis', *Media, Culture and Society* 29(1): 75–103.

——2007b 'Television is Happening: Methodological Considerations for Capturing Digital Television Reception', *European Journal of Cultural Studies* 10(4): 485–506.

——2009a *Talking with Television: Women, Talk Shows and Modern Self-Reflexivity*, Illinois: Illinois University Press.

——2009b 'Television: Tufte's Living with the Rubbish Queen', in F. Devine and S. Heath (eds) *Sociological Research Methods in Context*, London: Palgrave.

Chapter 5

Affect and ambiguity, not governmentality

In this chapter we question the main assumptions made in previous textual analyses of reality television that imply an uncomplicated reach of governmentality and pedagogy to audiences. The affective dimensions of reality television intervene in this otherwise linear picture and we employ ideas about affect to detail how our audiences make connections to reality television participants in order to: connect back and legitimate their own experiences, connect back to their own emotional histories by reaching into the affects experienced by others, and locate themselves in relation to their own and others' value practices.

> Affect is found in those intensities that pass body to body (human, non-human, part-body, and otherwise), in those resonances that circulate about, between, and sometimes stick to bodies and worlds, and in the very passages or variations between these intensities and resonances themselves.
>
> (Seigworth and Gregg 2010:1)

So far in the book we have been using the idea of affect in different ways. In its most abstract sense (as outlined in Chapter 2) we first examined the way affect has been used to produce new forms of value for capital: whereas sentiment and emotion have long been key markers of 'women's culture' in novels and film, we demonstrated how the manipulation of feeling has been extended and used to open out markets through what Illouz (2007) identified as 'cold intimacy'. In Chapter 3 we mapped this extension of intimacy onto the drive of the reality television format where the textual apparatus, and its mutating incursion into new intimate terrain, form a technology of intimacy. What was previously considered to be 'private', what Thompson (1996) calls 'the sphere of affect', is opened out as a form of spectacular, intense, often melodramatic entertainment, by which (as above) 'intensities pass from body to body' across the screen *and* as we will show between the screen and the viewer.

Affect is the name we give to those forces that can make us 'do things', move us, connect us to things, but which can also overwhelm us: 'affect is persistent proof of a body's never less than ongoing immersion in and amongst the world's obstinacies and rhythms, its refusals as much as its invitations' (Seigworth and

Gregg 2010). This is exactly what the next two chapters detail: they examine the resonances and intensities produced between the television and the viewer that make us do things and do nothing, creating connections as well as refusals. As we have suggested television can produce a 'beside-ness', a binding to others as well as a dramatic distancing, which is always produced through the social encounter, whether that encounter is with other people, media representations or through technology, in this case with the television.

Here we want to explore both the very specific incitement to affect and more generally how affect generates powerful social and political climates such as fear and ontological insecurity, allowing us to enter the debate about the political significance of affect. Two of the key points made by Spinoza (Deleuze and Deleuze 1978) in his exploration of the working of power is, first, how affect is connected to ideas, and, second, how negative affect leads to a diminished capacity to act. Hence it is important to think about how the affective incitements offered by reality television are connected to ideas about what we can do – our perceptions and capacity to act. Therefore when we think about our social location we also need to think about our access to discourses and narratives that enable us to make investments in ourselves and others, such as in the narrative of the 'good family'. Committing ourselves to the idea of the good mother, for instance, reveals not just the attachment to a relatively fixed ideology, but also shapes the conditions of possibility for how we live and move through social space.

Many readings of reality television have relied on theories of governmentality to support the genre's alignment with a very particular historical climate of neoliberal politics, but this assumes a rather different pedagogic relationship with audiences than that implied through the affective potential of reality television and we want to tease out the relationship between pedagogy and affect in this chapter. Larry Grossberg (1997, 2010b) has long argued that affect is the 'missing link' in the understanding of media and ideology. We argue that it is affect that enables us to understand how the contemporary conjuncture is structured and thus how to intervene if we hope to achieve social change. To ignore affect in these times of greed, avarice, cruelty and insecurity is to miss out key aspects of the political air we breathe. These feelings are not only part of the realm of the senses but are materialized; most obviously the affects of greed and competition that produced the current economic crisis are now producing fear and insecurity in the majority of the population. These affects, as Heather Nunn (2011) demonstrates, have trickle down effects that we can see on reality television, such as property programmes which shift their focus to notions of domestic security and havens from the heartless world rather than on profit making through property development.

Ben Highmore (2010) notes how the words for designating affective experience sit awkwardly on the borders of the material and immaterial, the physical and the metaphysical: we are *moved* by a sentiment; our *feelings* are hurt; I am *touched* by your presence. Terry Eagleton (1989) also describes affect as 'nothing less than the whole of our sensate life together – the business of affections and aversions, of how the world strikes the body on its sensory surfaces, of that which takes root in the gaze and the guts and all that arises from our most banal, biological insertion in to the world' (p.13). In this chapter therefore we want to capture the 'movements' our audiences make in their response to reality television between the sensual and the material. In television audience research Philip Schlesinger *et al.* (1992) have previously shown how the TV programme *Crimewatch* generated the powerful affect of fear. The programme which regularly focused on gratuitous representations of rape and attacks on women actually influenced people's everyday movement through social space as older women were more likely to stay at home rather than venture out after viewing.

Likewise, we know how the repetition of affects over time, such as shame and humiliation, will influence the spaces women are willing to occupy and those they avoid, thereby decreasing their capacity to act (Reay 2000; Skeggs 1997, 2009; Walkerdine 2010; Walkerdine and Lucey 1989, 2001). Affect not only influences how and where bodies can move, but it also materializes on bodies as they move through space. It accumulates and takes shape over time: affects of confidence and fear produce very different bodily presences, of entitlement or insecurity, in social spaces.

In the previous chapter we identified the development of our method, the 'affective textual encounter' which enabled us to identify the moments when our research respondents engaged with the television '*as if*' it was part of their lives, intervening in the social relationships of which they are a part. This connected to our understanding of the technology of it (outlined in Chapter 3) which focuses in more detail on how reality television as an affective medium (through its use of techniques such as melodrama) manipulates affect to incite particular responses, such as disgust. In this chapter we take this methodological development further through analysis of how affect enables us to understand television by distinguishing it from other processes such as 'reading representations'. Most available analyses of the affective dimensions of the media rely on close textual readings, such as Kavka (2008) and Gorton (2009), whereas we focus instead on audience encounters and interactions with the television through empirical research. Our data thus begins to flesh out the 'relay between performing and viewing' that Holmes (2008) suggests is heralded in by new forms of television. This relay, we argue, generates forms of co-extensivity and co-entanglements between the audience and television product. But before we begin this analysis we locate our work in relation to the dominant paradigm of reality television analysis – that of governmentality and its assumptions about the pedagogic invitation to the individual.

Locating governmentality

The arguments about the relationship between reality television and affect on the one hand, and the dominant reading of the genre in relation to forms of governmentality and the individualization thesis on the other, have rarely been satisfactorily thought through together. At the same time that reality television seems to have questioned the epistemological and ontological terrains of reality and truth, it has also given rise to a renewed interest across television and media scholarship into questioning the 'messages' of television. As we demonstrated in Chapter 1 many authors suggest that reality television invites viewers to take up the narratives of self-work and transformation necessary in neo-liberal political contexts. This is supported by a sustained thesis of 'governmentality' which is born from Rose's (1989) Foucauldian analysis that has shifted the theoretical terrain from thinking about a dominant ideology which comes from central sources – the ruling class, the State and its ideological apparatus – to more integrated bio-political imperatives in which the subject takes up the work of producing the self in their own interests. In this reading reality television expounds a pedagogic message which has largely been interpreted as part of a broader neo-liberal move to instrument individualization in countering the repeal of State support (Ouellette and Hay 2008).

This analysis assumes that viewers must learn to assess and judge others in a broader move towards assessing and judging themselves, where the call to the productive individual is founded upon asserting personal responsibility for one's own life choices and outcomes, what Heelas (2002) calls the 'self-work ethic' (that we develop in Chapter 7). So whilst a Foucauldian reading moves beyond 'ideology' in the Marxist sense, the message of self-work is a dominant motif which works in the interests of neo-liberal politics. There are some voices that are sceptical of the over-determinist way in which theories of governance seem to explain all. Grossberg (2010a) suggests that the theory is so well worked out in advance that they 'guarantee that they will find what they are looking for' (p.317) and David Morley (2010) points out that such a position leads to a form of functionalism. The problem is that a straight reading of governmentality 'creates a seamless web between capitalism (finance, post-Fordism, etc.), politics and subjectivity' (Grossberg 2010a:320) which to us is suggestive of the kind of research which has long been discredited for assuming the dominant 'effects' of media.

Grossberg (2010a) notes the assumption within governmentality analysis that television participants, and the huge audiences that follow these programmes alike, are bound up in the *same* neo-liberal project because 'it fails to distinguish between hegemonic constructions and distributions of the population and bio-political management of the population' (p.320). In Chapter 1 we discussed some of the work on reality television which *did* interrogate both hegemony and bio-politics (see also Thoburn (2007)). In Chapter 3 in our textual analyses we discussed how the resources available to participants to do the work of the self were unevenly distributed, not only through the detachment of participants from their history, social location and material forces, but also through the modes of textual production by which immediacy and intensity work to efface social histories. But like Grossberg, we see a problem with a lack of historic and contemporary specificity in many governmentality analyses when neo-liberalism comes to signify so many different practices. This is why, in Chapter 2, we set out the historical classed and gendered precedents for self-work which feed into the current conjuncture. But what then of the affective resonances of the melodrama of reality television as it enters into these histories and presents?

We are left with rather incongruent readings. On the one hand the affective potential of reality television 'opens up' any symbolic overloading through its excess and potential 'queering' (Kavka 2008), whilst on the other hand the governmentality thesis' reading suggests a 'closing down' of reality television into the straightforward mirroring of the workings of individualized neo-liberal culture. Kristyn Gorton (2008) does attempt to think through the relationship between these pedagogic elements and affect in her account of *Wife Swap*. In that programme she notes that the attempt to suggest that real social differences can be worked out through emotional investments (epitomized in the coming together of the two families at the end to work out what they have learned) only asks the audience to consider what the individual may have learned. She argues that, 'far from teaching the viewer or participant something, the programme perpetuated individualized response and this is what shuts down any real potential for social change' (Gorton 2009:109). In the end then, despite the potential opportunity opened up by affect in a programme like *Wife Swap*, the emphasis upon individual volition and disposition is what closes down any broader social understanding, and we are reminded of Bill Nichols' (1996) observations in Chapter 1 about the arresting potential of affect. Affect has the potential to both open up and close down understandings, it depends, as Spinoza maintained, on how it is hinged to ideas and to the capacity to act.

Gorton's analysis is primarily premised upon textual analysis, whereas the evidence from empirical audience research paints a rather more complex picture. In Annette Hill's (2005, 2007) large empirical research projects, she discusses in more detail the relationship between pedagogy and her viewers' understandings of what they might have 'learnt' from reality and factual television. She finds that viewers rarely actually associate reality television with direct pedagogic advice, instead, by positioning programming more closely to entertainment they engage in a debate about the *idea* of learning itself. This muddies the waters somewhat since it suggests that the terms of engagement, potentially the affects of entertainment, serve to question the pedagogic apparatus itself, and by extension we might suggest begin to undo some of the assumptions about the workings of governmentality.

There is a consistency in our data that does confirm a certain reading of governmentality based on social and cultural positioning. Our South Asian group from Clapham were much more likely to say in interviews that they took notice of some of the pedagogic elements of reality television.

> I work with my child myself and I use strategies with her. And it was interesting to see how you know she ended up using positive reinforcements and

positive attitude, rather than going into negative controlling attitude. That's right because that's where the parents were controlling things and you know the children here (referring to *Supernanny*) they got into control again, like I'm going to control you, you don't do that, and children rebel. Then they rebel, the more they control them, yes it becomes a circle, it's really difficult to break it off and find a connection. She seemed able to do them with the children and with the parents and make them do too. I learned a few things probably myself.

(Raazia, Clapham, Text in Action)

I like it because they actually tell you what you are eating that is wrong and what is causing all the health problems.

(Chabera, Clapham, interview talking about
You Are What You Eat)

Because actually I'm married I do have my married life, so I understanding that they send, you know, the wife to another home and you can deal with some other families, you know. ... You can understand these feelings. But when you go to some other home and you're kind of like 'oh my gosh' my home is much better than, you know, this. It's like a good lesson for us, like the married people.

(Sabeen, Clapham, interview talking about *Wife Swap*)

Yeah, yeah, I just like to know people and how you treat them and how can you understand each other better and compromise. So it's like you can just then use it for everyday life as well when you're at work, when you're with your friends, you can just see that how you can compromise in some ways and when it's better to be quiet, when it's better to say something, things like that, the relationships yeah. ...

Yes, some programmes are really good when they help people to like be better in relationships and with the kids especially, so it is quite helpful yes and it can be applied in everyday life and everyone, anyone who is watching can adopt things from that, it's good.

(Madiha, Clapham, interview talking about *Wife Swap*)

Bearing in mind our discussion in the last chapter about how our different methods allowed different modes of articulation, it is interesting that when many of our Clapham viewers are called to cognitively account for their relationship to television, they are keen to tell us what they have 'learnt' from television. Recall the discussion of Saj who was keen to present an image to the researcher about television's place in her adoption of British culture.

In one of the extracts above we see Madiha give one of her numerous accounts of what she thinks can be learnt from reality television. But this picture is much more complicated than an adoption of pedagogic advice, a technique in the weaponry of governmentality. As this interview unfolds, we see how her incorporation of her viewing is closely entwined with her migrant experience. Madiha is a student who has been living in London for three years having grown up in Pakistan; here she starts to talk about how she likes the programme *Get a New Life*:

BEV: Is that, I wonder is that because you could imagine yourself in that position, would you ever go and change your life entirely?

MADIHA: Actually I wouldn't change myself, my personality. I might change the country, like I did [laughs].

BEV: [Laughs] Yeah, yeah, how old were you when you came here?

MADIHA: I was 17 when I came here.

BEV: Oh right so that's quite a radical change?

MADIHA: Yeah, but obviously I stayed with the people of my country and I tried to make it very home, yeah very homely like as it was in Pakistan. But I would not change myself, my personality, for example I still wear my own cultural clothes, I will still follow my religion, I would not change myself as such. So it could be interesting though that people start to think to go somewhere and live.

...

BEV: I'd be too scared, but you know, that's a major transformation.

MADIHA: Yes. Like it kind of applies to me as well now, that I can see, I can see the things in that.

BEV: Yeah. So you read your experience into it?

MADIHA: Yes. ... It was quite hard as well for me, but it's settled down, slowly, gradually.

(TALKING ABOUT REALITY TELEVISION IN GENERAL AND WHY PEOPLE TAKE PART)

MADIHA: ... It's basically, it's more comfortable to watch these kind of things because you just think that it's like people like one of us, like us, they are us kind of thing. It's not imaginary or, yeah? Do you know what I mean?

BEV: Yeah, they're not actors.

MADIHA: They're not actors, they're not acting and if they're happy we can be like that, if they're not happy, what are the reasons and how can we change this, yeah. ... Yes. If it is for good, if they're doing it for good and they're not happy, they're not satisfied where they're living and they think they can have a better life, so it's worth taking like this kind of risk really. Well I came here and now I'm glad that I came here because I just gained so many things. I am studying now, I'm working as well, I have so much confidence now. (Clapham, interview)

In this articulation of a relationship to television, Madiha is using reality television as a post-hoc evaluation of her own particular narrative of change. Wanting to keep her personality and yet change her lifestyle she seems to adopt the language of much make-over television, but here it is not the instigator of change for the future in the 'seamless web' between politics and subjectivity, but it is deployed in the service of a much more complex attempt to narrativize the difficult experience of migration and dislocation. Therefore even where the pedagogic elements of reality television do at first sight seem to play a direct role in our interviewees' responses, for our Clapham viewers these are more often related to their position vis-à-vis their experience of British culture. These are played out rather differently in the text-in-action viewing sessions where the Clapham women can immediately 'perform' their relationship to reality television, as we go on to discuss in Chapter 6. The more interesting question for us is what else are they drawing on to make that knowledge useful to them in particular? And what makes them want to *articulate* their learning to us as researchers?

Much more common across the data from our other groups were numerous examples of women venting frustration at the pedagogic elements of reality and lifestyle television which echo Sender and Sullivan's (2008) survey research where their audiences of make-over programmes often critiqued the instructions of the experts. Here are a few examples from our data:

> No, I couldn't stand like someone telling me like how it should be all the time. And them not doing it, if they were mucking in together, but someone standing there telling you, you know how you should be doing this, you should be doing that, ah!
>
> (Michelle, Addington, interview talking about *Supernanny*)

> It was these two middle class women who I don't think have any sense of style anyway telling other people that how you're comfortable is wrong. It's just wrong.
>
> (Ruby 1, Brockley, interview talking about *What Not to Wear*)

There was quite a lot of resistance to the direct advice meted out by 'so called' experts and importantly there is also quite a lot of pleasure taken in that resistance. This can be seen in the collective feelings that emerged in focus groups:

SUSAN: That might be cool, that's not too bad, I'll go out and get one of those. And other times it's, 'God, what the *hell* has she got on, she needs to go on the programme herself!'

RUBY 1: [laughter]. Yeah, [inaudible 06.04], I don't watch it because it's like oh come on they're talking about these, you know –

SONIA: Trinny and whatever.

RUBY 1: Trinny and Susannah. [inaudible 6.15]

SONIA: That other woman, that's what I'm saying.

RUBY: Yeah, we should have someone telling *them* what to wear, have you seen some of the stuff she puts on lately?

UNIDENTIFIABLE THROUGH LAUGHTER: Tell me! [laughs].

GROUP: [laughter]

(Brockley, focus group talking about *What Not to Wear*)

Our viewers clearly understand the pedagogic elements of reality television, which certainly does not hide its lessons, foregrounding strongly the imperatives to self-work and transformation in its narrative structure. Viewers' appreciation of the benefits of television advice was often tied to a sense of narrative fulfilment in the transformation, rather than to a willingness to actually adopt the advice:

> Sometimes at the time you think 'oh no way' but no-I like the way they do all the makeup I think that can make such a difference and it certainly makes the people feel better. I think that's good because it's nice to see them happy. And it's nice to see them happy rather than how they were before when they were all depressed.
>
> (Sophie, Addington, interview talking about *What Not to Wear*).

Therefore what comes across from the data is the sensation of *pleasure* taken from the entertainment of modes of advice in the ability to ridicule experts, with an appreciation and *empathy* for participants *as part of* the dramatic resolution. This seems to confirm Hill's (2007) findings about the nature of pedagogy being bound to entertainment and we might want to add generated through affective reactions to reality television: 'it's nice to see them happy'. We think it is in the entertainment space of television that something other than reading messages is occurring which begins to undermine any overly straightforward account of governmentality.

Intimacy and affective actualizations: 'looking through'

As we have been keen to point out through our methodology, there are often numerous disparities between what viewers say in their interviews, the focus groups and the text-in-action session. Even viewers angry about being told what to do on reality television in the focus group, often admit to taking great pleasure from the same programmes in their interviews. Recall Ann in Chapter 4, whose articulation of distaste for the genre is complicated by the pleasure of the experience, and the pleasure of expressing distaste. Both Grossberg (1997), talking generally of 1990s postmodernity, and Gorton (2009) referencing recent developments in reality television, point to ambiguities in knowing that something is a bad object but taking curious pleasure in its affect. This contradictory response generated a great deal of attention from feminist media analysts throughout the 1990s and is exemplified in some developments in cultural studies, such as Brunsdon (1991). Such ambiguities opened up by television's affective register might seem to confirm the idea that reality television only calls us to engage as individuals – and individuals that are constantly changing. But to understand this we need to look closer at how the process of affect works socially in our reactions to reality television

As we have discussed, current writings on reality television argue that the form relies on a particular 'actuality' – a relationship to the real, which is played out in time and space in which the viewer feels moved by their proximity to the text (Kavka 2008; Hill 2007). In other audience studies much has been made of the audience's need to look for moments of 'genuine' emotion in television participants' performances (Hill 2005; Jones 2003). Those findings exist in our work too and therefore we will not rehearse those similarities here, although detecting the reactions of 'inauthenticity' were certainly a pleasure of the viewing encounter. Rather here we want to draw attention to the workings of proximity in audience relations with reality television in order to complicate some of the existing assumptions about the relationships between 'closeness' and 'feeling'.

First, let us demonstrate how our research respondent's awareness of reality television viewing is experienced as emotional 'presentness' in the interviews. For instance Sabeen talks about the revelation moment of the new house in *Extreme Makeover: Home Edition*:

> So in front of your eyes you're going to see it because before, the house it was like this, and they're doing it, just you know building it and doing it. And afterwards they're going to show how the family reacts, *you start crying as well sometimes … they were so real like you start crying oh my God* – She sacrificed all through the life and now she gains a home like that with her children.
>
> (Sabeen, Clapham, interview)

In another interview Ruby 1 shows how she shares in the emotional journey of *Wife Swap*, not just in terms of women participants, but also with all of the characters:

> Yes, 'cos I think sometimes you've got to go through all that anger and fighting and shouting and screaming at each other to, unfortunately you know you've got to go through it to find out the answer to solve the problem, it's part of the process. And yes we'd all love to be able to sit around a table and make notes and say well I disagree with this, and I just think OK I'm going to change but life ain't like that. You do have to scream and shout sometimes to be heard you know it's an invasion in your life, you know it's their home and someone's coming in, you know and saying right I'm going to change it. Well of course they scream and shout and there are tears and you know swearing and kids slamming doors and wives slamming doors and people saying they're going to walk out on it. But I think there's only one programme that I watched that there wasn't a proper conclusion, they had to stop filming or something, but they always come to the end, you know they sit round a table and its been a really emotional experience and *I really feel that, I feel that anger sometimes, and I feel that sadness … So I think I personally go through that journey with most people on the Wife Swap, not just the wives, but the husbands and the children, I go through-the family yeah.*
>
> (Ruby 1, Brockley, interview)

As we have previously discussed feminist audience research scholars argue for undoing the kind of the division in which emotion and sentiment is detached from critical engagement (Abu-Lughod 2005; Ang 1990; Mankekar 1999). For instance, Berlant (2008) details how women's culture has *always* been produced through the domain of affect and the expression of feelings. The distinction between the rational and the affective is resonant in previous discussions of documentary where emotional excess in factual television is associated directly with a lack of engagement with 'political' issues (Nichols 1991). Feminist re-appraisals of such distinctions between masculine rationality and feminine emotionality lead us like others to make a more sustained attempt at a politicized emotional analysis, asking what do affects *do*?

Applying a more critical analysis of affect to television audience research is of course not straightforward. The messy nature of feelings and their necessarily lack of attention to senses of cognitive order make them difficult to pin down in relation to the traditional sense of 'meaning' and 'interpretation' on which media studies often depend. Grossberg (1997) pointed out that much television does not operate at the level of the representational, but instead as style, making it resistant to traditional modes of ideological interpretation, operating through disconnection as an apparatus of indifference. Grossberg was addressing a particular 'postmodern' historical conjuncture of the late 80s and early 90s where emphasis on style and surface was considered to be the dominant aesthetic. We want to use his argument to suggest that we are now in a period of intimate intensity, not indifference, in which connection is incited and produced, not primarily through aesthetic drivers (as was postmodernism) but through a capitalist drive towards intimacy as a new way of extracting value in the political economy of television (and its multi-platform extensions).

Kavka (2008) for instance, suggests it is incitement to difference that pushes us to think further about how emotional excess creates attachments that 'matter' in which the viewer is called to share in the situation: 'I've been there' and 'this matters'. Reality television's call to emotional investment may undermine traditional structures of representation and forms of subject positioning usually determined by processes of signification. Recall the debates in Chapter 1 about how reality television operates more at the level of intervention and evocation rather than representation. For Kavka the viewer is not asked to consider the terms of representation 'this *is* a gay man' but rather 'this is *a* gay man' amongst the cacophony of other visible identity categorizations across television space. Thus the viewer is recurrently spoken to as an individual in an endlessly individuating experience, reflecting the broader transformation of intimacy in the public sphere (as we discussed in Chapter 2) and is, according to Kavka (2008), attached to public space through a series of 'nested boxes' rather than as a member of any particular group or minority.

For the time being, let us follow through this line of thinking in our audience research. Our methodology – through analysis of the affective textual encounter – enables us to see the process of affective connection at work. The following extract is taken from a text-in-action session with Liselle (from our Forest Hill middle class group) whilst watching an episode of *Wife Swap*. It shows how even when the reality television participants are viewed as a source of shock, disgust and humour to our viewer, clearly presented as extremely dysfunctional and politically racist, Liselle is able to '*look through*' the symbolic representation of the person to analyse and evaluate the relationship on display. In this instance, the television participants, David and Dee are an obese, white working class couple that constantly swear loudly, whose children behave badly, who express their aversion to mixed race marriages and are frequently pictured eating large amounts of junk food. They are swapped with a healthy, fit, semi-respectable black family, Lance and Sonia.[1] Yet when Liselle gets over her shock of their initial presentation she finds something endearing in their relationship:

Table 5.1

	Cue/Image	Television Text Wife Swap (Sonia and Dee)	Viewer comments Liselle (Forest Hill)
1 2 3	05:31 Images of hugging	**Voice over:** After 18 years of marriage roles in the Jackson household are equally well defined...	Liselle: Aaah. [laughs]
4 5 6	05:46	**David to camera:** She definitely wears the trousers, so to speak but I'm happy with that.	Aaah.
7 8 9 10	05:59 Images of David washing Dee's back	**David:** I wouldn't change her for the world.	Aaah.
11 12 13 14 15 16	06:12 Edited over close-ups on Dee's body as she gets out of bath	**David:** I haven't got a six pack, a six pack stomach maybe, but she took me as I was and I took her as she was. ... we're both quite big people and we're quite happy with each other	Aaah, oh my God. [laughs]
17 18 19	06:29	**Dee (to camera):** When I go to the new house I'm hoping that the guys is like David, bubbly like David.	
20 21 22 23 24 25 26	6.47 Edited over images of the fat couple eating large plates of food.	**Sonia as voice over and to camera:** I mean if he's a real slob that sits in a chair and wears a vest	Oh my goodness. What a picture, that is phenomenal. That is a performance. That is amazing That is two fat people with a huge amount of food [laughs] Oh my God.
27 28 29 30	8.11 Images of wives on car journeys to the swap	**Voice over:** It is the day of the swap. The couples hope that the swapping...	I think what is nice about it is that... yeah we can laugh at them, but there is actually...there is something *very genuine* between them

Table 5.1 (continued)

	Cue/Image	Television Text Wife Swap (Sonia and Dee)	Viewer comments Liselle (Forest Hill)
31	9.08	**Dee to camera:** This worst thing is if	
32		he's black. I will have a big problem I'm	
33		sorry to say.	Did she say if they are black I will have
34			a big problem?!
35	9.15	**Dee to camera:** I am not against coloured	
36		people far from it	Oh my God.
37		...but I don't believe in black and white	
38	9.23	together	Aaagh.
39			

Liselle moves in and out of different positions, first attributing value to the relationship even though everything about the couple has been negatively symbolically coded, and then displaying shock at the racism expressed on the programme. She challenges the bad language and rudeness of the older daughter towards the father and is critical of the manipulation of the swapped wife and of the programme format itself, whilst reading the husband/father's attempt to wield family power as a product of manipulation:

Table 5.2

	Cue/Image	Television Text Wife Swap (Sonia and Dee)	Viewer comments Liselle (Forest Hill)
1	49:35	**David:** I've had enough of Mary's	
2	Final	[daughter's] language. I told you long	
3	confrontation	before Christmas I have had enough of	
4	around a table	Mary's language. I want something to be	Mmm.
5		done about it...	
6	50:00	**David to Dee:** Things have to change	Ohhhhh!
7		round here!	
8	50:12		Jesus Christ! He has been
9			manipulated so much by her [Sonia].
10	50:22	**David:** I am asking you [to wife] to	Wow.
11		support me and back me that's something	
12		you won't do ...	
13		**Dee:** I'm not going to back you I'm going	
14		to get rid of you!	
15	50:42	**David:** If you want to chuck 18 years	
16		down the Swannee then go for it.	Wow.
17			
18			They were so together at the
19			beginning. Look at how together they
20			were.
21			Oh my God.
22			Oh God.

Liselle sees how the apparatus of the television 'set-up' provoked the destruction of David and Dee's relationship and is genuinely disturbed by what participation on the television programme has done. Before condemning the family, which seems likely due to the way in which they have been represented, she (through the viewing *process*) reaches for a point of connection by evoking memories of her similar experiences and considering herself within a similar social dynamic:

> But then again if I look at my family going 'bloody hell' that is the other thing, you can relate to it as well because I remember things like that you know, you know … I mean I can really relate to the girl who was manipulated by the black woman, because you just want to please the adults.
>
> (Liselle, Forest Hill, Text in Action)

To understand different types of attention, reaction and how we make connections to visual forms Vivian Sobchack (1999) suggests we look to the work of Belgian psychologist, Jean-Pierre Meunier. He describes how different types of attention are generated from different types of images, suggesting that some images are experienced as directly given to us, existing not 'elsewhere' which is usually suggested of film, but instead 'here' in the virtual world that is right 'there' before us. For Meunier, the intentional objective of documentary consciousness is comprehension, not evocation, whereas as Brunsdon (2003) suggested in Chapter 1 lifestyle television draws upon evocation.

We refer to examples like Liselle's above as instances of evocation, where viewers conjure a 'presence' in the text, in what Sobchack identifies as 'constitutive actualisations'. This phrase comes from her further discussion of the distinction between watching documentary and home videos. Documentary consciousness requires cognition, comprehension and learning, whereas home video requires the viewer to look through image via the experiential evocation of memory. In this process the images on the screen come to mean so much more than their object, they activate the viewer's sense of their relationships (constitutive) in the present (actuality), 'as if' they are intimately connected. We argue that reality television occupies a curious space between documentary and family video and that its particular verisimilitude and construction of intimacy and immediacy generates recognition in viewers beyond that available in traditional documentary forms.

Liselle 'sees through' the negative images of the couple and the manipulative elements of the programme format to contextualize and make the connections to her life, which is radically different in terms of class background.[2] In this instance it is the verisimilitude of the unfolding relationships (mother, father, daughter, wife, husband) that generates the type of *connections* she has to 'reality' television. Liselle is alert to how the different couples have been stereotypically valued and positioned and even repeats the positioning, but rather than judging and legitimating the stereotype, she instead judges the quality of the relationships. Liselle evokes a 'presence' in the text which is achieved through the structure of immanence made available through the drama of reality television.

How do we view Liselle's complex reach for understanding through making a situational comparison with herself? We argue that it is the verisimilitude of the performance of the intimate family relationships that enables a form of mimesis (a copy of the copy) to take place. The mimesis produces an emotional resonance based upon what Michael Taussig (1993) calls 'perspectival spectrality', the perspective we bring from our own experience to draw on that in front of our eyes in order to absorb and attribute the feeling of the relationship to ourselves. We have mostly at some time been shamed, humiliated, cared for and loved. We recognize the feelings played out in front of our eyes and this may be more powerful than all the negative symbolic loading which is placed on the characterization of the television participants. Traditional film analysis argues that visual representation reproduces a virtual space marked by 'proximity without presence' (Fleisch 1987), yet the very similarity of the emotions played out in front of our eyes to those we have experienced enable Liselle to make an actualization of resonance which is both proximate *and* present. We can see the potential such moments of connection, of affective actualization, have for aligning different people with each other if Liselle turned this connection into a political rather than personal understanding of her experience, broadening her perspective into one of power and injustice.

In many ways examples like these fit neatly with Kavka's (2008) 'theory of mattering' where reactions operate not at the level of signification, but of significance. Using Theresa Brennen's (2004) theory of affect we can see how feeling moves in ways that could otherwise be blocked by representation. In terms of a theory of ideology affective reactions cannot have any determined effect, the outcome is always uncertain and therefore any straightforward ideological process becomes uncertain and the text becomes open to a series of individuated responses:

> As a genre whose appeal is grounded in affect, reality TV cannot account in advance for the inter/personal alignment, discernments and knowledges that may arise amongst participants and/or viewers, whatever the producers' or editors intentions.
>
> (Kavka 2008:133)

Reminding us of the discussion in Chapter 1, it is the unknown quality of liveness that makes reality television an 'open ideological form' or in Kavka's more provocative analysis, a 'queer' form which 'jams the cognitive frequencies with tears and noise'. Yet before we get too wild with the positive political potential of reality television we are reminded of our previous research on queer television (Skeggs *et al.* 2004) which demonstrated that it was precisely the affective resonances portrayed such as taunting, bullying, shaming, rejection and fantasies of community, revenge, belonging and love that shaped the past, present and future investments in making connections to the narratives and characters. Ideology was produced through affective actualizations that trigger a re-living of a previous experience, which are then re-coded into narrative fantasies which re-align into the capacity to act (as opposed to the prior experience of the incapacity to act). We explain this further below.

Individualized and duped?

In following these accounts of affect and television, the mobilization of affect can work against what might be presumed to be a more 'dominant' representational meaning in the text that reveals symbolic violence or pedagogic instructions in governmentality. Possibilities are opened up both within the text, but also within audiences' mobilization of affect. Meaning and mattering are not the same and this sidelines questions of ideology, as Kavka so eloquently puts it, 'reality television is not the handmaiden of the status quo' (2008:3). *Affects* are pre-linguistic bodily experiences that are produced through the social encounter: they only have the potential for emotion, they are feelings that are yet to be coded. *Emotions* are the linguistic expression of the affect, they are as Seigworth and Gregg (2010) describe at the beginning of this chapter, intensities and resonances produced through the social encounter. Therefore affects and emotions are not necessarily aligned: the relationship between the two is dependent upon their orientation to any particular object. We all have feelings but we may do very different things with them, or they may do very different things to us. To remain with Kavka's reading therefore this suggests that the object potential of affect is either not that interesting, or relatively uncertain, existing as it does, only in television's constantly shifting immediate present.

In Lynne Joyrich's (1991) critique of Grossberg's position, she is suspicious of the potential to separate out television's affective mechanisms from its ideological imperatives, noting the cultural analysis which has feminized the debates about the emotional as part of the problem (remember Nichols?). For Grossberg (1997) the affective economy of reality television sets free a mobile subject able to choose his identifications and invest emotions however he wishes – because affect has no grounding it also has no limitations. However, Joyrich asks us to consider these changed relations of subject and affect as *the* ideology of advanced capitalism: 'Rather, the dispersal of affect and positions of identification may itself be seen as ideological, cut to the demands of the power divisions and hierarchies that define today's society' (1991:32).

In a later clarification of his position Grossberg maintains that he is indeed describing a very particular political conjuncture – postmodernism – when the dominant media aesthetic was style 'you cannot separate out the structure of feeling from the conjuncture. Because what makes the current conjuncture *exactly what it is* are the affective articulations amongst various overdeterminations' (2010b:327, emphasis in original). Although Grossberg's argument is based on a plea for greater context to theories of affect, with which we agree, we also want to offer a caveat about making assumptions about the mapping of particular affective cultural moods onto lived experiences in a similar vein to our criticism of the assumptions made of the workings of governance. Berlant (2006) warns of the current 'turn to affect' noting that shifts in affect cannot necessarily be correlated with changing worlds in any way. Just as Probyn (2004) maintains we need to be very specific about how different affects make us feel, think and act in different ways which requires a good deal of empirical evidence.

Here we want to look more closely at the *forms* immediacy takes in reality television viewing. It is the object-potential of any affect that concerns us – how do emotional reactions become oriented to any broader set of social relations? Or in Spinoza's terms, how do affects become connected to ideas. As we began to demonstrate in Chapter 4, affect was often speedily connected to passing moral judgement. Perhaps part of the answer as to how to interpret the evocation of the personal might lie in a more sustained interrogation of the terms of ambiguity suggested here. The availability of more than one position in the text is suggestive of the ability to cut the cloth to suit in doing the work of personalization (whether one reads that as an ideological or queer pursuit or not). But we want to draw attention to the idea that perhaps the ambiguities and the ability to *move* between positions tells us about the processes at work in the relationships between reality television and affect. Affective responses reveal the moments where our respondents are virtually subject to judgement: the programme positions them 'as if' they are the television participants. Both are participants and respondents are positioned by and respond to the regimes of value and the judgements they entail about investments, value and personhood. Teresa Brennan (2004) maintains that judgement is critical to making affects matter to the person: it is in the projection or introjection of a judgement that the moment of transmission of affect to the person takes place. We might consider reality television to be a synoptic medium of multiple judgements that mirrors wider social relations. However, like the potential for refraction offered by the mirror, this is not a straightforward process.

Ambivalence refers to a form of double coding and being of two minds about something that suggests that there is some space in between. We know that our audiences with their different types, compositions and volumes of value, attempt to accrue and defend their own value as well as disperse value relationally. E-motion itself refers to the process of being 'moved' – from one state (affect) to another (codification) and in our research we want to draw attention to the *processes and circuits* in which our audience is located, in order to understand the conditions of possibility for their reactions, for what they can *do* with the affect triggered by judgement on television.

Interrogating ambiguity: 'It's just sad'

Taking one emotion, 'sadness', and looking for its expression across all types of our empirical data was revealing. In semantics the word 'sad' has two meanings:

the first refers to an act of sorrow, to be mournful or causing sorrow, and the second is a derogatory slight, 'shocking, deplorably bad, incorrigible' (Oxford English Dictionary). Thus the first meaning refers to an emotion, 'feeling sad', and the second refers to a particular action, to 'judge' another as sad. We were drawn to this term by its repetition across our data. The most common way that it was used refers to an emotional and empathetic positioning with the participants on reality television. For example when Kathy is talking about the programme *Little Angels*, in which a child psychologist helps parents to cope with their children, she can see how much easier it is for couples to parent in partnership which makes her empathize with the single parents:

> ... Looking how hard it is as parents looking after children and you see a lot of single parents who have to do both of these roles which is really (?) sad you know ...
>
> (Kathy, Brockley, interview talking about *Little Angels*)

There also are many examples from our text-in-action sessions where viewers identified moments that were 'sad' and moved them to feel sad. When Vicky and Mel were watching *Wife Swap* they empathize with the woman who only has one child and then swaps her domestic situation for looking after six unruly children. During a scene where she was getting distraught at trying to control the children, they say:

VICKY: Not used to it is she
MEL: No, she's not
VICKY: Sad, and sad that she's not seen her little girl
MEL: Yeah
VICKY: Especially as she's been seeing her [the other wife's] kids all day
(Vicky and Mel, Addington, Text in Action)

Often, however, the use of the term 'sad' refers to the second meaning, a judgement made about those on reality television. For instance, Joan refers to the early contestants who audition for *The X Factor* as 'sad cases'. Or when Lucy talks about not liking the programmes that follow British package holidays, as in the programme *Club Reps* she says:

> 'Cos its sad [laughs] well it's all the-how young English people behave abroad. It's sad and it depresses me. You know it's like watching those police camera ones, those police camera ones and boozy Britain and all that.
>
> (Lucy, Forest Hill, interview)

But often, a distinction between empathy and a moral judgement is not so clear. Similarly in a text-in-action session with *What Not to Wear* the respondents' conversation suggests a similar ambiguity in the meaning of 'sad'. At the point in the programme where the experts, Trinny and Susannah, have thrown away all of the clothes in the participant (Michalena's) wardrobe, they become shocked by the way she isn't taking it seriously enough:

> All the clothes gone!
> How can she be laughing?
> How sad is that?
> Her problem is that she has no self-esteem.
>
> (Razia, Sabeen and Sheeba, Clapham, Text in Action)

The women, not surprisingly given the way Michalena is pathologized by the programme, are making a judgement about her lack of recognition of just how bad her wardrobe is, followed by a more empathetic position, whereby they suggest that this might be related to a lack of self-esteem. The phrase 'How sad is that?' seems to occupy both positions simultaneously. This discursive movement is common and returns in the focus groups, for example:

> I don't know it depends if you-you can see some programmes and you feel for the person and you think, 'ah you know you need help, sort yourself out' but in other ones you just think 'you're sad – get a life'.
>
> (Sarah, Brockley, focus group)

What we can see here is that the intimate incitement to feel empathy, the route to connection, is intricately bound up with evaluations of worth and value. It is often not necessarily a case of *either* care for participants *or* the moral judgement of them, but that viewers move in and out of care for participants, even often occupying both modes simultaneously.

Recall our discussion in Chapter 2 about the contemporary drive to constant emotional management via the rise of therapy culture which unites the intimate sphere with moral rules, etiquette, and the models for mating – the terms of relationships and intimate engagement (Berlant 1997; Illouz 1997; White 1992). And as we develop in Chapter 7 the focus upon the self-work ethic and the emotional management of the micro-politics of the performance of everyday life on reality television nourishes the developing needs of commodification, opening out new markets for capital and new forms of governmentality. Therefore, we argue that through a history of gendered emotional labour, women are positioned more immanently to the immediate concerns of reality television, and just like the traditional arguments about soap operas, women's cultural competences are at the centre of drama.

The focus of such arguments about emotional management is about how calculative techniques encroach into intimate worlds extending the historical process of the organization of femininity for both commodification (fashioning the aesthetic female body, servicing the family) and governance (disciplining the family). As Hochschild's (1983) research on female flight attendants' showed, the commercialization of intimacy produced different models for emotional well-being with women ideologically positioned differently to men as potential suppliers of care and empathy; affects designated as supposedly natural to women. Remember Thompson's (1996) model of the spheres of interest and influence accorded to femininity (affect) and masculinity (calculative rationality) in the 1800s and its ideological naturalization. Thus the emotional labour of gender is usually hidden and often fetishized.

However, the spectacular visualization of the labour is no longer hidden but made explicit and subject to performance management. Hochschild argues that as the emotional world has been opened out into public life it 'opens the family home to a larger world of feeling rules' (Hochschild: 1983:160). The larger world of feeling rules in this instance is characterized by a television genre in which we are called to make attachments and respond to the constant evocation of feeling. Every intimate practice is subject to the codification of value.

Lucy goes on to suggest when she talks about the make-over programmes *What Not to Wear* and *10 Years Younger:*

> Yeah 'cos at least if it's American, I can go 'oh well they're American', but if it's set here, it's like oh no I don't, you know 'cos that's quite sad ... it's taking people who are sad with their lives, sad with how they look and I know they have to diet and they have to exercise and stuff, but surgically making them look better so that their friends and family suddenly love them. It's like how sad is that, it's just like it's quite sad, I find it quite cringey.
>
> (Lucy, Forest Hill, interview)

The empathy that Lucy articulates about those who are 'sad with their lives' is inextricably tied to what might be seen as the impossibility of a make-over to suddenly make people love them, and thus the 'sad' depthlessness of the TV genre. Similarly when Liselle is watching *Wife Swap*, she moves swiftly from suggesting that a particularly emotional moment 'is very sad' to feeling uncomfortable with the invasion into intimate domestic lives on the programme 'I think it is very sad ... I think the whole thing is voyeuristic'. Empathy, judgement of others, and a critique of the televisual intervention into these intimacies, are interwoven in the women's discussions.

Therefore the response of 'it's just sad' is vitally connected to the regimes of value associated with the mediation of intimacy *and* with the genre itself. As Holmes and Jermyn (2004) point out, and we mentioned in Chapter 1, the broader debates about 'cultural value' which surround these programmes are often shaped by notions of 'quality' which are themselves couched in distinctions premised on gender and class. It is clear from our discussions that the cultural value attached to reality television reverberates through the emotional management at work and the critical distancing done by our middle class view-ers. Therefore when women are called to recognize the emotional labour involved in the pleasures of watching reality television, they must also recognize themselves as flawed. 'Putting the "me" into seeing "you"', as Hochschild (1983) describes it, is therefore an uncomfortable process as the women are located in the same circuits of labour and evaluation as the television participants. In watching reality television and empathizing with those on television, the women ultimately also recognize themselves as 'sad'. For example when Sally from Brockley talks about the programme *Ladette to Lady*, it is couched in the broader recognition that 'ain't I sad cause I've watched every one of them'.

In terms of the emotional labour at work here the women in our study are moving between immediate affective reactions related to their sympathy/empathy with those that they are seeing on television, whilst also making moral and ethi-cal decisions provoked by the genre in order to make cognitive judgements of those that they see. Both of these moves operate within the broader frameworks of cultural value in which the genre is a devalued and denigrated form of pop-ular culture, resonant of women's culture more generally (Van Zoonen 1994). In doing so they put themselves in the picture which connects to an understanding of their investments and their own (perhaps sometimes painful) position in the regimes of rational and relational value.

Reality television's call to perform emotional management invites women in particular to process a set of ambivalent investments in relation to care, moral judgement, aesthetics, intimacy and a denigrated genre that can be located as an extension of a longer history of gendered instruction than available entirely through the neo-liberal thesis of governmentality. For the governmentality thesis to operate unproblematically there would not be such disjuncture between affect and cognized articulation. Recall Liselle's constitutive actualization that mobi-lized an affective reach beyond the ideological coding of the text to 'connect' with reality television's participants. Rather, we argue that these very dis-junctures, ambiguities and complexities *reveal* the various investments made by women in the making of gender.

Ambiguities we think are closely tied to the text's intensities. In Molly Haskell's (1974) discussion of female over-identification with the image in relation to other feminine genres which rely on melodrama, like the soap opera and the women's picture, the female spectator is incited to feel the experience of her own sacrifices made in marriage. The body is so close and so excessive that the 'tears and wet wasted afternoons' of watching women's films involve a level of masochism. Women return again and again to the stories that make them cry, feel sad, or recognize their own limitations and take pleasure in that repetitious cycle (Gorton 2009). We might see Sally's *'ain't I sad because I've watched everyone of them'* in a similar vein, since we see how closely the terms of the reality television drama are tied the women's own personal investments involving some level of personal risk and time wasted, at the same time as pleasure, rather than operating at a level of safe critical distance.

Their movement between positions displays the women's ambivalent relationships with reality television as they navigate their own personal intimate terrain within broader discursive narratives of value which demand judgement. Like Gray (1992) and Seiter's (1990) audience research our respondent's sought to legitimate their responses. Where the middle class women of the Forest Hill group pressed upon us their knowledge of cultural taste and their ironic relationship to the medium, our working class respondents, like Sally, devalue their engagement in the telling. They all reveal ambivalence but account for it in different ways, and we explore the processes of legitimation in the next chapter. As feminist theorists such as Emily Martin (1989) have demonstrated in relation to gender, post-colonial theorists such as Homi Bhabha (1994) in relation to race, and queer theorists in relation to sexuality (Halperin 2003), *ambiguity* signals intensities and is key to the making and reproduction of all structured inequalities.[3]

Conclusion

In this chapter through our empirical audience research we have complicated the theories of governmentality that have dominated textual analyses of reality television. We show how even those who present themselves as apparently most subject to the pedagogic elements of reality television, do so through a complex mode of articulation related to the process of migration. They do not just internalize the lessons and become the good subject/citizen/individual, but bring their lives into play and assess the 'teaching' accordingly. This process suggests a temporality of relating back through prior investments rather than learning for the future. Pedagogical imperatives in the programmes for other viewers produce pleasures through television participant's resistance to experts or through narrative or formula recognition, or a recalcitrant rejection of 'advice' – not necessarily bearing any connection to the neo-liberal 'moral of the story'.

We also found many examples of affective 'reach', like the example from Liselle, where our respondents express care for television participants as they are bound up in the same web of emotions that often take them beyond (or around) the symbolic loading of representation. However, it is not enough to leave it there and assume that affects play no part in the social. Our data reveals, through the particular stages of the methodology, that viewers constantly move between positions, between and within the different research methods, and from affective states to cognitive states. It is therefore not so much the consistencies that interest us, but the inconsistencies, the contradictions exposed by the affective reactions that generate unpredictable responses which require explanation beyond individualization, psychology and governmentality. When we look closer at these ambiguities we can see how they are tied to histories of migration, race, gender and class, such as the performance of emotional labour which binds empathy with morality. Therefore whilst we cannot predict what affects will do, how people will feel (and we have certainly been surprised in our data by the consistent pursuit of care despite the symbolic violence of reality television texts), we might be able to predict what social factors come to bear upon viewer's struggles for value and certainty.

We can suggest how affect is connected to ideas and narratives and how these feed into and out of people's social position and their pre-dispositions to act. Our respondents come to the viewing encounter with substantive forms of investment and disinvestment in ways of being, their person-value, with their ontology shaped through their experience of social conditions. We know that as a result of this positioning and experience they are located in similar circuits of evaluation and judgement to the television participants (as well as the genre itself) and thus locate themselves through connection and disconnection to the experiences and narratives on display. We begin to suggest how ambiguities set in motion a search for security, for a way to channel contradictions, which we explore in our next chapter. Whilst in this chapter we have concentrated on how affective connections are made, how care is evoked and ambiguity experienced, in the next chapter we concentrate on how affect is made political in the struggle over judgements and the claims for moral authority and value.

Notes

1 We add the prefix 'semi' here because we are told that Vince, the husband, spends £50 per week on weed.
2 Liselle empirically identifies herself as 'middle class' through a discussion of her education, housing, family and aspirations.
3 See a fully developed debate in Skeggs (2004).

References

Abu-Lughod, L. 2005 *Dramas of Nationhood: The Politics of Television in Egypt*, Chicago and London: University of Chicago Press.

Ang, I. 1990 'Melodramatic Identifications: Television Fiction and Women's Fantasy', in M. E. Brown (ed.) *Television and Women's Culture: The Politics of the Popular*, London: Sage.

Berlant, L. 1997 *The Queen of America Goes to Washington City: Essays on Sex and Citizenship*, Durham and London: Duke University Press.

——2006 'Cruel Optimism', *Differences: A Journal of Feminist Cultural Studies* 17(3): 20–36.

——2008 *The Female Complaint: The Unfinished Business of Sentimentality in American Culture*, London and Durham: Duke University Press.

Bhabha, H. 1994 *The Location of Culture*, London: Routledge.

Brennan, T. 2004 *The Transmission of Affect*, Ithaca, NY: Cornell University Press.

Brunsdon, C. 1991 'Pedagogies of the Feminine: Feminist Teaching and Women's Genres', *Screen* 32(4): 364–82.

——2003 'Lifestyling Britain: The 8–9 Slot on British Television', *International Journal of Cultural Studies* 6(1): 5–23.

Deleuze, E. and Deleuze, J. 1978 'Giles Deleuze: Lecture Transcripts on Spinoza's Concept of *Affect*', Vol. 2006: http://www.webdeleuze.com/php/sommaire.html.

Eagleton, T. 1989 'The Ideology of the Aesthetic', in P. Hernadi (ed.) *The Rhetoric of Interpretation and the Interpretation of Rhetoric*, Durham and London: Duke University Press.

Fleisch, W. 1987 'Proximity and Power: Shakespearean and Cinematic Space', *Theatre Journal* 4: 277–93.

Gorton, K. 2009 *Media Audiences: Television, Meaning and Emotion*, Edinburgh: Edinburgh University Press.

Gray, A. 1992 *Video Playtime*, London: Routledge.

Grossberg, L. 1997 *Bringing it All Back Home*, Durham and London: Duke University Press.

——2010a *Cultural Studies in the Future Tense*, Durham and London: Duke University Press.

——2010b 'Interview with Larry Grossberg with Melissa Seigworth and Gregg', in M. Gregg and G. J. Seigworth (eds) *The Affect Theory Reader*, Durham and London: Duke University Press.

Halperin, D. 2003 'Monsters from the Id: Gay Sex, Psychoanalysis and the Inner Life of Male Homosexuality' *Sexuality after Foucault*, Conference, at Manchester University.

Haskell, M. 1974 *From Reverence to Rape: The Treatment of Women in the Movies*, New York: Holt Rinehart and Winston.

Heelas, P. 2002 'Work Ethics, Soft Capitalism and the "Turn to Life"', in P. du Gay and M. Pryke (eds) *Cultural Economy*, London: Sage.

Highmore, B. 2010 'Bitter after Taste: Affect, Food and Social Aesthetics', in M. Gregg and G. J. Seigworth (eds) *The Affect Theory Reader*, Durham and London: Duke University Press.

Hill, A. 2005 *Reality TV: Audiences and Popular Factual Television*, London: Routledge.

——2007 *Restyling Factual TV: Audiences and News, Documentary and Reality Genres*, London: Routledge.

Hochschild, A. 1983 *The Managed Heart: Commercialisation of Human Feeling*, Berkeley, CA: University of California Press.

Holmes, S. 2008 '"A Term Rather too General to be Helpful": Struggling with Genre in Reality TV', in L. Geraghty and M. Jancovich (eds) *The Shifting Definitions of Genre: Generic Cannons*: Jefferson, NC: McFarland.

Holmes, S. and Jermyn, D. (eds) 2004 *Understanding Reality Television*, London: Routledge.

Illouz, E. 1997 *Consuming the Romantic Utopia: Love and the Cultural Contradictions of Capitalism*, Berkeley and Los Angeles: University of California Press.

——2007 *Cold Intimacies: The Making of Emotional Capitalism*, Cambridge: Polity.

Jones, J. 2003 'Show Your Real Face', *New Media and Society* 5(3): 400–21.

Joyrich, L. 1991 'Going through the E/Motions: Gender, Postmodernism, and Affect in Television Studies', *Discourse* 14(1): 23–40.

Kavka, M. 2008 *Reality Television, Affect and Intimacy: Reality Matters*, London: Palgrave Macmillan.

Mankekar, P. 1999 *Screening Culture, Viewing Politics: An Ethnography of Television, Womanhood, and Nation in Postcolonial India*, Durham and London: Duke University Press.

Martin, E. 1989 *The Woman in the Body*, London: Routledge.

Morley, D. 2010 'Mediated Class-ifications: Representations of Class and Culture in Contemporary British Television', *European Journal of Cultural Studies* 12(4): 487–508.

Nichols, B. 1991 *Representing Reality: Issues and Concepts of Documentary*, Bloomington and Indianapolis: Indiana University Press.

——1994 *Blurred Boundaries: Questions of Meaning in Contemporary Culture*, Indianapolis: Indiana University Press.

Nunn, H. 2011 'Investing in the "Forever Home": From Property Programming to "Retreat TV"', in H. Wood and B. Skeggs (eds) *Reality Television and Class*, London: BFI/Palgrave.

Ouellette, L. and Hay, J. 2008 *Better Living Through Reality Television*, Oxford: Blackwell.

Probyn, E. 2004 'Shame in the Habitus' in L. Adkins and B. Skeggs (eds) *Feminism After Bourdieu*, Oxford: Blackwell.

Reay, D. 2000 'Children's Urban Landscapes: Configurations of Class and Place', in S. Munt (ed.) *Cultural Studies and the Working Class: Subject to Change*, London: Cassell.

Rose, N. 1989 *Governing the Soul: The Shaping of the Private Self*, London: Routledge.

Schlesinger, P., Dobash, R. and Dobash, R. 1992 *Women Viewing Violence Watching Televison: Screening Crimewatch*, London: BFI.

Seigworth, G. J. and Gregg, M. 2010 'An Inventory of Shimmers', in M. Gregg and G. J. Seigworth (eds) *The Affect Theory Reader*, Durham and London: Duke University Press.

Seiter, E. 1990 'Making Distinctions in TV Audience Research: a Case Study of a Troubling Interview', *Cultural Studies* 4(1): 61–85.

Sender, K. and Sullivan, M. 2008 'Epidemics of Will, Failures of Self-esteem: Responding to Fat Bodies in *The Biggest Loser* and *What not to Wear*', *Continuum: Journal of Media and Cultural Studies* 22(4): 573–85.

Skeggs, B. 1997 *Formations of Class and Gender: Becoming Respectable*, London: Sage.

——2004 'Introducing Pierre Bourdieu's Analysis of Class, Gender and Sexuality', in L. Adkins and B. Skeggs (eds) *Feminism After Bourdieu*, Oxford: Blackwell.

——2009 'Haunted by the Spectre of Judgement: Respectability, Value and Affect in Class Relations', in K. Sveinsson (ed.) *Who Cares about the White Working Class*, London: Runnymede Trust.

Skeggs, B., Moran, L., Tyrer, P. and Binnie, J. 2004 'Queer as Folk: Producing the Real of Urban Space', *Urban Studies* 41(9): 1839–56.

Sobchack, V. 1999 'Towards a Phenomenology of Nonfictional Film Experience', in J. Gaines and M. Renow (eds) *Collecting Visible Evidence*, Minneapolis, Minnesota: Minnesota University Press.

Taussig, M. 1993 *Mimesis and Alterity: A Particular History of the Senses*, London: Routledge.

Thoburn, N. 2007 'Patterns of Production: Cultural Studies after Hegemony', *Theory, Culture and Society* 24(79): 79–94.

Thompson, J. 1996 *Models of Value: Eighteenth Century Political Economy and the Novel*, Durham, NC: Duke University Press.

Van Zoonen, L. 1994 *Feminist Media Studies*, London: Sage.

Walkerdine, V. 2010 'Shame on you! Intergenerational trauma and working-class femininity on reality television', in H. Wood and B. Skeggs (eds) *Reality Television and Class*, London: BFI/Palgrave.

Walkerdine, V. and Lucey, H. 1989 *Democracy in the Kitchen: Regulating Mothers and Socialising Daughters*, London: Virago.

——2001 *Growing up Girl: Psychosocial Explorations of Gender and Class*, London: Palgrave.

White, M. 1992 *Tele-Advising: Therapeutic Discourse In American Television*, Chapel Hill and London: University of North Carolina Press.

Chapter 6

From affect to authority

The making of the moral person

Recent interest in affect emerges from understanding its role in political formation: what affect does and what it makes people do. But also from an interest in a return to the social rather than a focus on the individual (see for instance Ahmed 2004 and Blackman and Venn 2010). In the last chapter we discussed the way affect has been inserted into an understanding of the politics of the encounter, of our capacity to act and do (or not) things. One of the key points made by Spinoza (Deleuze and Deleuze 1978) is how negative affect leads to a diminished capacity to act and the incapacity to act develops cumulatively over time and space. But also as we detailed in the last chapter, affect must always be connected to ideas for it to matter, or be effective. Hence we think it is important to think about how the affective incitements offered by reality television connect to ideas about a person's value and their social location.

Disgust is probably the most obvious example of how the incitement of an affect 'ugh, gross' is converted to an idea such as 'it's disgusting' which is then connected to groups of people 'they're disgusting', generating public consensus for social contempt, as ideas about disgust are learnt and repeated over time (Probyn 2004). Lawler (2005) for instance, shows how disgust shapes class relations and is an essential element in the making of middle class identities. This is why Ahmed (2004) speaks of an affective economy: feelings are distributed, but not in disparate ways, they are organized socially. She maintains that in affective economies, affects *do things*; importantly (for us) they align individuals with communities (or bodily space with social space) – or not – through the very intensity of their attachments.

As we began to demonstrate in Chapter 4, it was the reality programmes' incitement to judgement, often through the long held close-up, that provoked affective responses that were turned into forms of moral assessment of a person's value. We discussed the regularity with which our groups produced affective responses at the same moments in the text, but these generated very different judgements depending on the form of the connection and the way the connection was threaded back into their own life narratives and value positions. We use this frame to shift attention from the assumptions about the singular self-disciplining subject of some reality television analyses to an approach which addresses social circuits of value, to enable us to understand how people are positioned, pre-dispositioned, enabled or limited to make investments in their lives and the lives of others. These circuits of value establish the conditions for, and understandings of, the performances of personhood induced by reality television.

Thus, in this chapter we define the responses of our viewers as *acts* in which they *perform* the increasing mediation of experience whereby public understandings of distinction, disgust and social in/difference are repeatedly produced. We think that the 'as if' forms of connection induced by reality television, 'as if part of people's lives' enables us to explore wider social relationships. 'As if' has a doubling function: it works both 'as if' registering taking part in the mediated interaction, and 'as if' as in performing dissimulation – opening up the ambiguities of performing the relationships to television as if authority is accepted whereas in fact authority is challenged. In the previous chapter we pointed to the ambiguous reactions to the pedagogic imposition of 'advice' and we explored how similar ambiguities around 'it's just sad' reminded us of the longer and complicated histories of the classed and gendered politics of the different spheres and regimes of value.

Here we want to explore how ambiguity is converted through claims for value and authority. We explore how reality television incites affective connections that generate very differently resourced reactions: ranging from *schadenfreude*, to assertions of taste and cultural difference, to attempts to occupy the moral high ground by legitimating the life-choice of full-time motherhood. All these reactions reveal how what is provoked by reality television flows through wider circuits of value, revealed through the viewers' defence of their own personal investments.

Converting affect and ambiguity: *schadenfreude*

Let us return to our discussion in Chapter 3 about how contemporary class relations get configured in reality narratives of self-transformation. First, we argued that in removing a sense of history by calling television participants to act in the moment, programmes dislocate people from the histories of their making and the conditions of possibility that they inhabit. But we noted how the verisimilitude and liveness of the programmes locates viewers 'as if' they were in the setting and relationships of the television programme: dislocated from social conditions but located within the relationships of the programme. We then argued that processes of individualization are located *in* class structures, structures that establish the forms and types of resources (capitals) that people can call on to authorize themselves with value. We detailed how authorising oneself was now considered to be a social necessity with the decline of traditional forms of authority such as the state and the church. However we noted how ideas about the good self and the proper person were premised upon people having specific compositions and types of culture and also how these forms of culture had to be displayed properly, such as the contemplative rationalized telling of the reflexive self. We analysed how different TV formats enable or make it im/possible for participants to authorize themselves. For instance, when mothers on *Supernanny* are subject to the 'judgement shot', they have to immediately account for their own and their child's behaviour. We then demonstrated how access to what is considered (in the dominant symbolic economy) to be complete and rounded architectures of the self are based on one's access to material and cultural resources. As we have maintained throughout this book individualization is not the undoing of class relations (as some have argued); rather, it is the reconfiguring of class relations via the language of selfhood. These are the newer discursive formations of class that deny not just the social and material conditions that constitute the person, but also eclipse the very techniques by which the person is able to make themselves from their positioning and resources. We now want to unpack – rather than hide – the mechanisms by which class is made through affective conversions in our audience responses.

In the last chapter we pointed to how ambiguity generates uncertainty and our data reveals many attempts to assuage insecurity through the production of certainty. In this section we explore the workings of *schadenfreude* before going on to explore how people use a variety of techniques to establish and stabilize their own authority. *Schadenfreude* – delight in another's misfortune – the condition which enables viewers to take pleasure in the difficulties others face, has been one of the most criticized aspects of the reality television genre and grounds the various claims about the genre's moral bankruptcy. It appeared with regularity in our research and our research respondents often reflected on their awareness of this process:

> Sort of revelling a bit in other people's, you know, not misfortune, but sort of kind of makes you think, well actually my kids aren't so bad.
>
> (Orlaine, Forest Hill, interview talking about *Supernanny*)

> Just to see because you think yours is the only hardest life, sometimes you think 'Oh my God', maybe I've got four children, it's killing me, you know, oh God I'm, rushing and doing things. But when you see others you think 'oh no my life isn't so bad as well' … so you can compare your life sometimes.
>
> (Lily, Clapham, interview talking about *Wife Swap*)

But what do reactions of *schadenfreude* reveal? Do we all like to feel better about our own lives in equal measure regardless of our personal histories? If *schadenfreude* is a powerful affect does it make us do anything? Steve Cross and Jo Littler (2010) interrogate the function of *schadenfreude*, suggesting it is a *zeitgeist* affect, one that tells us a lot about the contemporary political conjuncture, offering a political economy of the psyche (Deleuze and Guattari 1983). They move away from a more abstract notion of *schadenfreude* as an ahistorical or universal feature of the 'human condition' into considering it as a more trans-individual affective process of resentment. They maintain that *schadenfreude* represents a negative capacity in socially affective relations, one that desires equality, but is primarily unable to think of it as anything other than levelling through humiliation. It is certainly a revelation about one's position in regimes of value. But *schadenfreude* is also a claim for authority, for certainty, for knowing what is right and proper. We detail how it works through a range of different modalities.

Many of the women's comments refer to the incompetence, stupidity and inability of people to be able to do and handle aspects of lives, and are often preceded by the affective gasps and 'Oh my God' statements. Examples include: 'I look at the mess they've got themselves into and think "there but for the grace of God"' (Joan, Addington, interview); 'You just wonder where people are in their head sometimes, they just don't seem to know what they're doing' (Ruby 1, Brockley, interview), and 'I can't believe they did that, unbelievable, can't they see what they are doing?' (Sharon, Addington, interview). In these statements an assessment of what is required is made through comparison and evaluation. This might be thought of as '*in-between*' affect and emotions, what Sianne Ngai (2005) calls the mediations between the aesthetic and the political that act as knotted or condensed 'interpretations of predicaments' that are brought into place by affective responses. What statements of *schadenfreude do* is reveal both the attribution of value to self and others in the need for certainty, for the closure of ambiguity. They reveal the intensities that pass from body to body. Ngai calls these 'ugly feelings' which are canonically minor (as opposed to the high drama of hatred and passion), arguing that 'the unsuitability of these weakly intentional feelings for forceful or unambiguous action is precisely what amplifies their power to diagnose situations' (2005:28).

For our viewers *schadenfreude* enables the recouping of certainty and authority claims: they would never do, be, and appear like that, despite repeated recognition of the same feelings and situations. Grossberg (1997) in his earlier discussion of television affect suggests that we can incorporate the movement of individuals through television's affective landscape as a process of Gramscian struggle: 'People are constantly struggling, however, naively and ineffectively, to bring what they are given into their own contexts, to make something out if it that would give them a little more purchase on their lives, a little more control' (p.134). We argue therefore that the movement between affect and cognition reveals these moments of struggle because viewers, historically and immanently, are part of the circuits of value into which reality television enters and makes. *Schadenfreude* offers a respite for the judgements, evaluations and de-authorizations to which they are also constantly subject, offering a momentary position on the pedestal of the moral high-ground, a re-evaluation, what Ranciere (1983) calls a settling of accounts.

As we have discussed in Chapter 1, previous audience research (Hill 2005) provides evidence that although reality formats encourage viewers to make moral evaluations, but those readings were not necessarily indexed by the viewer's relationship to social positioning. In keeping with our findings from the methodology we found that moral reactions were made in socially differentiated ways dependent upon their social position because our respondents had uneven access to the resources required to establish moral authority. Our respondents connect with television after years of education, access to and possibilities for cultural, social and symbolic investments to generate very different capitals for generating value and authority.

Middle class reactions: commentary and taste (Forest Hill)

In the 'text in action' viewing sessions, where their immanent reactions to the programme were converted to reflexive commentary, our middle class participants' responses were shaped through assertions of cultural taste and knowledge about public/political debates of reality television. As part of a broader cultural skill to hold the form at a distance, they would often provide commentary during the TV programme. For example the extract below is from a Forest Hill respondent reacting to an episode of *Wife Swap,* one which evoked strong reactions in our working class viewers which we detail later.

Ruby 2 here does not seem to be making a kind of 'in a flash' judgement that Molly Haskell (1974) argues characterizes women's responses to melodrama, which is a response to their over-presence in the image and the emotion charge of the form. Instead she is deploying a rather detached explanation which is

Table 6.1

	Cue/Image	Television Text Wife Swap (Tracy and Kate)	Viewer comments Ruby 2 (Forest Hill)
1	34:20:00	**Voice over:** Things are also tense in the	
2		Thomas household as Tracy decides it's	
3		time for a break. Trevor has to put the	
4	Image of Tracy	kids to bed before heading off to work.	
5	reading a book	**Trevor:** Listen I want no talking Josie, no	
6		talking to Lucy you understand me it's	
7	Cut to Trevor	bedtime.	**Ruby2:** I think it's interesting that people say,
8	taking child out	Good night	you know they have got a full time job
9	of room:		or whatever, they have got a partner
10		**Child:** good night	that works at home and they feel that
11	Trevor to		they shouldn't have to do anything
12	camera		when they come home. I always think
13		**Trevor:** Sometimes like this I'm working	it is interesting that because- yes you
14		till about two – four thirty in the morning	do work really hard but you have a
15		just so I can get things done	family, do you know what I mean? So
16			if you are not willing to invest in the
17			family you might say "oh yeah well I
18	Shot of Trevor	**Trevor:** Right bye	am working all the hours and I am
19	going out of		providing for my family" but that also
20	door		means *time* as well and I think you
21			have got to weigh that up, do you know
22			what I mean?

more about an abstract concept of work–life balance. She never addresses the participants as 'you' directly but rather uses a more abstracted sense of 'you' as 'people' in general and enters into a theoretical debate about time use and investments. This discussion is addressed to the researcher as an invitation 'do you know what I mean?' to engage in a broader moral assessment of what matters and how time and energy use 'should' be considered.

Ang's (1985) audience work on *Dallas*, using Foucault, describes how commentary can be used to control the object on which it reports. Besnier (1990) claims this commentary is exemplary of how middle class discourse operates with a 'neutralising distance', establishing a 'middle of the road' ideology, to mark a distinction between the restrained and those who let themselves get carried away. This distancing process Bourdieu (1986) maintains is a cultural code that is acquired over time and through education and can be used to display one's value.

When middle class viewers *did* offer more heightened emotional responses they were often referenced by knowledge of specialized taste that challenged the authority of the TV 'experts'. In the next example viewers are watching the episode of *Faking It* where Leeds factory worker Mick is mentored by extravagant London designer David in order to 'pass' as a fashion designer (an example that we also discuss in Chapter 3):

Table 6.2

	Cue/Image	Television Text *Faking It (Mick –Fashion Designer)*	Viewer comments *Jemima, Deirdre, Vishni (Forest Hill)*
1	13:17	**David:** It's becoming apparent that he doesn't	
2	David: to	know a lot about fashion or about	
3	camera	designers he doesn't even particularly	
4		know what he likes, what does he like?	
5	Clothes on the	**David:** Marc Jacobs again that's a really	– What! [loud]
6	rails	famous designer that's a name that you	[Laughter and outrage noises]
7		really do have to learn.	– Ohh poor thing
8		**Mick:** Marc Jacobs	– And he looks like a (buffoon)!
9			– He probably does know what he likes
10			it's just (?) and quite simple quite (?)
11			– Yeah
12			– Not bright colors and –
13			– Yeah
14	13:36	Some of the stuff I saw today was ok	– If the mentor had done some
15	Mick to camera	some of the stuff was just completely off	legwork he'd have taken him to some
16		the wall you know unbelievable I can't	designers who are a bit more like that
17		believe that anybody would wear	than (?) simple (?) because that's what
18		something like that and then I met David	his style is
19		**Mick:** I didn't embarrass you too much	– But they just tried to choose
20	David and Mick	today then?	somebody outrageous
21	walking down	**David:** Not at all I never get	– They tend to look for really stark
22	London street	embarrassed do you think I'd look like	differences (?)
23		this if I got embarrassed	– Mmm – I suppose
24	Montage shots		– And on both sides really
25	of London		– You know a lot of people are
26	Streets		interested in clothes why not choose
			one of them

Table 6.2 (continued)

	Cue / Image	Television Text Faking It (Mick –Fashion Designer)	Viewer comments Jemima, Deirdre, Vishni (Forest Hill)
27	14:05	**Voice Over:** London's Brick Lane, the	
28		heart of cutting edge fashion, and where	– That's where erm Yasmin gets all her
29		Mick will be based for the next few	clothes from Brick Lane
30		weeks in his own studio.	– Is it?
31			Yeah but quite (?) It can be quite
32			(frumpy)
33			I find I get quite a few tops
34			We go to the market when normally we
35			shop
36	14:57	**David:** what you need to do now is to	
37	David and Mick	really start really looking at clothing, you	– The thing is he doesn't seem to realize
38	in design studio	know observe all the details then start	that he doesn't look that well dressed
39		utilizing them in your own design work	himself he doesn't actually look like a
40		**Voice Over:** For Mick to start designing	very – he doesn't look like anyone that
41		his own range of clothes he needs to	you would want to dress like
42		learn a whole new production process	– No
43		**David:** it's important to think about the	– You know you're not whereas there
44		concept I want you to gather together a	are people that do look really great
45		whole heap of things that are going to	aren't there.
46		influence you… once you've gathered	– Really inspiring yeh
47		this research then the design starts	– He looks sort of Boy George gone
48			slightly wrong
49			– [Laughter]

Here we can see how Vishni, Deirdre and Jemima feel compelled to defend Mick, the television participant, deploying a common motif of care and empathy for participants. They attack the expert's dress (which is not that difficult as he is clearly quite eccentric) but they offer critique and advice *for* the expert, suggesting he should have taken Mick to see different designers. They also reveal their knowledge of the programme techniques: 'they tend to look for stark differences'. But what is significant here is that their authority is resourced by their own cultural knowledge of fashion. London's fashionable 'Brick Lane', as it is presented in the programme as a contrast to Mick's experience of the North of England, is familiar and ordinary to these viewers. They say 'that's where Yasmin gets all her clothes from', where one of them gets 'quite a few tops' and where 'we go to the market' which allows them a platform from which they can critique the authority of the TV expert fashion designer, labelling him a 'Boy George gone wrong'.[1]

We do not want to imply that the middle class groups were less affectively 'involved' in reality television, they could easily move between commentary and affective reaction in the same session, but they were less likely to immediately connect themselves to participants 'as if' in the same circuit of evaluation. Rather here they produce forms of cultural knowledge to compete and critique the television expert and authorize themselves. Some middle class viewers did attempt to 'reach' for connections with the relationships on television in order to care about participants (as Liselle demonstrated in the previous chapter), but there was a visible and tangible difference between the ways these connections could be made in comparison to our other groups.

South Asian women's reactions: cultural difference

As we have suggested in Chapter 5, the Clapham group of South Asian women were more likely to talk of reality television in terms of getting 'tips', particularly on fashion and parenting. This type of response concurs with other audience research on lifestyle TV where advice and educative tips, particularly from the make-over are collected but not necessarily acted upon. This is one of the most direct examples of this kind of take-up as a direct response to the programme *What Not to Wear* about making over tired mothers – see Table 6.3.

In the programme as we detailed in Chapter 3, the experts focus on the forensic detailing of body parts and dispositions of the made-over participant: the neck, the face, even the lips, which is then mirrored by the viewers in that they declare that they like the hair, the shoulders, the face. Ultimately, as the evocative sense of the successful make-over reveal is contained through commodification, and the retailing and price details of the new trousers are displayed on the screen, the viewer at home declares: 'Wow! I'm gonna buy those trousers!' When watching *What Not to Wear* our Asian viewers often entered into the affective terms of the show, displaying shock at the failing women, and awe at the successful transformations, even here responding with an intention to follow the consumer advice.

However, this type of reaction was then often connected to a claim for moral authority based on cultural difference. Consider this extract from different viewers watching the same programme – see Table 6.4.

We can see here the way in which the women enjoin in a critique of the participant on the television programme and not the expert. They speak to participants directly: 'Why don't you do it yourself?' and 'Have you not thought [about] getting a bigger size then?' as the TV participants hold up examples of the 'failing' wardrobe, or squeeze into a pair of jeans that are too small. This is less a direct *schadenfreude* reaction; instead an engagement with the characters and the narrative. Notice how they are using the second personal pronoun addressing the participant directly as 'you', clearly referencing the presentness of the experience. They connect to their own experiences, 'I used to work a lot though then', and then resource their critique through cultural difference – 'I must say Asian women are hardly ever fat ... unless they are educated [and then] they don't do stuff'. They are referring to their discussion about how breast feeding and having to work helps to keep off baby weight-gain. Ultimately Lilly starts with a moral comparison about herself 'when *I* had *my* babies' but is cut off by a discussion of whether she is prepared to talk about breast feeding and working on tape. Their claim for moral authority therefore is framed through reference to cultural difference. Tips and cultural differences of honour and shame resourced many of the emotional reactions from our Clapham group and enabled them to both connect to and draw some distance from television participants and from the researchers, as we discussed in Chapter 4, where discussions were closed down with the refrain 'it's cultural difference' with little willingness to explain what this might be.

Table 6.3

	Cue / Image	Television Text What Not to Wear (Tired mothers)	Viewer comments Razia, Shabeen, Naazia (Clapham)
1	48.11	**Sarah:** .hh oh my God!	.- hh She looks much younger.
2	(Trinny and	Very, very different	
3	Susannah unveil	**Susannah:** You've sort of got this grace	– Her hair's...
4	the mirror to	from somewhere. You are *so* graceful.	
5	reveal the 'new'	It's the way you stand, your shoulders	
6	Sarah)	are back, your neck like Trinny says is	– What was that her hair!
7		very elegant. But it's the way you're	I also like the shoulders
8		holding your face, the way you're	
9		holding your lips, it's a very different	– And the face
10		human being.	It's sad that she's just looking over her
11		**Sarah:** My worry is that now that I'm	shoulder.
12		going to look too glamourous. I'm going	
13		to walk somewhere and I'm gonna stand	– Right
14		out because I look better than everyone	
15		else	
16	(sound of footsteps)		
17	(cut to Sarah	**Trinny:** See, I love you like this, it's so	– Wow! I'm gonna buy those trousers!
18	walking in the	feminine and pretty Sarah. It's a very	
19	room in a	different you though.	
20	different outfit.	**Sarah:** I think that's what it is. It's such a	– She's the same girl which was
21	Details appear	big change. I was obviously expecting a	wearing those clothes at the beginning.
22	on the screen of	change, but I'm just a completely	
23	the price and	different person now. It'll make a big	
24	shop the clothes	difference to me and Carl. You know I'll	
25	are from)	like going out, I think he'll be proud of	(laughter)
26		me.	

Table 6.4

	Cue/Image	Television Text *What Not to Wear (Tired Mothers)*	Viewer comments *Naked and Lilly (Clapham)*
1	02:43	**Woman:** ...and not the sexiest thing to	
2	Video tape of	wear in the bedroom perfect for feeding	
3	woman holding	the baby but no baby to feed so I don't	
4	up a saggy	know why I'm still wearing that	
5	nightie	**Susannah:** It's all about sexiness isn't it	
6		they're so so aware of what's wrong but	
7	Cut to Trinny	they don't know how to put it right.	– But I think, if you *know* that, why
8	and Susannah		don't you do it yourself?
9	on the couch	**Trinny:** yep	– Instead of getting sort of the telly to
10			do it
11	VT Michalena	**Michalena:** the- there is gap there	– yes
12	trying on	But that's how all me pants are look me	– Okay I would (always wear sexy
13	clothes with	bits	things)
14	some of her		
15	stomach		– Oh, my *God*. [Laughter]
16	sticking out of	.hhhh [sharp intake of breath, squeal	
17	her jeans	experts look horrified]	
18	Presenters shock	**Michalena:** I can manage to squeeze that	
19	edited over	in but it's not too painful I can just shove	
20	Michalena's VT	that down there like that and then put me	
21	Michalena	tops over	– Have you not thought of like getting a
22	shows how she	**Trinny:** we know she's going down	bigger size then?
23	dresses	don't we	– Yeah?
24			
25		**Susannah:** definitely [waves hand]	
26		**Trinny:** definitely	

Table 6.4 (continued)

	Cue/Image	Television Text *What Not to Wear (Tired Mothers)*	Viewer comments *Naheid and Lilly (Clapham)*
27			– Oh my God.
28			– I think I've seen this I think
29	03:28	**Trinny:** Their biggest issue obviously is	
30		after they've given birth got back their	
31		weight and everything has redistributed	– You know (Vy?) after she had a baby
32		in a way that their clothes don't fit them.	she was (?)
33		If they've put it on their thighs it has to	– I know but she was breast feeding that
34		come off and that's why I find you do	helps
35		end up in that stretch trouser you wore	– I used to work a lot though then – you
36		when you were pregnant.	used to
37		(other VTs)	– You were breast feeding
38		**Susannah:** it's amazing how they all	– No: I put them (on the bottle) it was
39		lose sight of the woman they were before	too hard
40		they had children.	– My –
41		…	– Heh, heh,
42			– No way!
43			– Especially (?) two babies.
44	04:06	[Trinny and Susannah on telephone the	– So that's the thing with Asian women
45		'winners']	I must say they are hardly ever fat. (I
46			think I know why) unless they are
47			educated they know then maybe they
48			don't do stuff
49			– When *I* had *my* babies I also had–
50			– This is on record
51			– Heh heh

Working class reactions: emotional responses to mothering

The dominant resource for the working class full-time mothers in our project to claim moral authority was motherhood. Here class and gender worked as more powerful determinants over racial differences. For instance when Razia, Shabeen and Naazia are watching that episode of *What Not to Wear*, when the experts apparently take on the lives of the TV participants for a day, one says, 'I don't think I'd quite like – you know, to let someone look after your babies. Some BBC woman to look after your babies!', thereby mitigating the authority of the expert as 'some BBC woman' – fashion and parenting are clearly very different forms of authority. And whilst Saj was watching *Supernanny* in a Text in Action (TIA) session where she did not seem to have much English, her tutting and gasps are converted into moral authority as she tells us of her parenting expertise whilst the television image shows the mum struggling with getting her child to bed:

SAJ: I say 9 o'clock bedtime.
NANCY: No problem?
SAJ: No problem. I say 'go to bed'.
NANCY: And they go?
SAJ: Yes. Discipline.

(Saj, Clapham, TIA)

Potentially because of their overwhelming choice of watching *Wife Swap*, the Addington and Brockley women make their most emotive reactions in relation to aspects of mothering. Half of the Addington group were full-time mothers and all but one of the Brockley group were mothers who were either not in paid work or working part time, and those that worked did so in the care industry or the service sector. This particular example is drawn from respondents watching the *Wife Swap* programme we discussed in Chapter 4 between a more affluent working class aspirational mother Tracy, who works as a legal secretary, and a less affluent working class mother of six children who stays at home, Kate – see Table 6.5.

Here our respondents prefer the less affluent wife, Kate, with six children, as more 'normal' and morally object to the apparent materialism of Tracy. They say, 'Don't you think that's saying more about *her*?' when she talks of her fear of going to a wealthy home, and show absolutely no empathy for her crying to camera when faced with the prospect of looking after six children – they do not make a connection, an affective reach or a constitutive actualization, to her predicament.

The Brockley viewers in the extract in Table 6.6 watching the same episode also take a dislike to Tracy's apparent aspirational airs and are outraged at her not getting home from work until her child has gone to bed. (Recall from Chapter 4 how the image of the small caravan as Tracy's new home in the swap provokes such responses.)

Table 6.5

	Cue/Image	Television Text Wife Swap (Tracy and Kate)	Viewer comments Vicki and Mel (Addington)
1	04:14		
2	Tracy	Voice over: It's the day of the swap and	
3	packing clothes	both wives are getting ready to leave.	
4		Because the Thomas house is so	
5		crammed full of kids Tracy (the swapped	
6	Cut to image of	wife) will be staying in the family	
7	caravan in the	caravan.	
8	garden		
9	Cut to Tracy to	Voice over Tracy: I'm worried that I'm	
10	camera	going to be going to a house	– Don't you think that's kind of saying
11		totally above my level you know sort of	more about *her*?
12		multi million pound house or something	– The other one seems more (.) *normal*
13	Trevor (husband of	going into this big house with nannies	– yeh
14	Kate) with	and a guy who's you know really	
15	shovel / Kate in	pompous	
16	caravan getting	Kate: I hope she thinks this is nice	
17	it ready	Trevor: Well this is a five star hotel if	
18		she moans I'm going to 'av a	
19			
20			
21	06.36	Voice Over: Kate and Tracy get to	
22	Tracy looking	explore their new homes before they	
23	round the house	meet the families	
24	looking stressed		– Seems like definitely she's not
25	as she sees the		actually for kids really
26	number of		– She's more mater-, like for material
27	childrens' beds		things and like fancy jumpers

Table 6.5 (continued)

	Cue / Image	Television Text Wife Swap (Tracy and Kate)	Viewer comments Vicki and Mel (Addington)
28	Kate looking around the other house	Kate: It looks like there is only one child	– Yeah
29			
30			
31	Back to Tracy	Tracy: It's different from my house I	
32		think somebody's having a joke heh, heh,	
33		oh dear [starts to break down]	
34	Back to Kate in child's bedroom	Oh what a diddy little bed	– Is she crying?
35	Tracy to camera		– Yeah, looks like it, [dismissively]
36			
37		I'm a bit worried there seem to be a lot of	
38		cots and beds with children's the the	
39		that's six I've seen so far six children	
40		hmm that's an awful lot of children gosh	
41	Kate walking down stairs	I don't think I could do it [looks scared]	
42	Tracy crying		
43			
44		Kate: going from one child to six is	
45		really hard I hope she's ok	
46			
47		Tracy to camera: I don't think I can look	
48		after all these children, ok?	

Table 6.6

	Cue/Image	Television Text *Wife Swap (Tracy and Kate)*	Viewer comments *Sally, Sonia, Sally Mc (Brockley)*
1	Tracy to camera	I'm an individual I've built up my career over the last twenty years or whatever	All: Laughter
2	Cut to shot of	You know Charlotte's lovely and	
3	Tracy going to	wonderful and I love her to bits but one	
4	work	day she's going to fly the nest when	
5	Cut back to	she's eighteen or twenty and I want to	
6	Tracy to camera	have a life left.	
7	Shot of Mark in	**Voice over:** As Tracy's work is two	
8	warehouse	hours away Mark has a local job so that	
9	Shot of Mark	he can pick her up from nursery. They	– He picks her up, he picks her up that's
10	collecting Lottie	have a routine and having only one child	right
11		works for them.	– You're only a bloody legal secretary
12	Tracy and Mark	**Tracy:** I've got friends who have more	do you know what I mean?
13	to camera	than one child and I've seen first hand	– But she has to be there EARLY IN
14		how it can affect your relationship	THE MORNING [shouting]
15		**Mark:** yeh	– Yeh, but she think she's on the *career*
16		**Tracy:** and that really worried us	ladder I know 'cos I am a legal
17		because eh you know Mark is my rock	secretary
18		and I don't want to lose that and	– No but what it is-
19		Charlotte is my second rock and I don't	– She's only a bloody legal secretary
20	...	want to lose her and I don't know how I	that's what I'm saying
21		could possibly have enough love for	– That is it, she's a PA and that's it
22		another child.	what's up with that anyway
23			– What, don't get home till baby's gone
24			to bed!
25			

Table 6.6 (continued)

	Cue/Image	Television Text Wife Swap (Tracy and Kate)	Viewer comments Sally, Sonia, Sally Mc (Brockley)
26	04:23	**Voice over:** Tracy is going to stay in	
27	Image of	the family caravan	
28	caravan in the	**Voice over Tracy:** I'm really worried	Hmmm
29	garden – cut to	that I'm going to be in a house totally	– See what I mean how does *she* know?
30	Tracy to camera	above my level you know sort of million	**All:** laughter
31		pound house or something going into this	– People have this thing about a legal
32		big house with nannies and a guy who's	secretary and she's *nothing* special
33	Kate in caravan	you know pompous	*nothing* special at all
34	getting it ready		
35			
36		**Kate:** I hope she thinks this is nice	

Our working class respondents undertake a heightened emotional performance in relation to reality television more freely. In the last extract they diminish Tracy's value 'You're only a bloody legal secretary' (line 12), and shout at the television, 'but she has to be there EARLY IN THE MORNING' (line 14) upset at Tracy's apparent prioritizing of her career over her child. For Sonia at home (who is also a legal secretary), Tracy on television emerges as 'nothing special', as all the viewers are outraged by her pretentiousness and lack of maternal care and perform a 'levelling out', or 'settling of accounts'. They use their own experience to authorize their analysis to demonstrate how Tracy is over-valuing herself (only a legal secretary) but also de-valuing her worth as a mother. There is something very different about the way in which reality television's presentness is felt and performed here. It intervenes immanently in their own circuits of value, producing no ambiguity in their responses and generating laughter at Tracy's caravan misfortune.

Working class masquerade

This was another surprise in our data: that the most verbally vitriolic acts of moral judgement were metered out by our working class viewers watching other working class women on *Wife Swap*. We want to use the possibilities opened up by the transcription process of our method to analyse these in more detail. The transcriptions in Table 6.7 offer more speech markers to show the animation in the level of performances of audience interactions.

This particular extract demonstrates the immanent mediation (immediation) generated through affect. The women begin with considerable empathy for Kate having not seen Tracy's child for having been at work all day. Kate's to camera distress is edited over the child sleeping which provokes this response: 'Oh no: she's crying' (line 17). They quickly convert this empathy to outrage directed to the more aspirational mother and in defence of the child 'that's not fair on that child!' (lines 23–4). There are moments of indignation when our working class viewers directly entered into the frame and narrative of the programme even inserting themselves into the role of the participants. Notice in the extract in Table 6.7 at line 28 Sonia even cues us into her shift in taking on the 'role': 'Mmm I'm taking the mother's role [performs] and when I woke you up and dragged you out of bed at six o'clock in the morning and dropped you off at seven o'clock', which is accompanied by some physical and bodily posturing. This is very different to the affective 'reach' made earlier by Liselle and by some other respondents in order to try and find a point of connection, a way to recognize and share an experience. Instead these instances are directly re-enacted and re-animated as of the same time and space in which the women viewers can immediately take part, whereby they enact their own and others' value.

Similarly, in the extract in Table 6.8 Sharon in the same Brockley viewing session directly mimics the reality television participant's 'hello' as she weakly tries to get the attention of the children.

Table 6.7

	Cue/Image	Television Text *Wife Swap (Tracy and Kate)*	Viewer comments *Sally, Sonia, Sally Mc (Brockley)*
1	18:19		
2	Image of car	**Voice over:** Unfamiliar with the journey	
3	clock	from Manchester it's taking Kate	
4		longer than	
5	Kate driving	expected to get ho:me which only adds to	
6	Kate to camera	her frustration.	
7	whilst driving	**Kate:** I ca:n't belie:ve it's eight o'clock	
8		and I left home thirteen ho:urs ago (1)	
9	Kate pulling	I've- no wonder I've got a headache its	
10	onto drive	just ridiculous	
11		**Voice over:** By the time Kate gets ho:me	
12	Kate enters the	its eight thirty.	
13	house / Lottie	**Kate:** How's Lottie?	
14	sleeping	**Mark:** She:'s fast asleep in bed (.)	
15		**Kate:** ah	
16		**Mark:** she's shattered	
17		**Kate:** Ah:::	**Sally:** Oh no: she's cry:ing, she's
18	Kate to Camera	**Kate:** [whispering to camera] I':m quite	having a ↑ mare of a day::.
19		disappointed that Lottie was in bed and I	**All:** Yeah.
20	Lottie sleeping	didn't get to bath her	**Sonia:** She's not had her all day really
21	Kate and Mark	I'm so tired	has she? I suppose with all them
22	in the living	**Kate:** My body feels re:ally ali:ve but	children ((?))
23	room	my head feels dead .hh quite often at	**Sal:** But (it's alright but) that's not fair
24		home it's the other way round. Hh hh	on that child!
25		**Mark:** Do you think Tracy would be	**Sonia:** Exa:ctly and that's what she's
26		feeling like that now?	feelin'
27	Cut to other		**Sal:** ((?))

Table 6.7 (continued)

	Cue/Image	Television Text *Wife Swap (Tracy and Kate)*	Viewer comments *Sally, Sonia, Sally Mc (Brockley)*
28	family		**Sonia:** mmm I'm taking the mother's
29			role **[performs]** and when I wo:ke you
30			up and dragged you out of bed at six
31			o'clock in the morning [and dropped
32			you off at <u>seven</u> o'clock
33			**Sal:** ⎯⎯ [to have you out by seven
34			**Sonia:** and now its eight thirty at night
35			and you ain't seen me all day::::
36			**Sal:** The <u>kid</u>'s in bed.
37			**Sonia:** How you gonna make up for
38			that?
39			**Sal:** You ca::n't
40			
41			
42			(6)

(*Underline for stress, CAPITALS for shouting, (in brackets for inaudible), (.) Length of pause in seconds, ↑ rising intonation, ::stretching of syllables, [overlapping speech)

Table 6.8

	Cue/Image	Television Text — Wife Swap (Tracy and Kate)	Viewer comments — Sally, Sonia, Sally Mc (Brockley)
1	15:47	**Tracy:** <u>Sit</u> down on the chair ple::↑ase	
2	Tracy trying to	**V/O:** Tracy's day is far from boring (.)	
3	order the	with the kids back from scho:ol its her	
4	children	first afternoon alone with them and its	
5		not going we:l	
6	Close up on	Tracy: Plea:?↑se	
7	Tracy	**[child screams]**	
8		**Child:** <u>sit</u> down <u>now</u> or I'm gonna <u>te:ll</u>	
9	Pan to children	daddy	[funny noise] ↑
10	Medium close	**[children screaming]**	hh hh hh hh hh hh
11	up Tracy	**Tracy:** If you- LOOK <u>listen</u>, <u>listen</u>	**Sharon: [mimicking Tracy]** hello:::
12	Pan to children	hello::: [hand gesture] <u>listen</u>, <u>listen</u>	(?)
13	Medium close	Children: hh hh hh	**Sal:** That's gonna get their <u>attention</u>
14	up Tracy	**Tracy:** ri::ght just- sit down **[looks with**	innit?
15		**dispair to camera crew]**	**Sharon**: hh hh you have to give me
16		**Child:** No:: Lucy SIT DOWN	permission to be in charge here
17		**V/O:** It ↓ doesn't take the kids long to	plea:::se
18		wo:rk out Tracy is a soft touch	
19	Pan to children	**Tracy:** Ri:ght I'm gonna get cross in a	
20		minute no:w will you <u>just</u> all be <u>quiet</u>	

In language analysis degrees of involvement are sometimes attached to relations of proximity given away through deixis (spatial and temporal markers of here now – this *is* happening/ it *is* here). In all of the extracts from the groups it is clear that the viewers use markers of temporal deixis – this *is* happening – and they share the present tense – a continual presentness. But in terms of spatial and social deixis, viewers from Forest Hill and from Clapham use the demonstratives 'that' rather than 'this', and television participants are referred to in the third person, he/she/they.

However in the examples above from our working class viewers this trend is transgressed when viewers 'replay' moments happening on the screen and take on the part of a television participant. In line 28 of Table 6.7, Sonia informs her audience that she is about to become the mother, replacing herself as the I and using *you* rather than *she*. Similarly in the last extract when Tracy is losing control in the Thomas house on television, the viewers make a noise mimicking Tracy's intonation and Sharon copies Tracy's 'hello:' and performs 'you have to give *me* permission to be in charge *here* please' (line 15). At heightened emotional moments in the viewing process there is a closer, shared deictic frame between the television and the audience.

These actions are performative acts which mark the viewer's exasperation with Tracy, and according to Edwards (1997) 'anger or exasperation, whether performed bodily or evoked linguistically [both here], can be used to signal that something is wrong or problematic about whatever they are directed at, functioning as shorthand formulations of the event' (p.170). Not only are the viewers reformulating events on screen for themselves as we have previously argued is a trait of watching talk shows (Wood 2009), but they are also directly 'replaying' them back – as in the case of mimicked hell:ooo. According to Besnier (1990) 'replaying' is an affective strategy which marks out one's moral position:

> Quotes, recreations of one's own and other's speech, and other types of replaying activities are affectively charged, in that they interweave the voices of different social entities and the replayer's moral agenda. They may mark the speakers' or writer's emotional involvement in the text, enhance the heteroglossic nature of discourse and [not so] subtly leak the reporter's stance on the replayed situation.
>
> (1990:426)

Whilst all of our women viewers demonstrate involvements in the text, which are related to their relationship to forms of emotion and melodrama, we argue that this is doubly meaningful for working class women in their over-representation on a show like *Wife Swap* which usually pits working class women (with different aspirations) against each other. In our textual analysis, we argued that much reality television assumes a normative middle class orientation (Savage 2003) and Samantha Lyle (2008) has argued that programmes like *Supernanny* invite a middle class gaze from viewers.

Unable to adopt a different classed gaze that will afford them a more distanced position, many of our working class women, particularly when watching *Wife Swap* enter into a 'masochism of over-identification' (Doane 1982). Mary Ann Doane's arguments about the female spectator suggest that women, in response to their location in dominant scopic regimes, must adopt femininity as a masquerade, and perform it in excess, in order to contain their own over-presence. Whilst the conditions of desire complicate the straightforward adoption of this schema to formations of class, given the histories of the monitoring of working class lives and submission to other socio/political scopic regimes, perhaps the analogy might have some force. Might it be possible to see these dramatic performances in response to reality television's presentness as masochistic (and pleasurable) masquerades of class relations?

The normative assumption of journalistic accounts of reality television's (mis)use of the working class for entertainment assumes that the middle class gaze necessarily encourages the ridicule and mockery of the working class. Whatever the producers intentions, in our findings at least, we see that our middle class group often deferred the potential 'meaning' in the programmes. Either they adopted a detached critical stance, or made an affective actualization through resonance and connection with moments of reality television, in order to show care for participants. Condemnations of reality television were more often evoked through the focus group and directed at the exploitative features of the genre, with some more veiled assumptions about 'the kind of people that go on' reality television. We explore this formulation in more detail in the next chapter, but these were less affective reactions and rather more straightforward snobbery related to taste.

The evocation of affect therefore seems to work in rather complex ways, ways that challenge Kavka's (2008) sense that reality television works to use time and space to create a sense of mediated community. We found mixes of community and misanthropy, connection, disconnection, reach and distancing, at different moments, which we suggest are oriented not only by time as a sense of immediate present but also by time and space in terms of our respondents' classed and gendered histories and location. The more powerful affective reactions converted to vitriol were made by our working class mothers towards aspirational 'non-caring' working class mothers. These are much more powerful expressions than the generalized derision our middle class respondents expressed towards the 'undeserving'.[2] They were much more immediate and proximate (in both time and space).

According to Ahmed (2004) emotions work to align subjects with some others and against other others. In this case the terms established by competitive motherhood (Thompson 2011) set those who have made different investments and have different positions and possibilities against each other. Tracy's expression of aspiration is seen to be both pretentious (a working class sin – as we have documented elsewhere (Skeggs 2004)) and a bad investment. Her lack of interest in children more generally (she just wants one because she also wants a 'life') is understood as a criticism. During the session Sonia tells us that she is also a legal secretary, having made difficult decisions about work and motherhood. The difference is produced by the emotional investments that can be seen to have been made by television participants that de/legitimate the choices and investments of viewers. Competitive motherhood and possibilities for value deter empathetic reach instead engaging respondents in a tournament of value and authority.

This shows how our respondents did not straightforwardly connect to participants who are more 'like them' which one might assume as we explore the potential divisiveness of reality television as a genre. In the last example Sonia's response is defiantly angry, and in emotional schema anger typically follows from a moral violation that infringes upon investments in person-value, leading to a desire for retribution (Lakoff and Kövecses 1987). In their work on the politics of affect, both Ahmed (2004) and Probyn (2004) suggest that there must be some contact or threat of contact in order for disgust, and the pulling away it involves to take place. The most emotive reactions reveal the intensity of respondents' investments and attachments that align with the desire to be seen to be a 'good mother'. As 'good mother' is one of the main ways in which working class women can gain value and authority, as we have argued in Chapter 2, this should not surprise us. But as 'good mother' is also one of the main domains in which they are subject to constant surveillance and judgement we should not be surprised if they deploy such judgements towards others: this is the competitive culture of mothering, promoted not just on reality television but across culture more generally (Jensen 2010).

Rachel Moseley (2000) suggested that by destabilizing the categories of viewer and participant, make-overs produce a potential dis-ease where the safest response is to retreat into a position of class- and taste-based superiority. That superiority can only be generated through material and cultural distinctions. *Wife Swap* is not a make-over programme and there are clearly generic differences which effect responses, but for Sonia there was no class-based or taste-based authority to take, unlike that offered to the middle classes watching *Faking It*, or the culturally superior position taken by members of the Clapham group as they watch *What Not to Wear*. For our working class participants the key resource, in the absence of other forms of value, was generated through their intense attachments to motherhood. In this way we are beginning to see how reality television viewing is shaped through an 'affective economy' – a phrase used by Ahmed (2004) to insist that emotions are distributed across social fields.

Affective politics

Emotive responses to reality television are thus resourced through structurally differentiated access to forms of moral authority: potentially made more intense by an over-presence of the image for working class women who recognize their positioning in regimes of value. Reality television therefore *does* enter into forms of sociality in which social structures are already in place. Unlike Kavka's (2008) free-floating and optimistic rendering of 'community' through reality television's frame, we want to suggest greater attention to the crux of the relationship between positioning and sociality. As we detailed in Chapter 2, Thrift's (2008) analysis is helpful for our overall framework in that he suggests that the politics of performance has become enhanced in mediated societies where we are constantly called to play out our relationships to one another. In his account of the 'misanthropic city', he argues:

> Though it hardly needs saying, sociality does not have to be the same thing as liking others. It includes all kinds of acts of kindness and compassion, certainly, but equally there are all the signs of active dislike being actively pursued, not just or even primarily as outbreaks of violence (for example road rage or Saturday night fights) but more particularly as malign gossip, endless complaint, the full spectrum of jealousy, petty snobbery, personal deprecation, pointless authoritarianism, various forms of *schadenfreude*, and all the other ritual *pleasures* of everyday life.
>
> (2008:208 our emphasis)

Elsewhere we and others have charted a substantive rise in the national affective noise of hatred, contempt, cynicism and derision (Garland 2001; Jones 2010; Lawler 2005; Mount 2004; Skeggs 2009; Tyler 2008; Wood and Skeggs 2011), into which the more generalized derisory responses of our middle class respondents fit. In an early essay, '*Only Entertainment*' about working class attachment to musical films, Richard Dyer (1977) argued that the affective sensibilities of the film texts – abundance, energy, transparency, intensity and community – were revelled in as direct responses to the social conditions of the time (the 1970s) of scarcity, exhaustion, dreariness, manipulation, fragmentation. The musical generated an affective sensibility that was closely tied to a working class sense of community. But the 'utopian sensibility' of Dyer's argument was generated through a gap between material reality and the fantasy of the entertainment world, whereas for our working class viewers in the case of *Wife Swap* the immanence of the form, the domestic verisimilitude of the settings, the intimacy of the relationships, and an over-presence of the image close that gap. Here the proximity and immediacy of reality television generates 'misanthropy' as well as 'community', and produces a range of movement from distancing to attachment for our respondents dependent upon their location in the economy of personhood.

Potentially, therefore, Dyer's arguments about working class community require reworking for late capitalism. For instance, government rhetoric and policy emphasizes us all re-orienting ourselves around the labour market and the UK has seen numerous government initiatives to get mothers back to work. In 2006 (the year most of our data was collected) the British government announced a multi-million pound 'parenting academy' because they perceived working classes to be failing at parenting. There are now a number of 'parenting orders' (IPOs) criminalizing poor parenting (Blakely 2011; Hunter and Nixon 2001; Nixon and Hunter 2009; Pitt 2002). But there is of course a longer history of blaming working class mothers for the failure of the nation (Dyhouse 1976, 1977; Lawler 2000; Skeggs 1997; Walkerdine and Lucey 1989). In which case affective pleasures (which include the negative affects of *schadenfreude* as well as the more positive affects of care) perhaps *do* offer a solution to contemporary social relations of the present capitalist conjuncture where working class mothers can take the high moral ground, even if only momentarily. This enables us to make sense of their intense affective reactions, which are converted into claims for moral authority and legitimacy. Yet as Cross and Littler (2010) maintain, this is a solution for capitalism not a critique of it: an ameliorative reaction to inequality that offers a momentary feeling of adjustment.

Conclusions

Taking as our starting point the very basic idea that television is an aesthetic affective medium par excellence we have made a more concerted attempt to detail the workings of affect in relation to reality television viewing than is currently available from textual readings of the genre. We also wanted to explore affect to demonstrate through our research, that affect is socialized, a social response that is not about the individual psyche but about the histories and positioning in regimes of value by which people understand their experiences and emotions. In this chapter we developed the argument made earlier in the book that viewer's relations to television occur through circuits of value in which co-extensivity and transindividualism are shaped through the very fabric of evaluative sociality. Our respondents saw themselves 'as if' they were the television participants and 'as not', in similar scenarios, exploring intimacy and domesticity through the narratives and characterizations of the programme. Motherhood is a key stabilizing narrative resplendent with promises of value that positions most women as rarely 'good enough' – but it is a narrative and institution of value in which women are both positioned automatically through reproduction but also one in which they invest. This investment in a relational practice, however, is one that is continually subject to judgement of official and non-official others. It is also an investment that has to be continually made through space and time – children grow.

Unlike our middle class mothers who had a range of sources of value, our working class mothers made motherhood *the* key source of value. In Bourdieu's terms they rejected that which they had been refused (capitals for certain forms of aspiration), investing all their time and energy in an alternative source of value. A huge amount of time and energy (labour) went into proving and performing good motherhood. This meant that they were often positioned in an ambivalent relationship both to themselves and others as well as to reality television. We saw this in their constant *movement* between care for and judgement of reality participants as they move between proximity and distance and between difference and indifference, depending on the constitutive actualizations and connections they made, based on prior investments.

In this sense we have begun to chart what affect *does*, rather than assuming what it can do. Affect enables connections to be made to the television participants and their characterizations, situations and position in narrative structures. What happens to these connections becomes significant: they can evoke judgement, replay morality, assuage ambivalence, generate self-criticism, produce affective reach, incite resonances, reproduce cultural in/difference. We agree with Joyrich (1991) and Grossberg's (1997) earlier call discussed in the last chapter that affect *is* the missing link in the analysis of ideology. Affect brings ideology into effect, by provoking tournaments of value in which prior investment has been made. But the form of affect is what makes us pay attention, or not (and this is what producers work so hard to achieve through the inflation of sensation). Without attention, as (Deleuze 1969/1990) notes, power would not be effective. This is why empirical audience research is so important because it can show what produces the attention and what patterns the reaction.

Indeed the role of affect in reality television complicates the working of ideology and pedagogy, since there is clearly a lack of certainty about any one group's particular *reading* of any particular programme. However, the *way* in which affective reactions are made and then cognized relies entirely on the access one has to cultural and material resources in order to justify one's own value when one is positioned 'as if' also subject to judgement. It was often easier for our middle class respondents and our South Asian women viewers to draw some distance from television participants in relation to cultural knowledge or cultural difference, but our most emotive responses came from working class women where their doubly coded over-presence in the image bursts through into emotive and angry reactions to those women most like themselves in masquerades of class. Some reactions were not so much 'as if' this were me, but rather 'this is me' in their performative re-enactments of particular moments in the programme. It is not that the social has disappeared in reality television's formation of immediacy and emotion, but rather that it is re-figured through affective registers: 'affect does not reside positively in the sign or commodity, but is produced only as an effect of its circulation' (Ahmed 2004:120). We are therefore able to see how affect brings power into effect through moral authorization. These relations would not be so complex if the governmentality visible in textual analysis of reality television texts did work completely in the lives of its audiences.

But we can also see how affect is connected more broadly to the specific conjuncture of capitalism, what Grossberg (2010) following Williams, calls the 'overdetermined structure of feeling' of the moment. Driven by political economy, the need for capital to generate more and more profit from television (as everything else), reality television is a key element in the national structure of feeling helping to shape the affect of the present, one strongly defined through judgement. As we have shown patterns of value can be discerned by which an economy of personhood can be seen in the making, through class, gender and race. Our research suggests that through the workings of affect people are constantly trying to generate (and defend) value for themselves *against* judgement. If reality television enshrines the 'performance principle' of late capitalism and urges individualization through the mediation of personhood, then the responses to it are figured in subject formations which have much longer and differentiated classed, gendered and raced histories that shape possibilities for being a person with value. In re-orienting our understanding of the work of audiences, not as readings, but as performances of value, as reality television's key mode of social intervention, we now turn to the most dominant signifier of value in our audience responses: labour.

Notes

1 1980s and 90s British pop star famous for his outlandish and feminine clothing.
2 Although we argue that because the middle class affects of derision and contempt fit into the dominant symbolic economy, where expressions of hatred (exemplified through the figure of the 'chav') become legitimate, they too are very powerful expressions of distinction which assert authority and taste through claims for superiority.

References

Ahmed, S. 2004 'Affective Economies', *Social Text* 22(2): 117–39.
Ang, I. 1985 *Watching Dallas: Soap Opera and the Melodramatic Imagination*, London: Routledge.
Besnier, N. 1990 'Language and Affect', *Annual Review of Anthropology* 19: 419–51.
Blackman, L. and Venn, C. 2010 'Affect', *Body and Society* 16(1): 7–28.
Blakely, H. 2011 'A Second Chance at Life: Labour, Love and Welfare on a South Wales Estate' *Sociology*, PhD, Cardiff: University of Cardiff.
Bourdieu, P. 1986 *Distinction: A Social Critique of the Judgement of Taste*, London: Routledge.
Cross, S. and Littler, J. 2010 'Schadenfreude: The Cultural Economy of Fame in Free Fall', *Cultural Studies* 24(3): 395–417.
Deleuze, E. and Deleuze, J. 1978 'Giles Deleuze: Lecture Transcripts on Spinoza's Concept of *Affect*', Vol. 2006: http:/www.webdeleuze.com/php/sommaire.html.
Deleuze, G. and Guattari, F. 1983 *Anti-Oedipus: Capitalism and Schizophrenia. Vol 1*, New York: The Viking Press.
Deleuze, J. 1969/1990 *The Logic of Sense*, New York: Columbia University Press.
Doane, M. A. 1982 'Film and Masquerade: Theorizing the Female Spectator', *Screen* 23 (3–4): 74–88.
Dyer, R. 1977 'Entertainment and Utopia', *Movie* 24 (Spring): no pages in original.
Dyhouse, C. 1976 'Social Darwinistic Ideas and the Development of Women's Education in England 1880–1920', *History of Education* 5(2): 41–58.
——1977 'Good Wives and Little Mothers: Social Anxieties and the Schoolgirls' Curriculum 1890–1920', *Oxford Review of Education* 3(1): 21–35.
Edwards, D. 1997 *Discourse and Cognition*, London: Sage.
Garland, D. 2001 *The Culture of Control: Crime and Social Order in Contemporary Society*, Oxford: Oxford University Press.
Grossberg, L. 1997 *Bringing it All Back Home*, Durham and London: Duke University Press.

——2010 'Interview with Larry Grossberg with Gregory Seigworth and Melissa Gregg', in M. Gregg and G. J. Seigworth (eds) *The Affect Theory Reader*, Durham and London: Duke University Press.

Haskell, M. 1974 *From Reverence to Rape: The Treatment of Women in the Movies*, New York: Holt Rinehart and Winston.

Hill, A. 2005 *Reality TV: Audiences and Popular Factual Television*, London: Routledge.

Hunter, C. and Nixon, J. 2001 'Taking the Blame and Losing the Home: Women and Anti-Social Behaviour', *Journal of Social Welfare and Family Law* 23(4): 395–401.

Jensen, T. 2010 'What Kind of Mum are You at the Moment? *Supernanny* and the Psychologising of Classed Embodiment', *Subjectivity* 3: 170–92.

Jones, O. 2010 *Chavs: the Demonisation of the Working Class*, London: Verso.

Joyrich, L. 1991 'Going Through the E/Motions: Gender, Postmodernism, and Affect in Television Studies', *Discourse* 14(1): 23–40.

Kavka, M. 2008 *Reality Television, Affect and Intimacy: Reality Matters*, London: Palgrave Macmillan.

Lakoff, G. and Kövecses, Z. 1987 'The Cognitive Model of Anger Inherent in American English', in D. Holland and N. Quinn (eds) *Cultural Models in Language and Thought*, Cambridge: Cambridge University Press.

Lawler, S. 2000 *Mothering the Self: Mothers, Daughters, Subjects*, London: Routledge.

——2005 'Disgusted Subjects: the Making of Middle-Class Identities', *The Sociological Review* 53(3): 429–46.

Lyle, S. A. 2008 '(Mis)recognition and the Middle-class/Bourgeois Gaze: A Case Study of *Wife Swap*', *Critical Discourse Studies* 5(4): 319–30.

Moseley, R. 2000 'Makeover Takeover on British Television', *Screen* 41(3): 299–314.

Mount, F. 2004 *Mind the Gap: Class in Britain Now*, London: Short Books.

Ngai, S. 2005 *Ugly Feelings*, Cambridge, MA and London: Harvard University Press.

Nixon, J. and Hunter, C. 2009 'Disciplining Women and the Governance of Conduct', in A. Millie (ed.) *Securing Respect: Behavioural Expectations and Anti-Social Behaviour in the UK*, Bristol: Policy Press.

Pitt, K. 2002 'Being a New Capitalist Mother', *Discourse and Society* 13: 251–67.

Probyn, E. 2004 'Shame in the Habitus', in L. Adkins and B. Skeggs (eds) *Feminism After Bourdieu*, Oxford: Blackwell.

Ranciere, J. 1983 *The Philosopher and his Poor*, Durham and London: Duke University Press.

Savage, M. 2003 'A New Class Paradigm? Review Article', *British Journal of Sociology of Education* 24(4): 535–41.

Skeggs, B. 1997 *Formations of Class and Gender: Becoming Respectable*, London: Sage.

——2004 *Class, Self, Culture*, London: Routledge.

——2009 'Haunted by the Spectre of Judgement: Respectability, Value and Affect in Class Relations', in K. Sveinsson (ed.) *Who Cares about the White Working Class*, London: Runnymede Trust.

Thompson, R. *et al.* 2011 *The Making of Modern Motherhood*, Bristol: The Policy Press.

Thrift, N. 2008 *Non-Representational Theory*, Abingdon, Oxon: Routledge.

Tyler, I. 2008 'Chav Mum Chav Scum: Class Disgust in Contemporary Britain', *Feminist Media Studies* 8(1): 17–34.

Walkerdine, V. and Lucey, H. 1989 *Democracy in the Kitchen: Regulating Mothers and Socialising Daughters*, London: Virago.

Wood, H. 2009 *Talking with Television: Women, Talk Shows and Modern Self-Reflexivity*, Illinois: Illinois University Press.

Wood, H. and Skeggs, B. (eds) 2011 *Reality Television and Class*, London: BFI/Palgrave.

Chapter 7

The productive person
Recognizing labour and value

In the previous chapters we argued that in looking for the affective reactions of our viewers to reality television, we were able to see the moments where they made particular connections with the text, which could take them beyond or around an interpretation of representation and a deconstruction of meaning. These reactions differed in style and content across our groups, patterned by the ways in which our respondents located themselves in circuits of value, which we were able to identify by comparing the different kinds of data collected across interviews, viewing sessions and focus groups. We unearthed a complex array of findings in which we found some considerable solidarity between women as they looked to 'care' for others, whilst we also uncovered a good degree of antipathy from women, often in situations where their own proximity to the experience of the television participants proved most threatening. Our findings support the ways affect can be seen as part of a social process, a way in which the appeal to the singular self can only be made in relation to wider social relations. This sustains our overall argument that the appeal to the individual of the kind described by the governmentality thesis can never be divorced from the social. We therefore contest Kavka's (2008) point that reality television's shift away from the straightforwardly representational is also a shift *beyond* the social. Rather we detail the way reality television invokes and *makes* the social in potentially more complicated but nevertheless divisive ways, which are always imbricated in circuits of value.

One of the key findings across our different types of research data is how differences emerged in the ways our research respondents located themselves in vectors of time and space. As we described in Chapter 4 these were localized familial relations for all the working class groups, whilst the middle class group were constantly engaged in accruing value which had future potential. This picture was complicated by the Clapham (South Asian working class) group's articulation of learning and getting 'tips' from reality television, which we think is framed by their deployment of difference as a means to access cultural value. But these different investments in time, and movement across social space, frame all of the women's affective and cognitive responses and we stress that these are part of the women's location in longer social histories of the kind we described in Chapter 2 that also pre-date neo-liberal regimes. This more differential picture can be made visible through drawing together the numerous ways in which the women's responses are located in various classed and gendered histories of labour which complicates their emerging relationship to the 'self-work ethic' constantly promoted by the self-transformation television programmes.

Labour and the productive self of neo-liberalism

As Stuart Hall (1998) remarks 'Not since the workhouse has labour been so fervently and single-mindedly valorised' (p.83). Since 1998 across the Western neo-liberal world the significance of labour has intensified in which the subject must constantly work on itself to increase its tradable value in different fields of social life, including the intimate, the aesthetic and the domestic, through consumption and paid work. Paul Heelas (2002) also notes the ever-increasing significance of work as an ethic. Identifying the different historical 'ideal-types' of work ethic from the protestant to the present day, he outlines a new form of 'soft-capitalism' which involves a 'turn to life' that assumes that work makes us more effective as a worker and as a person more generally, by which our life is enriched through enhancing commitment and motivation. Performing work is therefore always about *becoming*, not just *being*; developing potential that is always future-directed. He calls this the 'self-work ethic'. In this 'self-work ethic' it is life-itself in all its permutations that is called into effect on our reality television programmes that promote self-transformation. The individual must constantly work on themselves in order to add value to their future (and their family's future). This has become a particularly pertinent ethical imperative for mothering – for adding value to children – and for the reproduction of the workforce: as substantial research demonstrates (Briggs 2009; Buckingham and Scanlon 2003; Pitt 2002; Reay 1998; Rose 1989; Thomson *et al.* 2011; Walkerdine and Lucey 1989). This has led Angela McRobbie (2002) to suggest that, 'In exacting new resources of self-reliance on behalf of the working population, work appears to supplant, indeed hijack, the realm of the social' (p.99).

One of the major dynamics of capital in the present is how to guarantee the supply of labour into the future. David Staples (2007) argues that to maintain capital, it is not just the supply of labour (movement, biological reproduction and bio-politics more generally) that needs sustaining but also, he argues, entropic energy (unwilling labour, not yet mobilized labour, often domestic labour), which has to be converted into productive labour for capital. In parallel the state increasingly attempts to withdraw (in the UK) from sustaining the reproduction of the workforce, through privatization, and changes to welfare that force mothers into work. Feher (2009) notes the struggles between capital and the state in the Western economies since the 1970s as capital attempts to make the state pay for reproducing its workforce and the state tries not to do so. Both powerful forces attempt to make people pay for the costs of their own reproduction. The fervent valorization of labour can be seen as a response to these demands. What is odd is how ardently this imperative has been taken up on television which promotes labouring (on oneself, on others) as central to the production of the proper person as also entertainment. For instance, Ouellette and Hay (2008a) extensively discuss the ways in which a number of reality shows from *What Not to Wear* to *America's Next Top Model* present the self as a subject of constant reinvention mirroring the requirements of the flexible labour market of the neo-liberal economy. They encourage the numerous 'harsh pedagogic strategies' where programmes detail techniques to engineer minute details of the self, maximizing assets and minimizing shortcomings, for personal advantage in the market place. And not only are people encouraged to direct themselves towards paid work, they are also expected to mimic the dispositions of paid work throughout their lives. This type of critique leads a number of authors to refer to television's close alliance with workplace models of self-hood as the process of self-branding – to use Tyra Banks' oft cited phrase to be the 'CEO of me' (Hearn 2008a, 2008b; Ouellette and Hay 2008b).

We can see how reality television presents a vision of this entropic conversion, constantly requesting that those positioned as the entropic reorganize their energy into something worthwhile, to themselves, to their families, in relation to consumption, to the nation in claims to citizenship, and to capital more generally. This is presented as both a moral-governing and capital-enhancing project. Self-transformation is about becoming a constantly entropy-converting subject, willing and able to use one's labour in some productive way, never wasting energy or time. It is the production of ready, able, willing, capacity-rich subjects that are flexible and adaptable that is demanded by capital and governments working in the interests of capital.

Angela McRobbie (2002) documents the extensive raft of government 'welfare to work' schemes in the US and the UK in which the person who does not work becomes marked as the burden on the nation, the immoral individual who is not responsible and does not contribute. More recently McRobbie (2009) has noted how the responsibility for becoming the 'new' ethical subjects of the neo-liberal economy, those with the greatest potential to make their life anew, to make the 'right' choices and become the proper subject of the nation, are figured as young women. In Chapter 3 we argued that in many of our programmes we see the visualization of various permutations of labour to be performed as *the* responsibility of women. Many of the programmes in our sample focus on intimate, emotional and domestic labour, where it is assumed that women will and should also engage in paid work. This has a particularly historical gendered inflection because as we discussed in Chapter 1 women have long been subject to models of self-improvement which now apparently seem to 'mirror' neo-liberal solutions to flexible labour practices. They are now expected to be the ever-productive subjects of capital, entering the social relations of labour outside the home and engaging in multiple forms of cultural and biological reproduction, converting commodities into use-value in the home.

Labour of *all* kinds is presented as self-actualizing, something that is morally good for the person and the nation. The self-transformation reality television programmes that we examined, and in particular the make-over programmes, promote the idea of the woman as the ethical subject with full capacity to adjust, adapt and adopt new ways of performing labour and consumption in the formal economy. Her ability to 'choose' to perform her new freedom via work becomes a measure of her moral person-value and is often signified as feminist 'empowerment'. But it is one that she performs as a potential 'she' rather than a collective female 'we'; an individual 'she' in need of enhancement through her own labour in the name of her own choice and freedom.

This chapter details the different elements of labour that became significant to viewer reactions to and evaluations of a participant's performance of the 'self-work ethic' on reality television. Whilst for many writers TV is 'governing at a distance' and some even describe the audience member at home as the 'TV-viewer pupil' (Ouellette and Hay 2008a:109), as we have discussed in Chapter 5 our audiences' relationships to direct models of governance are often ambiguous and sometimes even downright hostile. We think this is because our viewers are located in longer histories of classed and gendered positioning that delimit the possibilities for investment in value which bring out a more complex range of ways in which our viewers react to the performance of labour on television.

The productive use of time

The insistence on labour as a sign of ethical worth and responsibility in which every activity is a value-generating activity makes time rather than space primary in the evaluation of labour performances. We were first alerted to very different class dispositions towards the use of time in our initial interviews where we asked about the use of television in people's lives generally. As we demonstrated in Chapter 4 we found radical differences between our middle class women's attitude towards turning on the television to that of our working class respondents from all three groups. The middle class women devised rules and strategies for controlling television's intervention in their lives in case their time was 'stolen from them' or wasted. This was very different from our working class respondents who had the television on all the time and were not at all worried about wasting time. For instance, note Deirdre's sense of time in her resistance to watching television:

DEIRDRE: I mean that's why I have moved it 'cos I thought no it's just taking up *too much time* … I wouldn't have just switched it on and left it on, I never did that …

BEV: Right you wouldn't watch it? Why don't you like it?

DEIRDRE: I just, well, it's the sense that it's *just a waste of time* … Why I wouldn't (watch it). Well very much again the sense of *a complete waste of my time*. When I was *sort of watching it, I mean this is the thing about television, I think it's rather hypnotic and I succumb to it*, so I start watching it, and I'm thinking getting involved, but actually thinking what an absolute load of shite basically, this is my feeling. *And so just a sense of having completely wasted time* and, you know, what on earth do people sort of, you know, want *to achieve*, I don't know.

(Deirdre, Forest Hill, interview)

The stress Deidre makes about the abuse of her time suggests she has a strong sense of what is good and bad time use and television fits into the latter. Wasting her time on something that she thinks has no value is an issue for her. The emphasis on wasted time and using time to achieve something is made even more specific by Ruby 2 who notes:

I just think *there's a lot more to life than TV* ... and there's other things that I'm doing with *regards to my work* and things that require me to focus. I just *try and find different things to do because there are different things to do in the world.*

(Ruby 2, Forest Hill, interview)

She goes on to establish rules for her use of time:

RUBY 2: I'm trying to get away from this TV thing ... I've got new rules.
NANCY: And so from what you said your TV's not always on in the background?
RUBY 2: No, it used to be, but again that's a habit I've chosen to break out of. I just think there's a lot more to life than TV ... and there's other things that I'm doing with regards to my work and things that require me to focus.

(Ruby 2, Forest Hill, interview)

Ruby 2 here is describing a journey of personal development away from television, 'breaking the habit' and connecting her time to her work. When we ask Ruby 2 what she does with her time, she is concerned to tell us that she spends all her time productively:

What do I do with my free time!? I try to go out as much as I possibly can, so I'll, you know, I mean part of my occupation what I do, kind of you know, when I go to the theatre sometimes it's not free time, I'm going there to catch a show or *network* a bit. But I go out, I see friends, I go to the gym, I work out, sometimes I do dance classes, sometimes I do singing classes, which is kind of a spare time thing, but it also helps, you know, my profession ... I'm trying to get into watching live music more, I do a little bit of that ... But yeah kind of, yeah ... doing a few classes. I read a lot and I suppose I do write in my spare time. Yeah kind of, I could go out to the theatre and cinema, that and do cultural things like going to the art galleries and things like that.

Every single activity in which Ruby 2 is involved (and we know she actually does what she says) converts her energy into productive potential and increases her overall person value through the accrual of capitals. She lives the self-work ethic where every energy output is a self-productive activity with an eye on the future. For Ruby 2 there is no gap between leisure and work (as for most of this group) and all activities are productive and convertible, making their time contribute towards the generation of the 'enterprising self', as described by du Gay (1986). She is the perfect ethical subject of soft capitalism, as were many of our middle class respondents.[1] For those with children the activities in which they are engaged convert their and their children's energy into capital, corresponding to what Annette Laureau (2003) calls 'concerted cultivation' – namely, growing into the self-work ethic.

Gender and time use: precious and wasted time

The responses above came about from discussing television in general in our interviews where our middle class interviewees carefully articulated a sense of the productive self. But if the arguments of governance are to be followed through to their functional extension then the 'TV-viewer-pupil' should not just apply to the middle classes, but must extend the messages of future accrual at every turn. As Ouellette and Hay (2008a) and Weber (2009) discuss, the gendering of discourses of self-transformation have particular inflections in the made-over female body of television as programmes pronounce 'aesthetic labour' as essential to advancement in the workplace, whereby the discourses of a programme like *What Not to Wear* become incorporated into the language of post-feminist female empowerment (Negra 2008; Negra and Holmes 2008; Negra and Tasker 2007).

But, as we alluded to in Chapter 5, it was actually relatively rare that we found viewers uncritical of the kind of advice espoused by *WNTW* expert hosts Trinny and Susannah, finding them too cruel and often preferring television participants who rebelled against them:

BEV: You don't think its useful for tips or anything?
NICOLA: No. The best one I saw, she was rebelling against everything they said and then they found this really nice dress for a premiere that she was going to with Chris or whatever and she just went entirely against them, she put the dress on for the big reveal but then just changed it in the car!

(Nicola, Addington, interview)

Nicola was typical of a straightforward rejection of the invitation to learn, and this type of rejection of pedagogic advice was also often read through an understanding of the time available for the labour required. As Michelle says about *What Not to Wear*:

Yeah, yeah. And you think … they forget that normal women have just got to go out and go to work and sort the kids out, and you know that does stuff your dresses up a bit.

(Michelle, Addington, interview)

Similarly Lucy, a mother from our Forest Hill group, during a text-in-action viewing session, speaks back to the *What Not to Wear* episode on making over tired mothers – see Table 7.1

Lucy assesses the advice of make-over experts Trinny and Susannah in terms of the presumed time available for labour. She begins by suggesting the conditions for childcare between the experts and participants are radically different, which leads her to de-authorize the experts in specific class terms as, 'stuck up posh bird' (lines 7/8). That the television participant has triplets makes Lucy, as a mother, even more sympathetic and protective towards her, hence the strong response, shouting at the television 'experts' in a direct challenge to their assessment and authority.

In a later section (see Table 7.2) she is more willing (momentarily) to listen to their advice. Lucy begins to think that Trinny understands the issue of clothing and childcare (line 6) but then realizes, as the programme develops, that the speech of the experts is different to their action, as they reveal that they really have no idea of the practicalities of the labour of childcare for other women. When the experts' impractical advice leads them to criticize the television participant, Lucy becomes enraged. The failure of the 'experts' to understand the labour requirements of different women's lives, and hence their time ('you have got enough to do', line 26) informs all of Lucy's responses.

Lucy's response would not surprise Bourdieu (1986) who notes:

> It is because the cultural capital that is effectively transmitted within the family itself depends *not only* on the quantity of cultural capital, itself *accumulated by spending time*, that the domestic group possess, but also on the *usable time* (particularly in the form of mother's free time) available to it.
>
> (Bourdieu 1986:253 our emphasis)

The gendering of time for labour is central to the connections made to both television experts and participants and this issue produced some degree of solidarity between women. It is also central to how reactions are informed by the conditions that generate class reproduction. For Marx (1967) it is time, energy and capacity that constitutes labour power and as he noted long ago 'socially necessary labour time' is precisely the time it takes to reproduce and service the workforce (although see feminist critiques which ask why biological and domestic labour was not factored into the fundamental analysis of capital value: Barrett 1982; Brenner and Ramas 1984; Glucksmann 2005; Hartmann and Sargent 1981; Steedman 2004). Our respondents understand the expenditure of time and energy and place themselves in relation to its possibility.

What is important to note, is that Lucy does not address the programme as if deconstructing a textual representation of characters as such, but makes a 'constitutive actualisation' (Sobchack 1999, 2004) (see Chapter 4) with the participant. She places herself in the situation as an arbiter of expertise, as neither the expert nor participant, but judge, by immanently assessing this advice for her

Table 7.1

	Cue / Image	Television Text *What Not to Wear (Tired Mothers)*	Viewer comments *Lucy (Forest Hill)*
1	2.23	**Trinny (introducing potential participants):**... the main offenders for closer inspection ...	**Lucy:** I bet they have got a nanny.
2			**Bev:** Yeah?
3			**Lucy:** I bet they have. I bet they have
4			got a nanny and it's all very well isn't
5			it?
5	4.27	**Trinny (on mothering):** There are all those juggling acts that are really tough	**Lucy:** Oh I think it's true but...But I
6			think that it's true but I don't think
7			people want to hear it from some stuck
8			up posh bird with a nanny. Do you
9			know what I mean
10	7.13	**Susannah:** it's Sarah, a mother of triplets who not surprisingly	**Lucy:** triplets?!
11			
12	7.19	**Trinny:** because they have triplets	**Lucy:** and no nanny.
13			**Bev:** mmm?
14			**Lucy:** and no nanny
15	7.45	**Trinny:** three kids at 23	
16	7.57	**Susannah:** ...drab, dull, uninteresting woman	**Lucy [shouting]:** NO YOU ARE EXHAUSTED YOU HAVE GOT
17			THREE KIDS!

Table 7.2

	Cue/Image	Television Text What Not to Wear (Tired Mothers)	Viewer comments Lucy (Forest Hill)
1	33.16	**Susannah:** Now we are suggesting	
2		clothes which are practical	
3		by being in a pattern that'll	
4		cover up sick, a bit of tomato	
5		ketchup…	
6			**Lucy:** (laughs) that is quite good.
7			
8	34.01	**Participant Claire:** I can't imagine I	
9		would ever wear that. I like the style but	
10		the whole colour	**Lucy:** Where is she going to wear that
11			though? She has got triplets? Where
12			exactly? You know, once a year to her
13			husband's Christmas do and it's not
14			going to hide sick is it?
15	35.2	**Trinny:** If you come back in the same	**Lucy:** She doesn't get it though does
16		clothes you are wearing now I will	she? (reference to Trinny). Why women
17		personally strangle you. You have	dress like that, it's practicality; you
18		£2,000	want stuff that washes and dries quick.
19			You want stuff that maybe doesn't need
20			ironing. I have got lovely dresses, I
21			don't wear them to school because I
22			would get snotted on and you know I
23			am getting up and down off the floor
24			and it…because I don't want to be
25			hand-washing and ironing and stuff, you
26			know you have got enough to do.
27			**Bev:** exactly
28			**Lucy:** they should be finding them nice
29			stuff that's easy care and it doesn't
30			seem to be.

own life as well as that of the television participants: 'I have got lovely dresses; I don't wear them to school because I would get snotted on ... I don't want to be hand-washing [etc.] ... ' (lines 20–26). The aesthetic labour of femininity, made explicit on programmes like *What Not to Wear* through the amount of effort, skill and knowledge required, was recognized by our respondents precisely *as* labour and not as natural and inevitable to an essential femininity, which is exposed in the contradictory governmental assumptions of the make-over.

The use of time and energy expended is also a key element in the adjudication of the effort made towards others in intimate relationships: are they worth it? This is a question participants are often invited to ask (by experts, by the experience of the swap in programmes like *Wife Swap*, or incited by those close-up to-camera moments which call for some assessment of a particular situation). As the subject of reality television is expected to perform the self-work ethic in all activities of their life, the objects to who they direct their attention are delineated as worthy or unworthy recipients, with relationships evaluated between necessary or wasted labour. In a particular episode of *Wife Swap* from series one with Carole and Peter and Michelle and Barry (discussed in Chapter 3), Barry remained in our audiences' memories long after the series had finished. The programme was first screened in 2003, regularly repeated and is often cited as an example of the absolute limit to women's love labour in intimate heterosexual relationships.

In the programme Michelle, who worked a 60-hour week, woke at five every morning to do all the housework, and lived with Barry, a man who did not have a job and seemed to barely do anything other than demand food – stunningly visualized in his large salad bowl filled with porridge that he insisted Michelle make for him every morning. She also washed his gym clothes everyday and drove him to the gym before going to her full-time paid work. In the evenings Barry goes to the pub with his mates whilst Michelle stays at home, sometimes with her teenage son, often doing more domestic work in preparation for the next day. Michelle swapped with Carole (an actress and theatre tutor), whose husband was in paid employment, helped with the housework and talked to her intimately and discussed her work. Michelle could barely believe the ease of her swapped life when she first moved into Carole's house. However, at the end of the swap we see Michelle (dramatically enclosed with Barry in a car on the Yorkshire Moors in the pouring rain) desperately trying to force him to admit on camera that he loves her. When Michelle and Carole face each other at the end of the swap, as usual, a verbal fight over household labour ensues when Michelle learns that Barry had made Carole a cup of tea: 'He's never made me a cup of tea in fifteen years,' shouts Michelle and Carole laughs.

For our respondents Michelle became a figure of pity and lack of hope, wasted time and a wasted life. She represents a bad investor (both in accrual and relational terms) as she resigns herself to her bad treatment, drudgery, lack of appreciation and ultimately becomes the symbol of the suffering and enduring wife. Barry was the epitome of a bad investment.[2] Such responses were epitomized by Ruby 1 in her Text in Action (TIA) session – see Table 7.3.

Table 7.3

	Cue / Image	Television text Wife Swap (Michelle and Carole)	Viewer Comments Ruby1 (Brockley)
1	9.25	**Voice over:** Back at the house Michelle is about to meet Peter...	
2			
3	10.1	**Voice over:** Finally Carole gets to meet Barry...	He doesn't like working does he?
4			He does nothing, but vegetate in a
5			massive bowl of porridge. Oh he's
6			nasty.
7			
8	20.11		He's got to get his arse off of the—, oh
9	Barry in the bath with paper		my God.
10	20.24		What a ghastly little man.
11	20.3		Look, he's eating it out of a fruit bowl
12	Barry eating porridge		for Christ's sake, oh my God.
13			*[Laughs]*.
14	22.4	**Voice over:** ...Every morning Michelle	Oh dear.
15		drives Barry to the gym, once she's	
16		packed his bag with clean sports wear...	
17		This is an essential part of Barry's daily	
18		routine.	
19			
20	22.5		Why would she stay? Why do people ...
21			his wife is slogging her guts out.
22	25.4	**Voice over:** ...although Barry	He is a really, really rude man. He needs
23		recognizes some of Carol's good	to get up off his backside and get a job.
24		qualities, she hasn't had much good to	He can't even feed himself.
25		say about him.	Even like there's the porridge, he's not
26			gonna go for more [laughs].
27			
28	35.22	**Voice over:** Carol has had enough of	'Cause he can.
29		Barry's methods, she wants to know why	
30		he behaves the way he does.	

Barry is positioned in the programme (note the effect of the voice-over) as the monstrous masculine. But what Ruby responds to is Barry's entropy, his lack of desire to work and his lack of appreciation of all of Michelle's labour. None of our participants placed themselves 'as if' in this relationship as they could not constitutively actualize themselves into this situation which would mean imagining themselves in such circumstances, powerless and hope-less, nor did they respond via *shadenfreude* (there was no ambivalence to channel). But our respondents judge and condemn Michelle for allowing herself to be exploited, asking: 'Why would she stay?' (line 20). To which Ruby replies to her own implied question, 'Why does he do it?' with "Cause he can' (line 28). Ruby responds with a clear feminist understanding of gendered power. Therefore, in keeping with Holmes and Jermyn's (2007) assessment of *Wife Swap,* the emphasis upon the performance of domestic labour, whilst condemning the entropy of some subjects, also allows for an analysis of women's investments in domestic, emotional, aesthetic and sexual labour.

Motherhood as an alternative source of value

Exactly where people 'chose' to perform their labour was an issue for many of our respondents. As we detailed in Chapter 5 our working class women in particular produced negative emotional responses to an aspirational woman in an episode of *Wife Swap* where Kate, mother of six, swaps with working mum of one, Tracy. Recall the anger produced in one of the Addington and one of Brockley TIA viewing sessions at Tracy's pretentiousness and lack of care for her child. First, they object to Tracy's crying to camera when faced with the prospect of looking after six children, they also take a dislike to Tracy's apparent aspirational airs, and are outraged when she prioritizes her formal work over her childcare.

The significance of motherhood therefore emerges as a key site in which the limits of the productive individual, in terms of formally entering the workplace, are resisted. (Although we might argue that programmes like *Supernanny* assert similar models through a notion of productive parenting). We discussed in Chapter 5 how this resistance offered the working class women in our study a route to moral authority outside of the pressure on women to return to work in low-paid employment as part of the neo-liberal political agenda. That time should be spent on the children also emerged as important for our Clapham focus group when talking about the paucity of South Asian families on reality television:

NAHEID: I can't remember their names. I remember once on *Wife Swap* there was an Asian family. Always remember it only because they were from a very rich background from Pakistan, so the guy had come in and they had brought in like servants with them ...

CHABERA: They used to go there (reference to an After School Club) straight from school. And those poor children used to come home and go to that centre, then come back and do work and their parents were always *working, working, working*, so that kind of, really, I felt really sorry for the children and the *Wife Swap* was a woman that came who was very like a stay-at-home mum and very laid back, and the children used to do everything fine. I felt so sorry for those children, like 'oh my God', what are they, about five, six. They were a really young age and, you know, they're taking out all the fun and I think maybe because it's an Asian family. I mean the servant woman was doing more for the children than the mum.

NAHEID: And the parents [inaudible 48.45] was like, 'Well we're doing this for their future.' 'You know so they can have a better future', *they don't understand that*. You know.

(Clapham, focus group)

Here 'working, working, working' for the future is seen to be a bad investment for women in both time and space, out of the home with no fun for the children. The value of the work ethic (even without the self-work ethic) is reversed and seen to be a negative use of energy and time. Our South Asian group, four of whom were full-time, stay-at-home mothers held a similar position to our other working class respondents for whom formal work offers few rewards in comparison to motherhood.

The value of the 'self-work ethic' was beginning to emerge in our research as a specific form of address to those who envisaged and could convert their energy, with access to the right resources, into future potential. It did not speak to those who are unlikely to have access to the means to generate value from the time and energy invested in low-paid work. This is why we need to understand the different sources and possibilities for value. Full-time motherhood both offsets the low value produced through low paid work, whilst also offering the potential for moral and affective value. Investment in motherhood is both a 'rational'[3] understanding of accrual potential as well as a *relational* investment which offers returns from love and giving: full time motherhood offers a future *with* value.

Enduring labour: 'just getting on with it'

The visual performance of labour that is often central to the dramatic action on reality television was *always* significant to the ways viewers assessed participants. 'Just getting on with it' was a regular positive criterion for assessing the moral value of reality participants for our working class groups. Below, one of the Addington focus groups debate the merits of a negatively loaded female figure of media derision, Jordan[4] on *I'm a Celebrity Get Me Out of Here*:

NICOLA: I always liked Jordan.
JOAN: I didn't.
VIK: I didn't either.
JOAN: I didn't like her.

MEL: Well not that I didn't like her, I didn't know her, I didn't know anything about her really just what I'd seen on the telly and I think she's got a bad, not a bad name but she adds up, well she did. I really did hear her talking and that, she had quite a lot to talk about, it weren't just about herself. She's quite a funny person as well. You think a person like her, 'cause she's got money and that and she's going to be spoilt: 'me me me', but she weren't. She was like –, she *did the tasks* and that, she didn't think, 'no I ain't doing that', like some of them said, 'I'm not going to do that', and *she just got on and did it.*

JOAN: She had to prove herself and she did.

(Addington 2, focus group)

Our participants' perception of a woman completely vilified in the British media transforms after they see her making an effort and not complaining. For Joan this means she has 'proven herself' to have value in their eyes. Jordan's uncomplaining labour is assessed through the same value system that our focus group apply to themselves. Here again we have an underlying assessment of pretension (those that complain that they are too good to do the tasks) alongside the practical labouring of 'just getting on with it'. Moaning, whingeing and complaining about having to do things are dispositions associated with those who think they have choice over what they can do, the spaces they can enter and the time they can spend, an entirely different perspective on life more generally. They see Jordan just getting on with things in the same way as they would. We could see this as a resignation to labour without complaint and/or we could see it as a critique of different dispositions to labour in relation to one's potential movement through time and space.

There is a good deal of discussion across our data, particularly from our working class participants, about the value attached to people 'coping'. Another vilified figure who achieved celebrity status through the reality genre was Lizzie Bardsley from the first series of *Wife Swap* who was unapologetically loud and engaged in a spectacular row with the other wife. Lizzie definitely did not promote the self-work ethic or the new subject of soft capitalism, instead she was entropy personified. The hugely negative symbolic portrayal of Lizzie on the show and in the press afterwards, represented her as irresponsible, lazy, unhealthy, and a 'benefit scrounger' with eight children supported by the state. However, rather than accept this negative value-loading, Sharon and Michelle from Addington describe the value they saw in watching how she 'coped' with her life.

SHARON: So you remember Lizzy?

MICHELLE: Just how she managed to cope with what she had. She had loads of children didn't she?

SHARON: Yeah, eight children.

MICHELLE: And she used to have to do all the dinners and I don't know, I couldn't do it myself.

(Sharon and Michelle, Addington, interview)

Instead of the condemnation invited by the programme and the press, Sharon and Michelle respond to the difficulties Lizzie must face in just feeding her eight children. The labour of their own lives is lived through the valorization of indefatigability and struggle that have a long history in working class culture, for example see Paul Willis' (1977) discussion of 'practical labour'. The indefatigability is not about a disposition to time-use to become a productive self for the future, but about finding value in one's likely conditions. Our working class respondents assess the where and the how of the labour performed, subjecting others to the judgements and they apply to themselves. This may also point to an historical inheritance, to a time when labour was dignified and endurance was considered to be a moral quality (Walkerdine 2010).

The performance of labour

As we have discussed in Chapter 1, appearing on reality television *as* labour has come to frame discussions about participants' working rights. For some this constitutes doing the 'work of being watched' (Andrejevic 2004) and protracted legal battles now ensue over the rights of reality television participants. Our working class groups supported the idea that there should be some direct financial reward for appearing on reality television. The Addington group were very sympathetic towards reality television participants who had used their appearance for commercial gain:

MICHELLE: If they make money out of it good luck to them. You know if they've had courage to go that far and have people see them and then to turn it on its head in other words and use the system to make money, why not?

HELEN: Why not. 'Cos one group got quite upset about that, one group were like, you know, 'They've done nothing really and now suddenly they've got'.

KAYLEIGH: But you get famous people who aren't really doing anything anyway. *But these people have been theirself –*, .

ALL: Yeah.

KAYLEIGH: And making money from it.

SHARON: Money from being themselves.

KAYLEIGH: – or whatever and got loads of money out of it and whatever, I mean, yeah those sort of people that, yeah but when *they like sort of come from nothing and they've made out of it from being themselves. Who are they harming?*

(Addington 1, focus group)

This group proposes that there should be some reward for exposing your *self* on television especially given the risk of ridicule that this entails. For our Brockley focus group, whose participants were Black and white working class, participating on reality television was seen as a realistic way of escaping the difficulties of providing for a family with economic constraints. Here the discussion focuses upon another vilified white working class woman – Jade Goody, who became famous for the vicious attacks made about her by *The Sun* tabloid newspaper and the responses they evoked. These were based on her lack of propriety: her colloquial direct speech, her size, her lack of education and her humour on the first series of *Big Brother*.[5]

SONIA: Don't get her started about Jade.

RUBY 1:   I kind of like Jade. I kind of like Jade. My little ghetto rat *made good*, you know what I mean [laughter]. I like her.

SALLY MC: [inaudible 14.32] reality TV. This is what it's done for a lot, the ghetto rats that you're all referring to.

SALLY: I like Jade.

SALLY MC: About *giving them a chance*?

RUBY 1:   Before you're struggling, ducking and diving, and then you get an *opportunity* through reality TV and then all of a sudden you're able to provide for yourself, provide for your family and not go to bed and … you know what I mean … And not wake up in the morning and think, 'Oh God, where is this going to come from, where am I going to get that from?' Reality TV does that.

SALLY: Yeah.

JANET: No, I like Jade.

MARIAN: I do actually.

RUBY: It's *only* Jade that I like. I think she's done very well.

MARIAN: She does her own shows.

(Brockley, focus group)

The connection to Jade is made through the evocation of similar social circumstances, struggling to provide, and an ironic commentary on the pathologizing of Black and white working class women in British culture. The repetition (nine times in the total discussion of Jade) of 'I like her' from all the focus group participants signals a defence against the negative value generally attributed to Jade and those like her (positioned as the abject working class – see Skeggs 2005; Tyler and Bennett 2010). That Ruby, Sally Mc and Sally are Black perhaps produces the particular articulation of 'ghetto rats', but it is through a shared sense of struggle that Jade's actual labour is valued. Her participation on reality television presents an opportunity structure, with the possibility of not having to worry constantly about providing for your family, as Sal and Ruby note:

SAL: About giving them a chance?

SAL: … ducking and diving, and you get an opportunity through reality TV and then all of a sudden you're able to provide for yourself, provide for your family and not go to bed- and … you know what I mean.

RUBY 1: Think about the dole queue the next morning, yeah

SAL: And not wake up in the morning and think, 'Oh God, where is this going to come from, where am I going to get that from?' Reality TV does that.

SEVERAL: Yeah.

(Brockley, focus group)

The women here directly inserted themselves into the lives that are on display on the television, they generate a fantasy of not struggling to provide for their families, projecting themselves into the comfort of the position of a successful television participant who can live without poverty. Reality television is not viewed as morally bad and exploitative (as it was by our middle class respondents) but as the remote but imagined possibility of a less constricted future: not as a textual ideological object but as a 'real' structure of opportunity. This says a lot about the current conjuncture where being humiliated on reality television and in the media can be converted into an opportunity, as it can set in motion other media avenues in the case of Jade: perhaps a brutal admission of the closure of other routes.

The fact that they assess Jade's (then[6]) success 'she's done well' as she did it herself (referring to her own television shows) by 'staying real' articulates a resistance to the forms of transformation that are promoted on reality television. Jordan, Lizzie and Jade represent that which is symbolically denigrated on television and in dominant culture more generally: loud, accented, sexual, large, fecund, local, excessive in every form, uncompromising and without pretensions. They all come from similar economic and cultural positions to the research respondents above and all are seen to be deserving of their success because they were not ashamed of, or apologized for, their culture. They are valued not just for labour but for unpretentiousness, coping and getting on with it. Just as indefatigability has a long history in working class culture so do critiques of pretension, following a long tradition of de-authorizing the imposition of middle class standards, identified by Vicinus (1974) and Bailey (1998), and continued to the present day in television, music and film (Hunt 1998; Skeggs 2004).[7]

This validation of the ability of working class television participants to extract value from their public performances becomes even more interesting when we see the very different responses from our middle class respondents. When Kayleigh from Addington asks of reality television participants 'who are they harming?' the answer is clearly answered in the responses we found in our middle class group – and potentially the bourgeois press. The Forest Hill group consider participation on reality television not as an opportunity structure but as 'getting something for nothing', as undeserving labour. Participation on reality television devalues their own investments in labour and education, by offering a public space to those who have no cultural or educational value. They use the similarly devalued phrase of celebrity to signal this lack of worth:

LISELLE: That's why I have a problem (with reality television). I think, because once it gets into getting something out of it –,

ANN: It's *humiliating*.

LISELLE: It says at what lengths you will go to and I think, I *think we start to think that you don't have to work hard at things* and we don't have to, it's like kids who just want to be famous, you know it doesn't matter what I do but I want to be famous. It takes away every sense of working hard at things and thinking about making a difference or it's just about this –,

ANN: Yeah.

ORLAINE: I think, I think it's called trash or trash is also about this celebrity thing isn't it? About *how people get famous and rich for not having any skills any more.* I mean *that's the trash label as well.* I think there's an element about that, people thinking, you know, that's just trashy that people can just get rich you know, just for doing –,

ANN: *Nothing.*

EMILY: I mean I think that the idea around celebrities is, because you know people are so *desperate* to get on television that they'll do anything, like TVs –, what do you call these morning programmes, that horrible man Jeremy –,

(Forest Hill, focus group)

In this conversation, labour is converted into a personality disposition, a person desperate to become a celebrity. An undeserving celebrity is a subject-position of an immoral person who should not be attributed with economic value because they have done nothing to deserve it. The middle class respondents challenge the rewards given to participants by appearance on television, because the value has not been 'earned' through either education or work. They do not have the right capitals to convert and accrue. According to Tyler and Bennett (2010) this particular formulation of a celebrity without value who provokes considerable derision in the press and blogosphere is usually a working class woman in the UK – the 'celebrity Chav'. For this group, of which Ruby 2 and Deidre (above) are a part, whose lives are devoted to converting all their energy into productive potential for the future in their self-work ethic, to be visibly confronted by those who have apparently made no effort other than to 'be themselves' is disconcerting and leads to the expression of outrage. For them being productive means accruing value through the investment of time and energy, which is very different to the quick fix gain on offer by reality television.[8]

Even though this group have incredible critical and abstract skills for analysing television programmes, understand its production pressures and political economy and have made affective reaches into the difficult relationships of some television participants lives, the restructuring of reward is a step too far. They detach the television participants from their social circumstances and read them as undeserving individuals in the focus group context. The Forest Hill group's investment in their own capitals and labour leads them to negatively assess others who have not invested in the same way, overlooking the fact that others may not have had access to the same benefits of education and work. They articulate a work ethic which values personal industry: '*I think we start to think that you don't have to work hard to get things*' and people '*get famous and rich for not having any skills any more*' that writers like Christopher Lasch (1979) suggest have collapsed in the new economy of entrepreneurialism. What they value and think matters are energies connected to the rewards of paid work, reliant on legitimate skills and education, reproducing a more traditional formulation of labour and a traditional value system. What we see expressed are concerns about how their own energy conversion (via labour and education) and their own values and investments are challenged by the celebrity potential of reality television.

To leave the picture here though is rather unfair as it relies on the type of performance and articulation that comes out of the focus group effect where our middle class respondents used their abstract knowledge of the cultural sector to explore the meaning of reality television which drew on circulating public narratives of the reality television genre. However, as we outlined before and in Chapter 5, when watching reality television and placed in an immanent relationship with the text, a very different picture sometimes emerges, further complicating the analysis.

Performing how

As we have discussed, the drama of many reality television programmes is generated by taking television participants out of their habituated lives and moving them into radically different environments (e.g. *Ladette to Lady, What the Butler Saw*, including the more successful *Wife Swap* and *Faking It*, or taking them into extreme circumstances e.g. *Survivor, I'm a Celebrity*) in order to see what they might learn in order to 'improve' themselves. As we discussed in Chapter 3 in *Faking It* contestants are 'trained' in skills, of which they have no previous knowledge, so a bike courier becomes a polo player, an army captain fakes a drag queen, and a 'choir girl' fakes being a 'rock chic'. We have discussed (in our textual analysis in Chapter 3) how the programme visualizes the difficulty of self-work to entirely 'become' something new. In the episode that we analysed we showed how the problems that Mick the factory worker to fashion-designer faced, in struggling with language and lifestyle, exemplified the impossibility of what Bourdieu (1986) calls the 'how' knowledge. How knowledge is the logic that underpins class practice producing the dispositions to enable cultural capital to be put into effect. These class practices are learnt over a lifetime and become embodied, revealed in bodily dispositions such as confidence, entitlement and anxiety.

Some of our Forest Hill respondents watched the same episode of *Faking It* and Mick the factory worker-come-fashion designer was an object of sympathy (and display of authority) with our research participants:

Table 7.4

Cue/Image	Television text Faking It (Mick Fashion Designer)	Viewer Comments Ann and Geraldine (Forest Hill)
1 2 12.36 3 Mick and mentor around 4 table	**Mick in close up:** I feel a bit pressured about it all... **Mentor:** do you think you can do it though?	
5	**Mick:** I don't know...	**Ann:** I am quite uncomfortable
6	Advertising break	**Geraldine:** I feel really sorry for that guy
7		**Ann:** Yeah
8		**Geraldine:** He is really uncomfortable
9		and he is very anxious
10		**Ann:** I feel really sorry for him...you
11		can see he had just no idea what is
12		going on
13 15.56	Mick embarrassed having to draw a nude	**Geraldine:** He comes across as a
14	woman	really sweet guy.
15 22.57	**Fashion show organizer:** Make sure you	
16 Behind the scenes	have got the next outfit	**Ann:** It's more the general lifestyle
17 at a fashion		isn't it than the skills itself.
18 show		
19		
20 29.49	Fashion expert grills Mick on his designs	
21 Design studio	and career. Mick struggles telling his	
22	career history	
23		
24	**Voice over:** They are not just selling their	**Ann:** It's a big thing isn't it
25	clothes they are selling their vision, Mick's	**Bev:** Mmm
26	vision needs work	**Geraldine:** He's not articulate in the
27		way he...
28		
29		
30		

Table 7.4 (continued)

	Cue/Image	Television text *Faking It (Mick Fashion Designer)*	Viewer Comments *Ann and Geraldine (Forest Hill)*
31	37.12	Mentor asks Mick series of questions related to his 'vision'.	**Geraldine:** Well I do feel he's under a lot of pressure
32	Mentor and		**Ann:** He is not using any kind of
33	designers		proper coaching techniques is he?
34	helping Mick cut	The helpers all laugh at Mick's responses.	**Geraldine:** I do wonder
35	his patterns	**Mentor:** I am so at the end of my tether	**Ann:** Yeah my friend's niece is in
36		today it is unbelievable.	fashion. She used to come home crying
37			every night, it was pretty cruel.
38			**Geraldine:** And I think he is quite a
39			positive person actually.
40			**Ann:** Yeah you do wonder why he is
41			...carried on doing it really because
42	38.56	**Mick to camera:** I am dreading the idea	he wasn't....
43		that I actually might fail and the fact that	**Geraldine:** If you have got nothing at
44		I'm struggling so much talking the talk is	stake, if he is not even paid for it...at
45		what's actually upsetting me. It's the	the end of it...
46		prospect of failure you know. I can't	**Bev:** Yeah
47		bear it.	**Ann:** I can't think why he
48			**Geraldine:** Yeah. But he did say didn't
49			he, failure, he is just scared of failure.
50			**Ann:** He is not convincing enough is
51			he?
52			**Geraldine:** He didn't have the
53			vocabulary, couldn't learn the
54	46.41	**Mick (making speech to convince jurors**	vocabulary in that time scale
55		**where he is struggling to explain**	**Ann:** He didn't have the kind of like
56		**himself):** Maybe one day get a	long standing conviction towards it.
57		sponsorship, train in New York or London	
58			
59			
60			

Our Forest Hill participants begin to see and respond to the distinction Bourdieu describes between skills and the underpinning episteme that enables skills to be operationalized. Mick is not seen to be the 'type' of person (does not have the logic of practice, the habitus) to be at ease in the world in which he is being tested. He had to make enormous efforts to both learn the specific skills (cutting material, assessing textures, measuring bodies) and the logic behind the skills, the confidence, the speech, the communication, the presentation of himself (cultural capital) and making contacts (social capital). But he lacks the 'right' dispositions to put his skills to work. His discomfort about his inability to live in a world without the knowledge of how to be at ease, is clearly visible, and is the point at which Ann and Geraldine respond with considerable sympathy. They say *'I really feel sorry for him'* (line 5) and enter the programme by connecting to the experience of their friend's niece who found fashion 'pretty cruel' (line 41).

Bourdieu and Waquant (1992) use the idea of schemata to refer to the 'mental and bodily' practices of classification that function as symbolic templates for the practical activities – conducts, thoughts, feelings and judgements – of social agents. Jorge Arditi (1999) develops Bourdieu's schemata through Foucault's episteme, focusing on the logic by which classification is structured in the first place, rather than the classification itself.[9] He shows how etiquette books function by their capacity to convey a sense of the infrastructure of social relations of the dominant social group. As we have discussed in other chapters we and others propose that reality television programmes also attempt to establish the 'order of things', whereby the historically established standards of the middle class generate a symbolic template for social relations. For, as Arditi (1999) notes, etiquette guides do not just encourage learning the specific skills – the manners – rather, the most important thing is to *master the logic instructing the manners*: it is to make the logic into a logic of practice, into a habit and habitus so that they make the specific skills look as if they are natural dispositions of the person.

In their post-programme discussion Geraldine and Ann's concern is eased when Mick returns home (even though he has successfully proven that he can 'fake it', if only for a television programme). They go on to assess the problems with language, stressing the problem of the schemata that connects to their own educational experience:

ANN: And I think on the factory floor … he is not going to be using language a lot. I think you know being a fashion designer, language is quite important, so I think. …

GERALDINE: It's so important in any job isn't it? Or in any walk of life it is important. If you can't learn it. The vocabulary

ANN: Yeah

GERALDINE: What's so scary about your training is that you don't have that

ANN: That is absolutely right

GERALDINE: And it doesn't matter what experience you have got behind you, like say from different ... from job to job, you know and as job descriptions change, you do use a different vocabulary, you have to make yourself understood in all kinds of different ways.

Ann and Geraldine grapple with the episteme, the logic behind the practice, to which they have also been subject and struggled in their own work. The debate hinges on effort, yet they attempt to constitutively actualize with the situation by placing themselves in it, trying to make a connection between this and 'any job'. It is this cultural underpinning that is almost made visible through failed performance, and it is the attempts to understand this unpredictable structuring absence that enables them, alongside an assessment of his labour, to keep sympathy for Mick's performance.

But as they continue this post-programme discussion about the gap between skills and logic, their practice with and knowledge of reflexive modes of articulation leads them to question their initial response to Mick's apparent ability to perform the practical skills in the first place:

ANN: The programme really simplified it

GERALDINE: Yeah, simplified it

ANN: Made it look I thought quite interesting, that anybody can do it

BEV: Mmmm. Is that a good thing or a bad thing?

GERALDINE: It is interesting, the pinning and the cutting

ANN: But the pattern cutting would be a big job, wouldn't it?

GERALDINE: I imagine that would be quite hard

ANN: And I think that was obviously a job taken over by somebody else isn't it? Who did the pattern cutting and then he cut round the pattern? But you didn't actually see him getting involved in the pattern cutting ... and that for me would be the main point of it all.

GERALDINE: The fabric, exactly that's right. And choosing the fabric that would be the ideal fabric for the design. That would be the scary bit for me I think, making the pattern and using the material. Basically he had a whole team of people around him didn't he?

ANN: Yeah. He had a lot of support.

GERALDINE: Yeah he did. But they took his drawings into something else didn't they so it was them.

This is interesting both methodologically and theoretically as the analysis occurs *after* watching the programme and after a detailed discussion; it is a position they develop. They begin to question Mick's skills that had earlier impressed them and by questioning editing techniques, suggest that the labour was not really done by him but by a whole team of people. Even his drawings, which initially impressed them, were not seen to be enough to convince. In a testing situation it is Mick's effort that is central to their assessment of his value and reflexively they become less convinced that he could do the *'hardest part'*. Is it the exposition of Mick's inability to correct the habitus that leads them to reflexively question his actual ability and labour? Or is it their attempt to include their own experiences into the discussion? They are not in the same class-based circuit of value as Mick (Ann is a lawyer and Geraldine is in arts education), but they understand what it means to be driven by the fear of failure, what it means to succeed and to invest in 'becoming'. Their post-hoc discussion re-aligns their investments with an understanding of television conventions. They did initially immanently reach for connection through sympathy, a reaction which is then mitigated by their post-hoc rationalization of the impossibility of class passing. Ann and Geraldine come to suggest that Mick actually had neither the skills nor the episteme.

This audience finding leads us to suggest that reality television operates with a different principle to that proposed by Arditi (1999) on etiquette guides. Instead of offering the logic *with* the skill, the episteme that underpins the practice, reality programmes *unhinge* the logic from the skill, repeating our findings from Chapter 3 about how reality television erases the historical production of the person, locating social issues as individualized dispositions. Rather than the self-work ethic of reality television attempting to educate the working class in the episteme, they make the episteme disappear, so that the failure to fully grasp what is required is visualized as a personalized psychological failure. This is the ultimate conceit of contemporary class relations in the era of mediatized performance.

Conclusion

Reality television appears to be involved, even if advertently, in the dramatic conversion of entropy into capital and in the making of governable subjects through the extension of self-work ethics into everyday forms of practice. Our textual analysis shows that through its intervention into many different forms of intimate, aesthetic, domestic, emotional and caring labour, reality television ensures the increasing valorization of labour. As capital extends its lines of flight into intimate fields it may enable, as Andrejevic (2004) documents, value to be extracted from the work of being watched. Reality television also enables exploitation via the promotion and display of suffering in a similar way to Eva Illouz's (2003, 2007) analysis of Oprah Winfrey. Television producers continue to find novel ways to extract profit from performances of personhood. By working in its own interests of capital accumulation it draws upon well established work ethics and repackages them in various forms but which ultimately require that people constantly labour in nearly every aspect of their lives (relationships, sex, communication).

But not all attempts to transmit this imperative to perform self-work, in the terms set out by theories of governance, work. The picture we paint here is much more complicated. By displaying the more complex rootedness of the classed and gendered histories of labour our respondents' reactions methodologically laid bare for us the difference between our textual and empirical analyses to demonstrate further to whom the call to governmentality speaks. The call to convert entropy into labour, to create self-propelling accruing subjects whose time is converted to enterprise, may only register with those audience members already invested in similar lives with achievable careers (not routine jobs), who can image a future rich with possibility. Our middle class viewers who rejected reality television's opportunity structure were attached to a work ethic which rewards traditional value accrual. They also see the futility in trying to generate a lifetime's habitus in the space of one labour performance for one television programme. Our research suggests that the take up of the self-work ethic is dependent upon the social location of the viewer and the possibilities, plausibility structure and value system offered by the histories of that social location. It speaks to those already invested, as an ideology for the already converted.

There were challenges to the contemporary expectations placed on women in terms of deploying aesthetic and emotional labour. Our respondents saw through the virtual call to transformation into the actual labour required, rejecting the symbolic violence done to participants, whilst simultaneously participating in the assessment of the labour performed, because they too are subject to similar judgements. Our respondents assessed the time, energy and type of labour required and located themselves as fellow labourers. If formal work offers no possibility for value accrual (and our groups range from those who enter 'working poor jobs' which have to be supplemented by state benefits to avoid child poverty, to those employed in legal and arts professions), or if their jobs are routinized (such as the legal secretary above), then women find other ways of generating value. The working class women emphasized 'just getting on with it' as opposed to 'becoming'; being uncomplaining and indefatigable; investing in motherhood as *the* source of value, and most definitely not being pretentious. Therefore different forms of labour are valued very differently according to history, positioning and investments. The working class women, in their acceptance of reality television as a structure of opportunity, embrace the possibility to erase the past (and why wouldn't they?) in order to reap the financial rewards of profiting from performing 'being oneself'. They were not convinced by the ideology of the self-work ethic. It only meant a lot of hard unrewarding work for little return.

It is therefore the different value systems that we explored in our introduction – accrual and relationality – which offer positions in the time/space vectors of past, present and future that mediate relationships to television, rather than a straightforward transmission of a neo-liberal self-work ethic through pedagogic strategies. Rarely does the viewer occupy the position of 'TV-viewer pupil'; rather, what surprised us from our research was how connections were made from research. respondent's own intimate positions in relationships (be it mothers, wives, partners) and how they did or did not make 'constitutive actualizations' through and/or back onto the television participant's relationships.

Knowing how reality television is designed to present morality in a particular way, as an episteme divorced from social context, they instead decide what matters.

Notes

1 See Skeggs and Wood (2011) for a further development of this argument.
2 For an extended discussion of the nature of exchange in this episode see Skeggs (2010).
3 We put 'rational' in inverted commas to signify that we do not think this is an entirely cognitive process, but a decision that emerges over time as the person learns that they cannot accrue value in particular ways.
4 At the time of the study, Jordan, aka Katie Price, is a British celebrity famous for her enormous breasts, relationships with footballers, her marriage to pop singer Peter Andre, and looking after her disabled child.
5 This focus group discussion took place before Jade was ejected from *Celebrity Big Brother* for attacking Shilpa Shetty, by calling her 'Shilpa Poppadom' and creating a national scandal, for which the then Labour Chancellor (and subsequently ex-Prime-Minister) Gordon Brown had to apologize for Jade and British racism to the Indian Prime Minister. See full transcript on http://newsvote.bbc.co.uk/mpapps/pagetools/print/news.bbc.co.uk/1/hi/enertainment. Downloaded on 15.08.07.
6 Following the 'racist' incident (see Tolson (2011) for a linguistic analysis) Jade was ejected from the house and lost her own shows on television. To reclaim her position in the public imagination, she made apologies, visited India and appeared in the Indian *Big Brother*, where she publically received the news of her cervical cancer. In March 2009 Jade Goody died, prompting the greatest display of media-instigated grief since the death of Princess Diana. The moral person value of Jade in life and death became a matter of national debate.
7 Producing the complex figure of the 'mockney' in English culture and the middle class tradition of 'slumming it' which is subject to enormous ridicule in working class communities and perfectly epitomized in Pulp's song 'Common People'.
8 In the US context Brenda Weber (2011) discusses the vitriol directed to Kate Gosselin, a reality celebrity mom, who is criticized on moral grounds for making money out of publicizing her children, flouting the rules of propriety around motherhood, whilst pursuing the American Dream.
9 Arditi (1999) suggests that structures of practice at different times also involve different logics of structuration, each necessitating a different logic of action from the people for whom these structures are material.

References

Andrejevic, M. 2004 *Reality TV: the Work of Being Watched*, Oxford: Rowman and Littlefield.
Arditi, J. 1999 'Etiquette Books, Discourse and the Deployment of an Order of Things', *Theory, Culture and Society* 16(4): 25–48.
Bailey, P. 1998 *Popular Culture and Performance in the Victorian City*, Cambridge: Cambridge University Press.
Barrett, M. 1982 *Women's Oppression Today: Problems in Marxist Feminist Analysis*, London: Verso/NLB.
Bourdieu, P. 1986 *Distinction: A Social Critique of the Judgement of Taste*, London: Routledge.
Bourdieu, P. and Waquant, L. 1992 *An Invitation to Reflexive Sociology*, Chicago: University of Chicago Press.

Brenner, J. and Ramas, M. 1984 'Rethinking Women's Oppression', *New Left Review* 144: 33–72.

Briggs, M. 2009 'BBC Children's Television, Parentcraft and Pedagogy: Towards the "Ethicalization of Existence"', *Media, Culture, Society* 31(1): 23–39.

Buckingham, D. and Scanlon, M. 2003 *Education, Entertainment and Learning in the Home*, Buckingham: Open University Press.

du Gay, P. 1986 *Consumption and Identity at Work*, London: Sage.

Feher, M. 2009 'Self-Appreciation; or, The Aspirations of Human Capital', *Public Culture* 21(1): 21–41.

Glucksmann, M. 2005 'Shifting Boundaries and Interconnections: Extending the "Total Social Organisation of Labour"', *Sociological Review* December: 19–36.

Hall, S. 1998 'The Going Nowhere Show', in A. Chadwick and R. Heffernan (eds) *The New Labour Reader*, Cambridge: Polity.

Hartmann, H. and Sargent, L. 1981 *The Unhappy Marriage of Marxism and Feminism*, London: Pluto.

Hearn, A. 2008a 'Variations on the Branded Self: Theme, Invention, Improvisation and Inventory', in D. Hesmondhalgh and J. Toynbee (eds) *The Media and Social Theory*, London: Routledge.

——2008b 'Insecure: Narratives and Economies of the Branded Self in Transformation Television', *Continuum: Journal of Media and Cultural Studies* 22(4): 495–505.

Heelas, P. 2002 'Work Ethics, Soft Capitalism and the "Turn to Life"', in P. du Gay and M. Pryke (eds) *Cultural Economy*, London: Sage.

Holmes, S. and Jermyn, D. 2007 '"Ask the Fastidious Woman from Serbiton to Hand-wash the Underpants of Aging Oldham Skinhead." Why not *Wife Swap?*', in T. Austin and W. de Jog (eds) *Rethinking Documentary: A Documentary Reader*, Buckingham: Open University Press.

Hunt, L. 1998 *British Low Culture: From Safari Suits to Sexploitation*, London: Routledge.

Illouz, E. 2003 *Oprah Winfrey and the Glamour of Misery*, New York: Columbia University Press.

——2007 *Cold Intimacies: The Making of Emotional Capitalism*, Cambridge: Polity.

Kavka, M. 2008 *Reality Television, Affect and Intimacy: Reality Matters*, London: Palgrave Macmillan.

Lareau, A. 2003 *Unequal Childhoods: Class, Race and Family Life*, Berkeley, CA.: University of California Press.

Lasch, C. 1979 *The Culture of Narcissism: American Life in the Age of Diminishing Expectations*, London and New York: Norton Press.

Marx, K. 1967 *Capital Volume 1*, New York: International Publishers.

McRobbie, A. 2002 'From Holloway to Hollywood: Happiness at Work in the New Cultural Economy', in P. du Gay and M. Pryke (eds) *Cultural Economy*, London: Sage.

——2009 *In the Aftermath of Feminism: Gender, Culture and Social Change*, London: Sage.

Negra, D. 2008 *What a Girl Wants? Fantasising the Reclamation of Self in Postmodernism*, London: Routledge.

Negra, D. and Holmes, S. 2008 'Introduction', *Genders Online Journal* (48).

Negra, D. and Tasker, Y. (eds) 2007 *Interrogating Postfeminism: Gender and the Politics of Popular Culture*, Durham and London: Duke University Press.

Ouellette, L. and Hay, J. 2008a *Better Living Through Reality Television*, Oxford: Blackwell.

——2008b 'Makeover Television, Governmentality and the Good Citizen', *Continuum: Journal of Media and Cultural Studies* 22(4): 471–85.

Pitt, K. 2002 'Being a New Capitalist Mother', *Discourse and Society* 13(2): 251–67.

Reay, D. 1998 *Class Work: Mother's Involvement in their Children's Primary Schooling*, London: UCL Press.

Rose, N. 1989 *Governing the Soul: The Shaping of the Private Self*, London: Routledge.

Skeggs, B. 2004 *Class, Self, Culture*, London: Routledge.

——2005 'The Making of Class and Gender through Visualising Moral Subject Formation', *Sociology* 39(5): 965–82.

——2010 'The Value of Relationships: Affective Scenes and Emotional Performances', *Feminist Legal Studies* 18(1): 29–51.

Skeggs, B. and Wood, H. 2011 'Turning it on is a Class Act: Immediated Object Relations with the Television', *Media, Culture and Society*, 33(6), 941–53.

Sobchack, V. 1999 'Towards a Phenomenology of Nonfictional Film Experience', in J. Gaines and M. Renow (eds) *Collecting Visible Evidence*, Minneapolis, Minnesota: Minnesota University Press.

——2004 *Carnal Thoughts: Embodiment and Moving Image Culture*, Berkeley and Los Angeles: University of California Press.

Staples, D. 2007 'Women's Work and the Ambivalent Gift of Entropy', in P. T. Clough and J. Halley (eds) *The Affective Turn: Theorising the Social*, Durham and London: Duke University Press.

Steedman, C. 2004 'The Servants Labour. The Business of Life, England 1760–1820', *Social History* 29(1): 1–29.

Thomson, R., Kehily, M. J., Hadfield, L. and Sharpe, S. 2011 *Making Modern Mothers*, Bristol: Policy Press.

Tolson, A. 2011 'I'm Common and My Talking is quite Abrupt' (Jade Goody): Language and Class in Celebrity Big Brother, in H. Wood and B. Skeggs (eds) *Reality Television and Class*, London: BFI/Palgrave.

Tyler, I. and Bennett, B. 2010 '"Celebrity Chav": Fame, Femininity and Social Class', *European Journal of Cultural Studies* 13(3): 375–93.

Vicinus, M. 1974 *The Industrial Muse: A Study of Nineteenth Century British Working Class Literature*, London: Croom Helm.

Walkerdine, V. 2010 'Communal Beingness and Affect: an Exploration of Trauma in an Ex-industrial Community', *Body and Society*, 16(1): 91–116.

Walkerdine, V. and Lucey, H. 1989 *Democracy in the Kitchen: Regulating Mothers and Socialising Daughters*, London: Virago.

Weber, B. 2009 *Makeover TV: Selfhood, Citizenship and Celebrity*, Durham, NC: Duke University Press.

——2011 'From All-American Mom to Super Bitch from Hell: Kate Gosselin and the Classed and Gendered Politics of Reality Television', in H. Wood and B. Skeggs (eds) *Reality Television and Class*, London: BFI/Palgrave.

Willis, P. 1977 *Learning to Labour: How Working Class Kids Get Working Class Jobs*, Farnborough, Hants: Saxon House.

Chapter 8

Conclusions

Intimacy, ideology, value and politics

Politics is first of all a sphere of appearance.

(Ranciere 2005)[1]

This book is the result of quite a journey. We began it as part of a project which sought to interrogate the shaping of identity and class through ethical scenarios on reality television. We were always hesitant about the term identity because of the difficulties it represented for understanding class formation: Skeggs' (1997) previous research had already alerted us to the fact that young women were likely to dis-identify rather than identify with a working class categorization because they understood how they were mis-recognized by judgemental 'others' as being valueless. As it transpired identity was not really an issue at all in the research: the middle class women identified as middle class straightforwardly through empirical criteria 'I went to private school', 'I have an MA', whilst the working class women all (but the older ones) did not know how to answer questions about class directly but instead framed the issue around questions of injustice, inequality and fairness. Hence a project on identity turned into a book about value.

Morality may operate as a form of cultural capital if it can be traded to gain a realizable capital value. For instance we have previously shown how in struggles over 'queer' space propriety can be converted into property (Moran and Skeggs 2001; Moran *et al.* 2004). We came to this focus via many routes. Our prior knowledge of feminist film and media theory meant that we were interested in reality television's melodramatic conventions and how they were deployed to heighten the moral force of the 'reality' entertainment. Early in the project we had a heated debate about the weight of the importance between the textual narrative or social relations in shaping audiences' reactions to television. Reality television's recruitment of so-called 'ordinary' people to be themselves, and its thorny relationship to the 'real' or perhaps the 'social', further complicates any accepted notion of a clear textual/social split. We have argued through the book for an approach which aims to recognize the role of textuality in the social *and* sociality in the text, drawing upon our combination of interests into media and social analysis. On re-reading Linda Williams' (2001) *Playing the Race Card* we began to realize that melodrama worked to structure class relations in UK in a similar way that Williams argued for race relations in the USA. As we progressed we came to understand that narrative is the hinge that holds hopes, expectations and ideology (family, motherhood, romance) together as people react to reality television from their position within social relations.

Our early viewing of the reality television genre and the impetus for our research funding application had alerted us to the very obvious symbolic violence of class representations developed and circulated in the British context during the mid-2000s. It was clear that working class participants were being recruited for entertainment purposes, which usually meant that their deficiencies were spectacularly visualized whilst normative (middle class) solutions were identified. Sometimes intense visual attention to abject bodies behaving badly was all that was required and *Ibiza Uncovered* was the most in/famous of these formats. Many programmes involved focusing on women's bodies as the constitutive limit to all propriety. The self-transformation formats such as *What Not to Wear* asked participants to participate in their own humiliation en route to personal and even 'feminist' empowerment (McRobbie 2004; Ringrose and Walkerdine 2008). We understood these forms of symbolic violence to be part of a longer history of shaming and a more general cultural trend of contempt and derision promoted by middle class cultural commentators, and we were concerned about the parallel rise of the circulation of the term 'Chav' in the UK to performatively bring into effect the recognition of a pathological, useless, abject working class subject (Chav became the Oxford English Dictionary word of 2004).[2]

At this point our analysis was still fairly simple – reality television recruited excessive people, made them appear/perform badly, using various heightened dramatic techniques, filming and editing, to make them appear even more gross and extreme and in need of a moral pedagogy of propriety. Cultural intermediaries were stepping in to teach them to eat less, smoke less, wear beige and communicate quietly, thereby generating entertainment from curbing precisely the reason for which they had been recruited: their excess. That the narrative emphasis was on how they achieved (or not) this propriety enabled the focus to be placed upon their own psy-dispositions in order to explain their failure by which participants experience considerable shame. Hence our intuitive position, also often mirrored in the bourgeois press, was of reality television's role as a ritual theatre of humiliation and cruelty, a position which has since been predominantly theorized as a broader neo-liberal governmental address to promote the 'self-work ethic' in the nation.

Having to continually present papers throughout the project meant we were tested at every turn and this became useful. We had to work out why the dominant theories of governmentality and performativity did not work for us in our audience research when they worked for other, mainly textual analyses (see Chapter 5). And we had to continually defend why we were studying class and affect (see later for the full explanation). We also had to learn to write together, bringing very different styles, disciplinary conventions and politics. It has been a challenge and a struggle and undoubtedly it would have been quicker to write two separate books. But ultimately we had to work out what was *at stake*, driven by the kind of work advocated by Stuart Hall (1996) to keep the 'tension' between the theoretical and the political by holding on to the 'worldliness' of textual practices, even though the strain between the two is (productively) irresolvable. This is what this conclusion hopes to establish: we want to show how reality television has become a phenomenon that can tell us a great deal about the workings of governance, performance, ideology, personhood and value in the current conjuncture.

Visualizing class and gender relations

We began the book by taking up Turner's (2010) point that the media now works in its own interests (as opposed to those of the state) and those interests are largely driven by profit. Changes in the political economy of television, and its now diverse platforms, have led to an explosion of cheap formats whereby reality television has come to dominate the schedules. But this tells us little about the *appeal* of reality television and exactly why it has proved so lucrative. In Chapter 1 we discussed the way in which its *form* capitalized on the particular effects of the medium, drawing upon television's complicated relationship to immediacy and 'liveness' in which it has been characterized as a medium of 'presence' (Morse 1998). Reality television's various attempts to capture, construct and create reality has led commentators to consider its impact as much at the level of 'intervention' as at the level of representation, where viewers are intensely implicated in the immediate drama of the moment. Therefore the profit motive is neatly fuelled by the appeal and the imperative of the form as the demand for output has led to the proliferation of reality programmes which are conveniently able to draw upon *and* develop broader social changes in public legitimacy. These changes refer to the way in which a person's moral value is no longer validated by the state or religion but through the public performance of their own value in a display of 'compulsory individuality' tuned to the needs of capital.

How reality television has arrived at this conjuncture is often explained through theories of governance and neo-liberalism whereby the shift to the focus on the individual is seen to eradicate other (social) distinctions which is also of benefit to the shrinking role of the state and the increased significance of the market. Many social and media theorists have noted the pervasiveness of this demand to 'self-work' across television in its reach into many aspects of personal life. In Chapter 3 we mapped how reality television provided a theatre of intimacy for the performance of personhood, as formats mutate and expand television participants were often (although not always in the case of more documentary-type programmes) recruited for their ripeness for transformation. Television websites advertised for the spectacularly bad, excessive, out of control people in need of re-education in many spheres of life. These already symbolically denigrated recruits were used as models to display the constitutive limit to proper personhood. And it is at this point that ideology first intervenes in our analysis at the level of *content*, as bourgeois standards of domesticity, femininity and individualism are offered as *the* normative standards to which the bad recruits should aspire.

But we think it is important to know where these standards come from and how they have become historically produced if we are to fully understand the current conjuncture. In Chapter 1 we discussed the classed and gendered legacies of other mediated expositions of 'ordinary lives' and of the visualization of personal and intimate terrains. Here the working classes and women have an uneven relationship to modes of (self-)presentation that are carried into the present neo-liberal moment and bound to the textual legacies of documentary and melodrama. Reality television's imposition of 'normative standards' can be seen as the extension of older forms of legitimation. As we outlined in Chapter 2, standards have worked to justify the interests of a particular class – the bourgeoisie – as they attempted to wrestle power from the aristocracy. We can therefore see how reality television works as a theatre of intimacy with its good and bad 'person-characters', which both *re-iterates* the drama of class and gender struggles over which people and standards count and matter, at the same time that it attempts to *deny* them through the (neo-liberal) emphasis upon the individual and the naturalization of the market.

We have described this as *the* structuring conceit of much reality television whereby the historical and material 'realities' of the social are at once evoked and suppressed. Therefore we have made a case for closer attention to the conditions of possibility by which performances and intimacies are enabled across reality television away from a straightforward politics of recognition. The formats for self-transformation programmes used the verisimilitude of recognizable everyday settings to make spectacular domestic and intimate relationships. We noted how conditions were set through particular editing, scripting and camera shots, as well as through narrative structure and dramatic conventions drawn from a particular blending of melodrama with documentary. The organization of time and space within the programmes was absolutely central to how personhood could be played out as either expansive or constricted (which parallels broader class spatial relationships): the middle class participants were given longer time-spans to tell their stories and to perform reflexivity (in programmes like *Get a New Life*), whereas the working class participants were expected to react to dramatic moments, divorced from the larger stories of their lives (in programmes like *Wife Swap*). Through the textual organization of time and space we illustrated how in the drama of the moment only some participants had the requisite knowledge, language and capacity to direct the action and the emphasis for some on reaction rather than action revealed their lack of control, self-determinism and ultimately individualized failure.

By detaching certain groups of participants from their historical and material circumstances, which might otherwise explain their motivations and actions, focus is directed onto their psychological dispositions, so that morality is accounted for through the grammar of performance. In a culture of the 'self-work ethic', where the person is a project which should be continually worked upon and displayed, those revealing a lack of control and self-determinism are located firmly as inadequate, not having made proper investments or the right choices in the production of the proper self.

If as Beck (1992) and Giddens (1991) propose, the reflexive telling of the self is *the* method of individualization disconnected from other forms of social connection, we can see how reality television legitimates this broader social move. The focus on the performance of one's own value revealed the lack of access to techniques for reflexive telling (although not reflexive practice; see Skeggs 2002) on the part of the working class participants – see our discussion of *Faking It*. But once this is located within a longer classed history of 'forced telling' (Chapter 2) reality television becomes another medium for making the working class perform their lack of person-value publicly. Whereas in the past it was legal welfare interlocuters that incited the public telling of the redemptive story of subjectivity, in the present 'forced telling' extends into 'forced performances' and the religious narrative of redemption has morphed into the performance of psychologized moral interiority. By drawing upon the political legacies of the past, we can expose the ideological mask of individualization conjured in the present, whereby the televised performance of pathology has become a mechanism for public judgement via the entertainment industry in the interests of capital.

Performing intimacy

At this point we have dealt with *some* of the propositions with which we began our research project about the significance of processes of individualization to class and gender formations in reality television texts. Our textual mapping in Chapter 3 detailed how the format reached into so many areas of our intimate and personal lives. We showed how texts forensically broke down persons and situations into component parts, whereby elements of bodies, gestures and material objects came to signify the failings of the person in a form of 'metonymic morality'. What this does not yet quite deal with is the *way* in which the intricacies of these intimacies are shepherded into modes of performance which might resonate with broader pressures now placed on people to legitimate themselves through the incitement to publicly perform their value.

The inwardness of the intimate, Berlant (2000) notes is always met by a corresponding publicness. When Kipnis (2003) writes about love, she argued that the US nation is in a state of advanced intimacy, what she defines as 'the somewhat metaphysical belief in our own interiority, an inside that has an almost quasi-medical status of something inside waiting to get out (leeches and bleeding served similar purposes in previous models of society)' (p.75). Substantial research has documented how, particularly in the US, therapeutic culture, also advanced across television, saturates how we are expected to relate to others and our 'selves' (Nolan 1998; White 1992). White (1992), for instance, proposed some time ago that many variants of television (dramatic series, home shopping and soap operas) are all part of a pervasive discursive therapeutic and confessional strategy in contemporary American television that engages viewers in the narrative and narrational strategies of the shows. Both capital and the state offer therapeutic remedies, with 'self-help' operating as a multi-billion pound global industry which enables state services also to be privatized (Blackman 2004).

Similarly across other sites such as the state, welfare, law, work and consumption, arguments are made about the way the performance of intimacy is made subject to quantification and calculation in ways that are made dramatic and explicit on reality television. Law, jurisprudence in particular, for instance, has taken on an intimate therapeutic function as it interprets and adjudicates relationships (Zelizer 2005).[3] We learn of the cost of our behaviour, of the loss to ourselves *and* the nation if we do not invest in ourselves properly, through labouring for the future in every single area of our lives. This is why it is argued that the 'performance principle' identified by Marcuse (1964) has extended into all areas of intimate life, by which all practices can be subject to normative standardization and economic quantification, giving fuel to the many areas of intimate terrain that the TV format can reach. But whereas Marcuse argues that performance has become performative (that is standardized, normalized and made unconscious), we argue the opposite: reality television breaks down the (unconscious) performative into a full-blown conscious performance, so that so many of our behaviours, choices, gestures and feelings are *acted out* and *acted up* for evaluation.

Aesthetics, in particular art, *has always* played a role making visible intimate possibilities (or not), in codifying the performative with value: the development of literature (such as Austen and Gissing) has been highly significant for generating intimate expectations of others, conceiving of the possibilities of attachment and potentials of relationships, for mapping forms of exchange. Generating expectations of standards and attributing value (and cost) to each intimate practice metaphorically is one of the modern ways in which ideology works on reality television. But there are limits to the performances required. Dull banality is rarely incited as it does not make good viewing. In this sense if we apply Bourdieu's (2000) analysis of fields, reality televisions' field of performance has limits and rules for practice: these establish the terms of exchange in which participants enter.

It is here in the elements of performance that our more straightforward content-driven picture of the dominant ideology of reality television begins to get muddied. Particularly as we begin to theorize how these governmental messages get passed on to audiences. Reality television's reliance on the performance of the everyday makes it the perfect stage for encompassing all the senses, the affects and embodiment that make up intimate relations. Performance contains more than just statements and visibilities (circa Foucault), it also combines speech, movement, aesthetics and gestures into an affective scene to which we as audience make connections: we may 'feel' the discomfort of the performance, laugh at the ridiculousness of bodies, and celebrate the endurance of participants. We enter into a realm of the senses whereby the outcome may be guessed at but never fully known in advance.

Therefore, the codifications and iterations of the (bourgeois) normative performative that we have described that provide the grounds upon which governmentality proceed, are called into question once they are revealed *as* performances. In maintaining and constantly reiterating normative standards the constitutive limits have to be detailed in all their glory, and it is the spectacularization of this excess and pathology that is used to generate audience attention (and ultimately advertisers). Many of our audience respondents were also positioned at some distance from the normative and were therefore potentially subject to the same judgement calls to reform as the television participants. Governmentality analysis would suggest that they respond to the pedagogical invitation to self-transformation as the 'viewer-pupil', but our empirical research suggested otherwise. We propose that there is a contradiction between what the televised field of exchange demands (heightened performance for sensation and attracting viewers for profit) and the demands of governmentality (inciting self-regulation) which opens up a gap into which many of our viewer's reactions enter.

We saw how class differences were particularly stark in reactions to 'expert' advice. Our middle class respondents did not believe that advice was directed to them, and our working class respondents often became outraged by the advice on offer. They did sometimes like 'tips' but only if these fitted into their aesthetic, social and domestic lives. They detached these elements from the overall narrative framework, which was usually about transformation, aspiration and improvement, just as they resisted the impositions of authority by those whom they refused to authorize, and they often took great pleasure in doing so as a viewing practice. Donzelot (1979) proposes that advice is a form of positive power, disciplining, rewarding and manipulating the conscience. We instead insist that this process is not straightforward: our respondents were rarely persuaded, challenging the attempts to put them in their place, defending their own culture, experience and value. They recognized and revalidated their own investments in standards, and these sometimes cut across class and drew upon gendered experiences of labour, rather than fitting into models proposed by experts. They de-authorized those whose knowledge was clearly based on very different economies of time (such as those who could afford nannies). They were able to do this because they reacted to the advice given to television participants 'as if' it was given to them. They 'constitutively actualized' (Sobchack 1999) themselves into the same situation because the programmes activated their own histories, positioning, investments and hopes.

The women's reactions that challenged the invitation to reform therefore revealed the habituated nature of gender and class performativity. We see how reality television makes conscious the unconscious iteration that holds the inequalities of class and gender in place. Rarely, in other areas of our lives, do we watch the performative broken down *and* staged over time and space. Usually we are too busy doing gender through our everyday iterations. Production techniques such as the long held close up 'judgement shot' gave our audiences time to evaluate people's reactions, making explicit and visible that which is so habituated that it is not often recognizable. The judgement shot offered audiences the position of *the* judge, but this also often revealed that they were also in the position of the *judged*, simultaneously revealing very different perspectives taken from different positions.

The invitation to the viewer to unpack person performance thus offered up moments for critical attention: 'why would she do that?' The exposure of the elements of the normative performative is, we argue, one of the logical (if unintended and inadvertently radical) results of reality television as it makes almost every practice subject to performance evaluation. In doing so we see how governmentality does not work. The intense attention given by reality television to the performative, where repetitive habit is broken down into its minute elements, is displayed in the encounter between both the participants *and* the audience who are both positioned by normative performativity. Attempts to put back behavioural elements after breaking them down (through the trope of self-transformation) enables audiences to see how utterly incoherent, contradictory and unstable the production of subjectivity and normativity is, and thus reveals to us the impossibility of the governmentality project, at least in having any straightforward determined 'effect'. It appears that the pernicious pedagogical nature of the texts (as we detailed in Chapter 3) have very little straightforward impact, but what the programmes did were incite value struggles about what *matters* and what counts.

Affective disruption

Any over-easy imposition of the governmentality thesis is further resisted by closer attention to those questions posed by reality television's *form*: that is its emphasis upon affect and immediacy, which for writers like Kavka (2008) evoke a theory of 'mattering' over a theory of 'meaning'. We have described the way in which reality television's intervention in what Thompson (1996) named 'the sphere of affect' fits with other drives by which affect has produced new forms of value for capital exploitation, alongside the recognition that this has long been a key ingredient of 'women's culture'. Reality television is a form of spectacular, intense, affective melodramatic entertainment, by which intensities pass from person to person across the screen *and* between the screen and the viewer.

Affect is a force which can make us 'do things', move us, connect us to things, but which can also overwhelm us: 'affect is persistent proof of a body's never less than ongoing immersion in and amongst the world's obstinacies and rhythms, its refusals as much as its invitations' (Seigworth and Gregg 2010). The key points made by Spinoza (Deleuze and Deleuze 1978) in his exploration of the working of power are, first, how affect is connected to ideas, and, second, how negative affect can limit our capacity to act. Our bodies are continually inscribed with the politics of our experiences. If we experience long histories of shaming, our bodies are likely to reveal our lack of confidence. As Bourdieu (1986) notes, our bodies carry our histories of experience, our long-lasting dispositions, as practice is converted through ideas. In this way we have insisted that affect is not purely an individualistic and biological experience because only we feel it, but it is ultimately a *social* experience because it marks our very connections to and relations with others – in a 'socius' of feeling. Affects are always social as they are produced from the sociality of the body as it inhabits the world (Dawney 2011).

As we demonstrated in Chapter 4, the use of our multi-levelled methodology allowed us to explore audience responses across different types of data, where we could compare reflexive accounts produced through interviews, with accounts generated through public discussion in focus groups, with immediate responses which captured reactions in text-in-action viewing sessions. This meant that we could compare types of data more usually gathered in audience research, that produce more sedimented ideas and connections to broader discourses, with immanent affective reactions of the viewing *experience* as it takes place *in time*.

As we demonstrated in Chapter 4, the use of our new method the 'Affective Textual Encounter' enabled us to map exactly where affect made our respondents do things. It was the reality programmes' incitement to judgement through the technical manipulation of affect, often through the long held close-up, the use of dramatic music, that provoked affective responses (such as disgust) that were turned into forms of alignment and non-alignment, into assessment of a person's value. We mapped how our groups produced affective responses at the same moments in the text, but how these generated very different judgements depending on the form of the connection and the way the connection was threaded back into their own life narratives and value positions 'as if' they were subject to the same judgements as the television participants. We think that the 'as if' forms of connection induced by reality television, 'as if part of people's lives' enables us to explore wider social relationships. 'As if' has a doubling function: it works both 'as if' taking part in the mediated interaction, and 'as if' taking a position (say performing dissimulation) – opening up the ambiguities of performing the relationships to television as if authority is accepted whereas in fact authority is challenged.

Our range of methods allowed us to further explore the role of ambiguity in audience responses, as viewers could move between positions both across and within methods. Ambiguity has long been of concern to television audience research since it questions what we can actually know about the relationship between texts and audiences if the television viewer is always located in a provisional and shifting position, as has been assumed by some of the interrogations of television as an affective medium (Grossberg 1987). The *form* of television, exacerbated by reality television according to Kavka (2008), opens up this potential further as the viewer in their identification of what 'matters' is not subject to any dominant positioning by the text. We saw in our audience research how responses like 'it's just sad' were coded in numerous ways as viewers moved between judgement and empathy and into evaluations of themselves. This process of accounting for their own ability to be *moved* by texts we located as a part of particular feminine competence associated with melodrama and we drew out women's longer relationship to this type of 'emotional labour' (Hochschild 1983). Some responses were based on questions of value accrual (how could they leave their house like that? – judgement) and some based on relational value (how can she let him treat her like that? – empathy) and these positions can simultaneously co-exist, and are therefore not easily corralled into a reading of ideology and/or governance.

We realized that because of the centrality of performing one's value (the performance principle) non-verbal actions of bodies and gestures were central to the incitement of judgement, key to the 'as if' connections. Gesture was a particularly powerful way to display dissimulation, an unspoken challenge to what was considered to be spurious authority transmitted through advice. The body with its minute movements became the place for the transmission of affects that were difficult to express, such as defiance, frustration, jealousy, depression, revenge, passion and desire. But our respondents noticed them and more often than not it moved them to make comparisons to their own lives, to how they had felt when placed in similar situations. Michael Herzfeld (2009) maintains that the members of a given society in recognizing the modalities of a culture must also generate a competence based on flaws and foibles, which he calls a 'fellowship of the flawed' (p.133). We suggest that it may be in the recognition of injustice that an understanding of relational value can be realized, through the shared experiences of humiliation and shame.

Affects also complicated a straightforward understanding of authority and de-authorization, because not all judgements were accepted or agreed upon and many forms of morality were contested from specific social positions (especially motherhood, which has a very long history of classed moral contestation (Gillies 2007; Lawler 2000; Reay 1998; Skeggs 1997; Thompson 2011; Walkerdine and Lucey 1989)). There was little consent over what constituted the proper and improper, or good or bad people, and the reception of the negative symbolic loading of representation was unpredictable. Some of our middle class respondents made an 'affective reach' into the lives of symbolically denigrated participants as they sought connections to participants via sharing the same types of feelings and relational value. Affective reactions, particularly those we found through our 'affective textual encounters', which captured the immediate intensity of reality television, could powerfully over-ride any 'reading' of content. The 'movement' of our audiences in response to situations and circumstances in which the *feelings* involved were recognizable is what enabled them to occupy multiple and often contradictory positions in relation to reality television and reality television participants. There are therefore limits to analyses of television that rely on textual analysis alone. As in the lessons learned from other audience research, we can understand the constitution of the dominant symbolic economy from representations, but we cannot predict in advance how audiences will respond. One of the other surprising results from our research was how the medium itself – because it relied on the production of affect to gain audience attention – destabilized its own pedagogical imperative.

Stabilizing authority

This affective positional shifting was not experienced in any way as disconcerting or confusing; rather it is part of the pleasurable experience of watching reality television. The ability to move between being both judge and judged afforded a range of emotions and attachments in which viewers' own lives really counted as valid authority. We began to realize that the numerous reactions revealed our respondents' investments, choices and aspirations as part of their continued and fluid engagement within 'circuits of value'. What was increasingly significant was the varying *intensity* of these attachments as viewers negotiate what really matters and the varying degrees of these passions alerted us to the political importance of what was at stake. This is why we used the idea of affective economy (Ahmed 2004) to understand how affective reactions are distributed, not in an ad hoc fashion, but organized socially. As we have seen, our respondents reactions align individuals with others – or bodily space with social space – (or not) through the very force of their attachments. Alignments can produce moral consensus, as Probyn (2004) notes, as ideas about disgust and the disgusting (who the affect of disgust is attached to) are learned and repeated over time. Likewise, Lawler (2005) shows how disgust shapes class relations and is an essential element in the distance drawn from others (non-alignment) in the making of middle class identities. But importantly, affect may also produce connections that we cannot anticipate in advance.

Extreme symbolic types such as Lizzy Bardsley from *Wife Swap* or David, Dee and Mary from *Wife Swap* who were used by television producers to generate horror and disgust actually provoked a lot of sympathy from our respondents for the labour and care they displayed towards others. Just as Jade Goody and Jordan (examples par excellence of British media symbolic violence) were also strongly defended because they had made the most of a difficult life. Therefore we maintain that understandings of injustice and unfairness in response to being (virtually and potentially) judged became central to the ways in which alignments and non-alignments were made to reality television participants.

Our working class respondents displayed considerable ambivalence towards the responsibility to 'perform' their value through models espoused through the 'self-work ethic', which generated feelings that were assuaged through comparison to others in order to explain that their lives were not 'so bad'. *Schadenfreude* revealed the attempts to channel the uncertainties and ambiguities set in motion by affect. We saw our respondents work to generate ontological security by attaching affective states of insecurity and anxiety to alternative positions of moral authority such as through motherhood. Perhaps surprisingly some of our working class participants displayed their most angry reactions to those with experiences most like themselves, complicating our initial understanding of the straightforward divisive nature of reality television along class fault lines, and alerting us to the significance of intensities.

This is because reality television's evocation of affect operated immanently for some groups rather than others. In heightened emotional moments our working class respondents directly shared the same deictic frame as the television, so close to the image that they take part in a class 'masquerade'. This masquerade can account for the women's feelings as they react to their over-presence in the image (in a programme like *Wife Swap*) by claiming authority for their invest-ments in maternal martyrdom. These reactions can be understood within cur-rent UK neo-liberal politics where good motherhood is represented as a state of unconditional full time care *but* where full-time mothers are depicted as a drain on the nation.

On the other hand, Bourdieu's (1986) point about how the middle class use distanced speculation to control people and objects made perfect sense when analysing some of the reactions of our middle class respondents who were able to display a wealth of cultural capital in their responses, in a way similar to media theorists. They often used abstraction and reflexivity to structure their responses and could sometimes demonstrate their mastery over the immanence of reality television in the viewing sessions. They were comfortable running the focus group like a university seminar, questioning the authority of one of us, ques-tioning the expertise of television presenters, and drawing on social capital (the television producers they knew) to evidence their answers. They were able to display considerable 'affective reach' by employing a model of care for partici-pants which was often quite patrician, but the implications of the moral invective of reality television did not bear down upon them in the same way.

The middle class group became most animated in the focus group around discussions about reality television participants 'getting something for nothing', which we think reveals their anxiety about their own investments in education and labour. Although often sympathetic towards the predicaments of reality tel-evision participants, they were worried about the overall message of gaining reward from simply 'performing oneself': a position that would bring into ques-tion their own access to entitlements and investments. This was not an immedi-ate response to a particular text or television participant, but a more sedimented assessment of the general cultural values of reality television as they engaged in critical commentary of the value of celebrity culture and labour. On the other hand our working class focus groups considered reality television to be a potential structure of opportunity placing considerable economic value on the labour of 'being oneself' on television as an accelerated route to material and cultural advantage.

This is part of a more complex picture in which our audiences displayed their relationship to broader classed and gendered models of labour, discussed in Chapter 7. The value of gendered labour powerfully intervened in evaluations of the 'self-work ethic' on reality television across our groups, but assessments of investments in time and energy around the use of the television set and in relation to investments in culture and education revealed concrete distinctions between classes. Whilst the working classes espoused more concerted attachments to relational value around the immediate needs of friends and family and the value of the enduring labour of 'just getting on with it', the middle classes revealed a position paradoxically *closer* to the lessons promoted by reality television of the 'productive individual' who invests in their future. Whilst disavowing reality television's ability to offer a quick fix, they displayed their attachment to a work ethic in which they are able to compose, invest and accrue their own value *over time*.

These findings therefore are not about just reading representations, but they are also about what television sets in motion, about what it invites us to participate in, and *do* (Wood 2009). Here for us, reality television is about experiencing a social encounter in which the viewer is implicated through their location in circuits of value. This encounter involves a gamut of emotions around empathy and judgement in which audiences are engaged in both shared amities and combative tournaments of moral value. Affective ambiguities are only assuaged through access to different resources of authorization: assertions of taste for our middle class respondents and motherhood for our working class audiences. The more intense the assertions of those authorizations, the more revealing of their own personal investments in moral value. This is an ongoing process of investing, stabilizing, securing and defending their lives, which does not begin or end with the viewing of reality television.

Valuation as ideology

If we refer back to our understanding of value formations in the introduction we can see how these structure the different reactions of our audiences. We argued for two main ways for gaining person value – the first accrual and the second relational. The former was constantly replayed by our middle class respondents' desires never to waste time and to constantly look to the future to increase their capitals. When their investments were challenged, or even publicly restructured through the 'celebrity' reward system of reality television, they become outraged. We also saw how our working class respondents powerfully defended their prior investments demonstrating how the relational route to person value enables all those invested in motherhood to be automatically connected to the future offering the working class women an alternative value source to that of capital accrual. Whereas middle class mothers have access to *both* capital accrual for future conversion, and relational value through sociality and maternity, our working class groups only had access to the latter. They therefore make the most of what they have, defending and authorizing their investments against that to which they have been denied access, as Bourdieu notes, refusing what they have been refused. This is why we saw intense verbal vitriol directed towards Tracy in *Wife Swap* in Chapter 6, because she valorized paid work as *the* route to person value, devaluing the investments of our working class respondents who are full-time mothers. Our middle class respondents were much less concerned to defend value; instead they displayed their value through their knowledge and cultural taste. And our South Asian group both defended motherhood and protected themselves from our intrusions into investigations of their value by the constant refrain of 'it's cultural difference'.

If we return to Jane Feuer's (1983) seminal essay, 'The Concept of Live Television: Ontology as Ideology', she shows how the 'mode of address' of television which continually asserts its features of 'liveness' even whilst not necessarily actually being 'live', cannot be divorced from arguments about content and ideology. The suturing of the viewer into the text helps to generate a sense of community and familiarity which can, especially in the case of US morning television, confirm an ideological positioning around heteronormativity and the uniformity of the family: 'It seems to me that the ideology of "liveness" must surely act to suppress contradictions' (p.20). Our work has concentrated on the way in which the *form* of reality television, its exacerbation of the immanence of melodrama, draws the viewer into the text which *sets in motion* and then invites the viewer to *assuage* contradictions through the establishment of moral value. Like Feuer, we argue that ideology is not only present in the symbolic content of television, but we also want to take this a stage further to suggest that it is not just in the mode of address that ideology operates, but in what that address asks the viewer *to do*. In our arguments about the affective reactions of our viewers, we showed how these could sometimes circumvent potential ideological messages of governance, but we *do not* imply that this translates into a set of attachments by which the individual is set-free in some postmodern rendering of subjectivity. Rather we have seen the ways affect calls upon a range of intensities by which audiences are engaged in *social* processes of evaluation, in struggles over ontology and value where we can see what is politically at stake.

Whereas Spinoza insists that affect only matters when it is connected to an idea, we want to suggest that affect really matters when it is connected to an idea that is loaded with value. We think it is value that is the most significant element in making affect count, because struggles for value connect people to investments in life course narratives securing their consent to the dominant order. This is why we think that reality television *is* ideological after all: because it attributes value to specific practices, legitimates these practices, and importantly establishes *as dramatic* the value struggles in which people are engaged. Even if responses do not always confirm the symbolic connotations of the text, they do confirm an engagement in the *process* of value attribution via the focus on performance. We therefore disagree with Nichols (1994) who locates the production of affect within banality:

The very intensity of feelings, emotion, sensation, involvement that reality TV produces is also discharged harmlessly within its dramatic envelope of banality. The historical referent, the magnitudes that exceed the text, the narratives that speak of conduct in the world, of face-to-face encounters, bodily risk and ethical engagement ground themselves harmlessly in circuits devoted to an endless flux of the very sensations they run to ground.

(p.57)

We do not think our audience reactions are harmless groundings, but that they are intense and immanent connections made to living injustices and inequalities. As Berlant (2008) notes, the displacement of politics to the realm of feeling both opens up a scene for the analysis of the operations of injustice, and shows the obstacles to social change that emerge when politics becomes privatized.

Valuation now pervades so many areas of life that bodies and the relations they enter into offer ever more possibilities for inscription. Even Marx noted how the representation of value never comes to an end. The detailed value coding of practices ensures that exchange value is not always directly apparent but it is often embedded in relationships.[4] And it is in intimate relationships – relational value – that our working class participants and respondents find ways of organizing value practices differently. Reality television engages audiences in a constant process of e/valuation of every aspect of life that it un/covers and it is in the *mechanics* of this process generated through form as much as content that ideology is at work.

This process is a product of the current historical conjuncture. From the beginnings of capitalism we can trace a complex relationship between capital, emotion and intimacy, be it in the negative emotions described by social theorists, such as the alienation of Marx, the anomie of Durkheim or the disenchantment of Weber, where emotions both drive and represent the individual's relation to capitalism. We now think we are in a period of what Illouz (2007) describes as emotional capitalism, in which the emergent spheres of political economy and domesticity that generated expectations of gender normativity have merged, both infecting each other with their methods of calculation and affect. The promotion of self-interest became a device that helped the spread of this infection through its use in both political economy and psychology. As bodies and practices are opened up to scrutiny, new variations and combinations of behaviours and bodies are de-and re-assembled in which intimate bodies, parts and practices are opened out to integrated moral, relational *and* economic evaluation, to what counts as worthwhile and good, what counts as the performance of propriety in the making of the good and proper person.[5]

Reality television therefore opens up an economy that not only produces value through traditional forms of exploitation such as providing audiences for advertisers, or through newer forms of exploitation, such as aspects of surveillance identified by Andrejevic (2004). But it may also enable exploitation via the promotion and display of suffering and misery on talk shows such as *Oprah*, as Illouz

(2003, 2007) charts. Or through the promotion of moral entrepreneurship (Illouz and Wilf 2008) which mobilizes viewers as moral actors: with *Oprah* extracting millions from advertisers by intimately connecting moral to economic value. Hollows and Jones (2010) also note the spread and marketability of 'the moral entrepreneur' as a new category of media celebrity whose value is produced through promoting both morality *and* products. It is the harnessing of people to value struggles which serve the interests of capital that we believe to be ideological, because that harnessing ultimately sutures people to their location in vectors of time and space as they can only find value from what they have available – resources which are historically and socially produced.

Value, ideology and temporality

One of the key features of an ideological analysis of reality television is to show how forms of individuality are encouraged (through historical legacies and technologies of the self) and through which 'self-determination' is encoded as natural and normal. Couldry (2011) further discusses the way in which reality television normalizes the mechanisms of judgement so that the apparatus themselves are rarely questioned. The structuring of competition between people has long been seen to be central to the reproduction of the interests of the powerful. Where people are defined against others, their competition serves to entrench their positions whilst obscuring the real fault line between profit and labour. This is why we consider governmentality to be a technique of ideology: it works to instantiate and legitimate middle class interests.

Nevertheless, the entwined roles of performance and affect work to expose some of the contradictions that governmentality may hold in place, which has led some theorists to herald reality television as potentially progressive through its indeterminacy and public iteration of the everyday. But we think (like Feuer) that ideologies also work to reconcile contradictions and ambiguities, but to also reconcile people to the positions they are likely to inhabit. This is a particularly powerful effect and one of the ways in which it is achieved is through incitements to develop positions and dispositions (such as the good mother) that offer a source of authority and value. But positions and dispositions are not just inhabited momentarily, they are developed over time, revealing possibilities and constraints that combine incitements to invest alongside punishments for non-investment. Caring is a gendered disposition that is encouraged and developed over time, institutionalized in motherhood, but a source of value for those with limited access to other sources with its lack pathologized.

Heterosexuality is the most obvious normalized long-term investment that is promoted from birth and involves a complex assemblage of incentives and punishments, but also, importantly, hope. The naturalization of the couple is one of the most powerful ideological norms that has often been promoted on (reality) television: struggling and suffering and hopefully reforming a bad husband is more valued than being single.[6] The narrative of romance mirrors the progress of investment over time through possibility and constraint as it reconciles women to investments in heterosexuality. As Walkerdine (1984) notes, at a very early age stories of being rescued by Prince Charming pre-dispose young girls to invest in the heterosexual contract via generating an affective *hope for the future*. The ideologies of romance, motherhood and normative family are all powerful hope machines that involve the continual deferral of the future promise: 'in the future you will control your lives/ be secure/have a happy family'. This is what Berlant (2006) calls 'cruel optimism' which describes our attachments to a cluster of promises that maintains our endurance for an object (person) or a fantasy (security) that is always ultimately deferred, often taking the form '*I* endure in the hope that *you* will change'.[7]

We know from Skeggs' previous research that many women repeatedly orientate themselves to the future in which they fantasize that their partner in whom they have invested will indeed change and become employed, successful, considerate, loving, everything that s/he is not in the present (Skeggs 1997). This is why Berlant (2008) describes gender as a genre, which operates like the narrative of romance, constantly interrupted, stumbling to fruition, subject to forces beyond one's control.[8] For Berlant it is future hope and optimism that *secures consent* in the present: 'Cruel optimism names a relation of attachment to *compromised conditions of possibility*' (p.21 our italics), what Berlant has also called a 'technology of patience', and what we through our audience research suggest is more dramatically a 'technology of endurance'.

However we do not think gender is played out in such a generalized form, rather that class relations cut through gendered investments to produce different dispositions towards time (past, present, future). For instance, if we think about endurance it was a highly valued disposition for our working class respondents in their assessments of reality television participants such as vilified Jordan who was able to endure all the tasks without complaint on *I'm a Celebrity*. Just as they valued Jordan's lack of pretence they also praised her capacity for endurance. We think the praise for endurance and indefatigability reveals a working class ontology, a form of being in the world in which investment is made in the present, in coping, or as our respondents put it 'ducking and diving, struggling and surviving'.[9] Their potential for future-focus was restricted by this very presentist orientation, produced from the possibilities they inhabited and the potentials they lacked as a result of social positioning. They valued endurance for what it did, enabling them to put a floor on their circumstances in order to make it into the future. They defended their choice of full-time mothering against aspirational futures for the intrinsic relational affective value it offered. They were not anxious about wasting time because for them time was not a precious resource that could be converted into a value practice.

This was very different from our always future pointing middle class group who were continually investing in value practices in the present in order to increase their value in the future. Their positioning and experience of very different time and space vectors, which offered distinctly middle class possibilities for accruing value and authority, produced a very different ontology, a very different way of being in the world. Inheriting and living with precarity or potential are two ends of an ontological scale which influence the investments that people can make. From an accident of birth some people inherit access to capitals and potential in opposition to those who are denied access to capitals and inherit precarity. Potential opens out time, enabling investments in accrual that can be maximized and owned. It also puts people in a potential position of loss (as they have something they can lose, be it objects, property or time) which is why they must continually secure their investments. At the other end of the scale people have less to access but also less to lose.

This may be why the working class women saw reality television as an opportunity structure in opposition to our middle class respondents who were angered by the 'something for nothing rewards of reality television'. Reality television offers a potential opportunity for those who have not had access to any. Yet for those who have had access to advantage and have constantly laboured to enhance their opportunities, the immediate rewards of reality television devalue all their prior education, labour and investments: they have something to lose.

This may also be why the pedagogic address of reality television did not work for our working class respondents. It does not speak to their ontological conditions, to their conditions of possibility generated over time, to the investment they have made and the hopes they have. They challenged the ideology of the ever-enterprising self because they know they have (had) no access to the capitals or the fields of exchange for becoming so. Yet to make this challenge they authorize themselves through another ideology – motherhood – one to which they are pre-disposed through years of incitement to care. But it is an ideology through which they can claim value. This is not just a matter of consent but of positive embrace.

Therefore, we want to signal how the pedagogic governmentality of reality television which calls for self-transformation may secure ideological consent not through a straightforward transmission to the viewer pupil, but though its reverse, by inciting audience resistance which takes the form of struggles for value. In generating defensive responses from those excluded from traditional sources of value, reality television offers a scene for struggle over what matters. Ideological production is not secured through the adoption of middle class standards, as most understanding of reality television suggest, but for reconciliation to, even celebration of, the cramped spaces by which the working class are already positioned: they put themselves in their place.

Ideology thus works through continually shaping time horizons for investment in different possibilities that are plausible. It engages people in a tournament of value, offering either survival, hope, maintenance of privilege, or to generate alternative value practices, by offering some respite from the constant but implausible invitation to accrue value through traditional capital (social, symbolic, economic, cultural) forms. Ideology is secured once an investment is made in gaining value.

As a stage for self-performance reality television visualizes spectacularly the expectations, requirements and measurements to which we are now subject. Foucault (1977) described us entering an age of infinite examination and McKenzie (2001) describes an extensive compulsion to perform. Deleuze (1990) identifies this continual opening out as an attempt to simultaneously generate new lines of flight for capital and create new ways of being and becoming that are open to ceaseless value extraction and control.

Reality television has become a sustainable form of intervention into the public evaluation of people. Therefore we suggest that a great deal more serious attention needs paying to exactly how reality television works not only with audiences but with evaluating personhood more generally. Dismissing reality television as trash television conceals rather than reveals it to be *precisely* a site where new understandings of value and ideology are coming into effect. Reality television finds new ways to generate profit from the 'free' performances of self inspection, emotion, failure and sometimes even success, and in so doing it valorizes and makes spectacular a great deal of women's emotional and domestic labour. In valorizing the process of valuation itself, through an affective register of immanence, it provokes audiences to react over what matters and what counts. Located in circuits of value, our audiences were subject to varying intensities generated by their own investments which are socially determined and where there is much at stake.

This is a process of ideology which did not necessarily engage subjects through forms of identification, interpellation and misrecognition (in the way in which ideology has been traditionally theorized) but asked them to take part in tournaments of value, circulating and distributing value to persons more generally. By metonymically mapping failure and lack of value reality television incited our audiences to defend and prove their *own*, and in this reaction their investment in the ideological mechanism of value struggle itself was secured.

Notes

1 Blechman, M., Chari, A. and Hasan, R. 2005 'Democracy, Dissensus and the Aesthetics of Class Struggle: An Exchange with Jacques Ranciere', *Historical Materialism* 13(4): 285–301.

2 For an analysis of the public legitimation and circulation of contempt about working class culture see: Mount 2004; Skeggs 2009; Tyler 2008; Tyler and Bennett 2010; Jones 2010.

3 Law has also always been reliant on the performance, not just evaluations of intimacy, but of the exchange value of persons, made explicit in disputations over the contracts of maids in particular (see Steedman, C. 2004 'The Servants Labour. The Business of Life, England 1760–1820', *Social History* 29(1): 1–29; Steedman, C. 2007 *Master and Servant: Love and Labour in the English Industrial Age*, Cambridge: Cambridge University Press).

4 The most obvious hidden form of value is the invisibility of labour in the commodity, hence Marx's identification of the 'commodity fetish'. Freud likewise argues that fetishes exist to hide drives.

5 A 'fit and proper person' is a legal category of personhood in Britain, first used in the seventeenth century to assess a man named Lascelles in order to ascertain his capability for owning slaves.
6 In our previous ethnography 'couple culture' was named as the most excluding form of social organization, much more pernicious in securing adjustment to the normative than ideologies of domesticity and motherhood (Skeggs 1997).
7 Thanks to Kirsty Campbell and David Oswell for all the great discussions about ideology.
8 In film noir films it was more likely that the woman would be killed than fulfil her 'potential' through love, marriage, domestication (Place 1998). Although unlike reality television programmes, the film noir star always had a good time.
9 We contrast this working class form of survival with the genre of entertainment called 'extreme sports' where usually upper and middle class men, such as Ranulph Fiennes and Bear Grylls, purposefully put themselves in extreme conditions in order to display how supposedly clever they are: survival as spectacular sport and adventure rather than everyday reality.

References

Ahmed, S. 2004 'Affective Economies', *Social Text* 22(2): 117–39.
Andrejevic, M. 2004 *Reality TV: the Work of Being Watched*, Oxford: Rowman and Littlefield.
Beck, U. 1992 *Risk Society: Towards a New Modernity*, London: Sage.
Berlant, L. 2000 'The Subject of True Feeling: Pain, Privacy, Politics', in S. Ahmed, J. Kilby, C. Lury, M. McNeil and B. Skeggs (eds) *Transformations: Thinking Through Feminism*, London: Routledge.
——2006 'Cruel Optimism', *Differences: A Journal of Feminist Cultural Studies* 17(3): 20–36.
——2008 *The Female Complaint: The Unfinished Business of Sentimentality in American Culture*, London and Durham: Duke University Press.
Blackman, L. 2004 'Self-help, Media Cultures and the Production of Female Psychopathology', *Cultural Studies* 7(2): 219–56.
Bourdieu, P. 1986 *Distinction: A Social Critique of the Judgement of Taste*, London: Routledge.
——2000 *Pascalian Meditations*, Cambridge: Polity.
Couldry, N. 2011 'Class and Contemporary Forms of "Reality" Production or Hidden Injuries of Class 2', in H. Wood and B. Skeggs (eds) *Reality Television and Class*, London: BFI/Palgrave.
Dawney, L. 2011 'Social Imaginaries and Therapeutic Self-Work: The Ethics of the Embodied Imagination', *The Sociological Review* 59(3): 536–53.
Deleuze, E. and Deleuze, J. 1978 'Giles Deleuze: Lecture Transcripts on Spinoza's Concept of *Affect*', Vol. 2006: http://www.webdeleuze.com/php/sommaire.html.
Deleuze, G. 1990 'Control and Becoming', in G. Deleuze (ed.) *Negotiations*, New York: Columbia University Press.
Donzelot, J. 1979 *The Policing of Families: Welfare versus the State*, London: Hutchinson.
Feuer, J. 1983 'The Concept of Live Television: Ontology as Ideology', in E. A. Kaplan (ed.) *Regarding Television: Critical Approaches – An Anthology*, Los Angeles: American Film Institute.
Foucault, M. 1977 *Discipline and Punish: The Birth of the Prison*, London: Allen Lane/Penguin.
Giddens, A. 1991 *Modernity and Self-Identity; Self and Society in the Late Modern Age*, Cambridge: Polity.

Gillies, V. 2007 *Marginalised Mothers: Exploring Working-Class Experiences of Parenting*, London: Routledge.

Grossberg, L. 1987 'The In-difference of Television', *Screen* 28(2): 28–45.

Hall, S. 1996 'Cultural Studies and its Theoretical Legacies', in D. Morley and K. H. Chen (eds) *Stuart Hall: Critical Dialogues*, London: Routledge.

Herzfeld, M. 2009 'The Cultural Politics of Gesture: Reflections on the Embodiment of Ethnographic Practice', *Ethnography* 10(2): 131–52.

Hollows, J. and Jones, S. 2010 '"At least he's doing something": Moral Entrepreneurship and Individual Responsibility in *Jamie's Ministry of Food*', *European Journal of Cultural Studies* 13(3): 307–22.

Hochschild, A. 1983 *The Managed Heart: Commercialisation of Human Feeling*, Berkeley, CA: University of California Press.

——2003 *The Commercial Spirit of Intimate Life and Other Essays*, San Fransisco and Los Angeles: University of California Press.

Illouz, E. 2003 *Oprah Winfrey and the Glamour of Misery*, New York: Columbia University Press.

——2007 *Cold Intimacies: The Making of Emotional Capitalism*, Cambridge: Polity.

Illouz, E. and Wilf, E. 2008 'Oprah Winfrey and the Co-production of Market and Morality', *Women and Performance: A Journal of Feminist Theory* 18(1): 1–7.

Jones, O. 2010 *Chavs: the Demonisation of the Working Class*, London: Verso.

Kavka, M. 2008 *Reality Television, Affect and Intimacy: Reality Matters*, London: Palgrave Macmillan.

Kipnis, L. 2003 *Against Love: a Polemic*, New York: Vintage Books.

Lawler, S. 2000 *Mothering the Self: Mothers, Daughters, Subjects*, London: Routledge.

——2005 'Disgusted Subjects: the Making of Middle-Class Identities', *The Sociological Review* 53(3): 429–46.

Marcuse, H. 1964 *One Dimensional Man: The Ideology of Industrial Society*, London: Sphere Books.

McKenzie, J. 2001 *Perform or Else; From Discipline to Performance*, New York and London: Routledge.

McRobbie, A. 2004 'Notes on "What Not to Wear" and Post-Feminist Symbolic Violence', in L. Adkins and B. Skeggs (eds) *Feminism after Bourdieu*, Oxford: Blackwell.

Moran, L. and Skeggs, B. 2001 'Property and Propriety: Fear and Safety in Gay Space', *Social and Cultural Geography* 2(4): 407–20.

Moran, L., Skeggs, B., Tyrer, P. and Corteen, K. 2004 *Sexuality and the Politics of Violence and Safety*, London: Routledge.

Morse, M. 1998 *Virtualities: Television, Media Art, and Cyberculture*, Indiananapolis, IN: Indiana University Press.

Mount, F. 2004 *Mind the Gap: Class in Britain Now*, London: Short Books.

Nichols, B. 1994 *Blurred Boundaries: Questions of Meaning in Contemporary Culture*, Indianapolis IN: Indiana University Press.

Nolan, J. L. 1998 *The Theraputic State*, New York: New York University Press.

Place, J. 1998 'Women in Film Noir', in E. Kaplan (ed.) *Women in Film Noir*, London: BFI.

Probyn, E. 2004 'Shame in the Habitus', in L. Adkin and B. Skeggs (eds), *Feminism After Bourdieu*, Oxford: Blackwell.

Reay, D. 1998 *Class Work: Mother's Involvement in their Children's Primary Schooling*, London: UCL Press.

Ringrose, J. and Walkerdine, V. 2008 'Regulating the Abject: The TV Make-over as a site of Neo-Liberal Reinvention towards Bourgeois Femininity', *Feminist Media Studies* 8(3): 227–46.

Seigworth, G. J. and Gregg, M. 2010 'An Inventory of Shimmers', in M. Gregg and G. J. Seigworth (eds) *The Affect Theory Reader*, Durham and London: Duke University Press.

Skeggs, B. 1997 *Formations of Class and Gender: Becoming Respectable*, London: Sage.

——2002 'Techniques for Telling the Reflexive Self', in T. May (ed.) *Qualitative Research in Action*, London: Sage.

——2009 'Haunted by the Spectre of Judgement: Respectability, Value and Affect in Class Relations', in K. Sveinsson (ed.) *Who Cares about the White Working Class*, London: Runnymede Trust.

Sobchack, V. 1999 'Towards a Phenomenology of Nonfictional Film Experience', in J. Gaines and M. Renow (eds) *Collecting Visible Evidence*, Minneapolis, Minnesota: Minnesota University Press.

Thompson, J. 1996 *Models of Value: Eighteenth Century Political Economy and the Novel*, Durham, N.C.: Duke University Press.

Thompson, R. *et al.* 2011 *The Making of Modern Motherhood*, Bristol: The Policy Press.

Turner, G. 2010 *Ordinary People and the Media: The Demotic Turn*, London: Sage.

Tyler, I. 2008 'Chav Mum Chav Scum: Class Disgust in Contemporary Britain', *Feminist Media Studies* 8(1): 17–34.

Tyler, I. and Bennett, B. 2010 '"Celebrity Chav": Fame, Femininity and Social Class', *European Journal of Cultural Studies* 13(3): 375–93.

Walkerdine, V. 1984 'Some Day my Prince will come', in A. McRobbie and M. Nava (eds) *Gender and Generation*, London: Macmillan.

Walkerdine, V. and Lucey, H. 1989 *Democracy in the Kitchen: Regulating Mothers and Socialising Daughters*, London: Virago.

White, M. 1992 *Tele-Advising: Therapeutic Discourse in American Television*, Chapel Hill: University of North Carolina Press.

Williams, L. 2001 *Playing the Race Card: Melodramas of Black and White from Uncle Tom to O.J. Simpson*, Princeton: Princeton University Press.

Wood, H. 2009 *Talking with Television: Women, Talk Shows and Modern Self-Reflexivity*, Illinois: Illinois University Press.

Zelizer, V. A. 2005 *The Purchase of Intimacy*, Princeton: Princeton University Press.

Index

Please note that page numbers relating to Notes will have the letter 'n' following the page number.